# CONTENTS

# ACKNOWLEDGMENTS

Many people have helped bring this project to reality. I could not have done it without the support and love of my family: Jon, Christopher, and Amanda, who put up with so much, including endless pizzas on the evenings I worked late on this manuscript. And many thanks go to all the great people at the city, county, and state parks who cheerfully answered my incessant questions. I especially appreciate my walk- (and bicycle-) loving friends who ventured forth with me, sometimes on a moment's notice: Bob, Jeanne, and Elise Harshbarger; Angela Smale; Clare Meeker; Brooke Thacker; Emily O'Neill; Chip Muller; Angela Ginorio; Emilia Muller-Ginorio; Pamela Smith; Janet Soares; Roshanak Clune and family; Chazz Hacking; Colin Hacking; Andy and Jan Dappen and daughters; Stacy Young; Jagoda Perich-Anderson; Janette Wray; and Adrienne Ross. For their many hours of sorting photographs, I am indebted to Amanda Hacking and Daryl Harshbarger. And last, heartfelt thanks to Joan Gregory at Sasquatch Books for her encouragement and invaluable editorial comments on the second edition.

When the time came for the third edition, I had a new round of helpers. Because I was on an extended trip overseas I sought, and received, the invaluable support of Laura Jean Wilcox, who, together with her steadfast partner, Mike Miller, and her dog, Chica, ventured forth in the Pacific Northwest winter weather to seek out new trails. I returned to the Northwest in time to walk dry trails in July, and I want to thank my husband, Jon, for his companionship and his tireless driving of more than 2,000 miles in search of "the perfect new trail." Our daughter, Amanda, took time off between quarters at the University of Washington to join me on several walks and to throw her photographic talents into some great shots. Both Chip Muller and Angela Ginorio get warm thanks and big kudos for putting up with two vagrant travelers for many weeks while this new edition came to be. Pamela Smith joined us, once again, for some soul-refreshing walks in the forests around Issaquah. Kathryn Britton, a long-time friend and Northwest native, strolled lake and forest trails with us in Seattle. Lastly, thanks go to Whitney Ricketts and all the staff at Sasquatch Books for their help in creating a great third edition.

# INTRODUCTION

When my family was younger, taking a walk often meant going to the mountains—either for multiday backpacking excursions or long day hikes. When they were older and had active sports and social lives, taking a walk was something I squeezed in between soccer games, family taxi driving, appointments, and school volunteer time. Now that my time is more my own, I still find that I crave a good walk the way some folks crave their morning latte or a trip to the mall. But I don't want just any walk—I want cathedral-like forests, open meadows, rushing rivers, tranquil ponds, mountain and water views, birds and other wildlife. And I have found, through many hundreds of miles of walking, dozens of small sanctuaries of nature just a few minutes from home. What glorious freedom, if only for an hour or two, to step from my car and immerse myself in the gentle pace of foot travel.

Because of our mild Puget Sound climate, the walks described in this book are accessible year-round. In spring, the breezes through Hazel Wolf Wetlands are pungent with the scent of newly opened skunk cabbage, and fluffy Canada goslings can be seen parading with their parents on the banks of Lake Sammamish. In summer, sun-ripened salmonberries cluster along Des Moines Creek Trail and in the open forest of Soaring Eagle Regional Park. As the days cool, the trail in Seattle's Carkeek Park rustles underfoot with fallen maple leaves, while migrating birds flock to Green River Natural Resources Area and Olympia's Woodard Bay Preserve. In winter, sword ferns on Everett's Lord Hill and grasses along the Mercer Slough dress in necklaces of white frost. No visit ever repeats itself. Like the mountains and the ocean, even these tiny green spaces in and around our cities offer ever-changing dramas of wildlife, plants, and weather.

## How These Walks Were Chosen

This book is designed to help you select easy, short walks just minutes from your home or workplace, be it in Olympia, Seattle, Everett, Issaquah, or any of the cities in between. From its inception, the goal of the book was to have all walks lie within a half-hour drive of a major urban center. Urban sprawl and increased traffic have challenged that goal; in response, we have eliminated some of the more distant walks and added others, closer to the urban centers. The good news is that counties and cities have responded to the taxpayers' interests, and many new urban trails and parks have sprung up over the past decade. All walks are on public land.

My criteria for a good walking trail are that it be at least a mile in length, be surrounded by greenery or close to water, and allow no motorized vehicles. Most trails meet that minimum mile, and others are part of a larger system of trails within a park where you are limited only by your energy and time. A few small parks, such as Seattle's Schmitz Preserve, Tacoma's Sunrise

Beach Park, and Hazel Wolf Wetlands, may fall a bit short on trail length but equal others in beauty.

Most important is that every walk chosen travels through natural places—everything from lakeshores and saltwater beaches to meadows and forests.

## Keeping Updated

Since the second edition of this book, park maintenance crews and trail volunteers have paved old trails and created new ones. Landslides and floods have closed or diverted others. More railroad right-of-ways have been and are being acquired and converted to trails, and new nature preserves now add green spaces to the local maps. I've tried to stay up-to-date with changes and improvements, but nature and politics rule. Because of this constant growth and change, things may not be as I have portrayed them by the time you take some of these walks. With luck, the changes will be for the better.

## A Word About Regional and Sidewalk Trails

The Puget Sound Region is crisscrossed with many long "regional" trails, which are usually converted from abandoned railway lines, and are extremely popular with bicyclers. Some of these regional trails have always been included in this book: the very popular Burke-Gilman and its extension, the Sammamish River Trail, for example. Others, such as the Centennial Trail and the Chehalis Western Trail, "made the cut" because, though they are long, they include many short stretches that appeal to walkers.

To keep this book true to its goal of nearby walks in natural places, we've eliminated some regional trails that are too far afield, such as the Snoqualmie Valley and the Preston-Snoqualmie Valley Trails and others that are just not "natural enough," such as the East Lake Sammamish and the Interurban Trails.

For the third edition, some very well-loved and popular urban walks were eliminated: Alki Beach Trail, Lake Washington Boulevard, Everett's North and South View Trail, and Tacoma's Ruston Way. With streets right beside them, they just don't conform to our definition of walks in natural places. But they are wonderful places to walk: some of them right alongside the Sound with the scent of sea air, the call of gulls, and the views out over the water.

Just because these walks didn't make it into this edition doesn't mean they aren't great trails in their own right. An Internet search will direct you to the nearest trailhead. How lucky we are to live in a place where the number of parks, trails, and walks has increased over the years!

## Thoughts on Safety

Not every trail is as safe as a suburban sidewalk. Despite maintenance efforts, nature often prevails. Mudslides obliterate paths, rain erodes them, and fallen trees block them. Walking in natural places can be risky. Wear appropriate footgear, and try to walk with someone else, especially in the more remote parks. Take common sense, a cellphone, and anything else you need. You're on your own.

### Thoughts on Care and Preservation

I've had people beg me, on hearing that I was writing this book, not to reveal "their" special trail or park. One hiker told me, "We don't want a lot of city folks overrunning the trails, picking the flowers, and not picking up after their dogs." Sadly, the worst offenders are often the folks who live right by the park. They "know" the trails and let their dogs run off leash. Local kids on bikes sometimes think the forest is their playground. Proximity does not imply ownership or the right to abuse the forest. When I do witness misuse of the trails, I speak up. I don't hesitate to tell people if they are where they shouldn't be with a dog or a bicycle.

That being said, I've seen that most people who share the trails, whether they come from 5 or 50 minutes away, respect the natural areas and understand the need for preservation and care. When parents feel that way, they encourage the same feelings in their children. There is no "my park" or "your park." These are all our parks.

Whether parks are signposted or not, the same minimal courtesies are asked of all visitors:

1. Stay on the trail. As a Bellevue park sign says, "Plants grow by the inch, and die by the foot."
2. Keep pets on a leash unless in a designated off-leash area. Always clean up after your dog.
3. Keep children and pets out of salmon-spawning creeks.
4. Don't feed the waterfowl, squirrels, or other wildlife.
5. Take only memories and pictures. Leave only footprints.

With everyone's cooperation, we can preserve our trails for ourselves and as a heritage for generations to come.

## HOW TO USE THIS BOOK

The walks are arranged roughly from north to south, grouped in chapters according to six urban hubs: Everett; Seattle (including Mercer Island and Bainbridge Island); the Eastside (including Bellevue, Redmond, and Issaquah); the cities of Des Moines, Renton, and Kent; Tacoma (including Vashon Island); and Olympia. Each chapter begins with a locator map and list of walks so you can easily choose where to go.

Each walk begins with a brief location description that places the walk very generally, in reference to an urban center. Distances given are in driving miles (not as the crow flies), from an approximation of the city's "downtown" area.

Following the location, there is a brief description line that includes the setting and special attractions of the walk.

Following that is a summary of the walk, with the following headings:

| | |
|---|---|
| **TRAIL** | Approximate length in miles; type of surface (boardwalk, gravel, natural surface, paved) |
| **STEEPNESS** | Level (flat or nearly so), gentle (easy ups and downs), moderate (gets the heart rate up), or steep (stairs or equivalent steepness) |
| **OTHER USERS** | Who shares the trail with you, the pedestrian. This might be bicycles and/or horses. Although they are not noted, expect to share paved trails with skaters. None of these walks allow motorized vehicles (with the exception of park maintenance vehicles). |
| **DOGS** | Three possibilities: Leash and scoop, Not allowed, or Off-leash. (Designated "off-leash" areas may or may not include the trail.) |
| **CONNECTING TRAILS** | Trails that intersect the walk |
| **PARK AMENITIES** | Restrooms (including freestanding facilities), interpretive walks, picnic tables, playgrounds, playing fields, etc. (Refer to maps and driving directions for parking information.) |
| **DISABLED ACCESS** | Americans with Disabilities Act (ADA) access, for the trail and/or park. (Call the listed office for details: their definition of "accessible" and yours may differ.) |
| **SETTING ICONS** | These icons appear before each walk description. A walk may have more than one different setting characterized by the following icons: |

FOREST . . . . . . . . . .    RIVER/STREAM . . . . . . .

LAKESHORE . . . . . . .    MEADOW/FARMLAND . .

NATURE PRESERVE . . .    WETLAND/POND . . . . .

BEACH/SALT MARSH/
ESTUARY . . . . . . . . . .

Walk descriptions may include ecological, historical, and scenic information. They are not intended to be step-by-step trail guides; the goal is to entice and invite you to discover the pleasure of the walk on your own.

**GETTING THERE:** Driving directions from major interstates are included for each walk, under the assumption that drivers will also have a good road map with them in the car. Driving directions in this book are basic and brief; they will be of little help if you take a wrong turn. For bus connections, call your local transit authority. All parks listed are open daylight hours only unless otherwise noted.

**ADDRESS AND CONTACT:** The address listed is the street location of the park or trailhead, not a mailing address. You may be able to use this address for an Internet map search. Not all parks or trailheads have addresses. Contact numbers may be for the individual park's office or a central parks department office.

Each walk is accompanied by a map, which is intended to give a general sense of the layout of the park and trail. Do not rely on these to locate yourself in complex parks such as Cougar Mountain, Lord Hill, Paradise Valley, Soaring Eagle, and others with extensive trail systems or many unofficial trails. Keep in mind that parks departments discourage use of these unofficial paths due to erosion and potential hazards.

All maps are oriented with north as "up" and are not drawn to scale (refer to the listed trail length to gauge the size of the park). The difference between paved, gravel, and natural surface trails is not indicated on the maps due to constantly changing conditions.

## Map Legend

| | | | |
|---|---|---|---|
| ═══ | ROAD | – – | TRAIL |
| ▰▰▰ | DOCK/BOAT LAUNCH | Ⓟ | PARKING |
| ℞ | RESTROOM | ⌂ | PICNIC AREA |
| ∧ | CAMPSITES | +++ | RAILWAY |
| ▬•••▬ | PARK BOUNDARY | ⊟ | BRIDGE |
| ⬆ | FOREST | | WATER (RIVER, LAKE, SOUND, WETLAND/MARSH) |

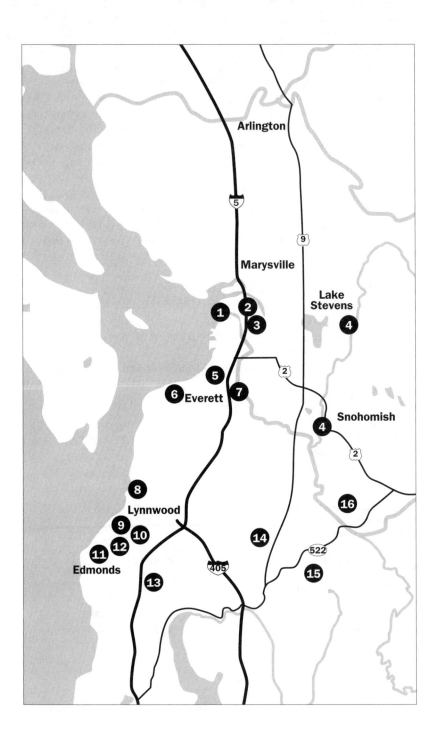

# IN AND AROUND **EVERETT**

# JETTY ISLAND

**1.5 miles northwest of downtown Everett**

*Bird-watch along Port Gardner Bay's salt marshes, beaches, and sand dunes.*

| | |
|---|---|
| **TRAIL** | 2–4 miles, depending on tide; natural surface |
| **OTHER USERS** | Pedestrians only; no pets |
| **DOGS** | Not allowed |
| **STEEPNESS** | Level |
| **CONNECTING TRAILS** | None |
| **PARK AMENITIES** | Restrooms, boating, picnic tables<br>Summer only: classes, guided interpretive walks, free ferry mid-July to Labor Day |
| **DISABLED ACCESS** | None |

Built almost a hundred years ago at the mouth of the Snohomish River to create a freshwater harbor in Puget Sound, this man-made island has succeeded in ways its creators probably never imagined. A southerly breeze cools the western shore, carrying the scent of seaweed and the barks of California sea lions. Sand-

pipers sprint on the mudflats; ospreys soar above. Around the Scotch broom, swallows dart and dive for their insect meals. Near the shore, crabs scurry for shelter under rocks. In the salt marsh, salt crystals glisten on the stems of the pickleweed.

Measuring 2 miles long and a half mile wide, this wildlife preserve just three minutes from the Everett marina is the city's summer pride. For seven or eight weeks each summer, Wednesday through Sunday, the 80-passenger ferry run by the Mosquito Fleet fills to capacity to take families, walkers, and bird lovers across the Snohomish River channel to the dock on Jetty Island. From there they disperse, though the majority cluster around the picnic tables on the western shore. To find solitude, walk either north or south for three or four minutes. You'll think you're on a deserted island—just you, the terns, herons, and swallows—and the shimmering, slippery, pungent sea lettuce that lines the beach.

At low tide you can circumnavigate the island on the mudflats, though you have to be willing to get your feet squishy with mud. On the western side, a berm built by the Army Corps of Engineers has created a new salt marsh. Here you are likely to see many of the more than 40 species of birds that visit or nest on the island. In early summer, expect to be dive-bombed by protective mother gulls warning you away from their nests.

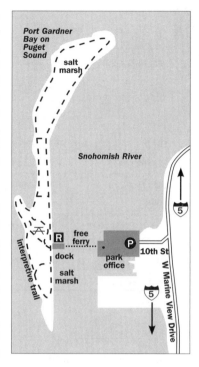

**GETTING THERE:** From I-5 in Everett, southbound, take exit 194 (SR 2, Wenatchee, Everett Ave). Turn right (west) on Everett Ave and go over the hill through town to W Marine View Drive. Turn right (north) and go 1.75 miles. Turn left (west) at 10th St into 10th St Boat Launch and Marine Park.

### What Is That?

Find out by joining a naturalist-led walk. Most are free. Call your city or county parks department for information. Parks also offer classes in outdoor-related topics such as gardening, birding, geology, animal care, naturalist studies, and science. Fees may apply.

From I-5 in Everett, northbound, take exit 192 (Broadway). Go north on Broadway about 1.9 miles and turn left (west) on Everett Ave. Go 0.6 miles. Turn right (north) on W Marine View Drive. Go 1.5 miles, and then proceed as above. Parking fee is $3 on Friday and weekends.

**ADDRESS:** 10th Street Boat Launch and Marine Park, Everett
**CONTACT:** Everett Parks (425) 257-8300; www.everettwa.org/parks

# LANGUS RIVERFRONT PARK

**6 miles east of downtown Everett**

*Cascades views and bird-watching abound along the Snohomish River and Union Slough.*

| | |
|---|---|
| **TRAIL** | 3.6-mile loop; gravel, paved |
| **STEEPNESS** | Level |
| **OTHER USERS** | Bicycles |
| **DOGS** | Leash and scoop |
| **CONNECTING TRAILS** | Spencer Island (Walk #3; no bicycles or pets allowed) |
| **PARK AMENITIES** | Restrooms, picnic tables |
| **DISABLED ACCESS** | Trail, restrooms, picnic area |

Old barges docked forever against the bank of the smooth-flowing Snohomish River recall days gone by when rivers and lakes, not roads, united the Northwest. Well-tended lawns and a paved walkway seem so genteel compared to the stalwart pilings of old docks. Great blue herons and belted kingfishers feed from the river—one on foot, the other on the wing—and migrating waterfowl rest in the reeds along the shore.

Enjoy Langus Riverfront Park with a civilized promenade along the riverfront, a hefty mile out and back, from the northern end—or with a 3-mile

triangular loop walk along the Snohomish River and Union Slough. For the longer loop, continue south after the pavement ends, passing under the imposing I-5 freeway bridge. The first stretch follows the river, where fishing boats, tugs, tourist boats, and an occasional log boom float by. At the southernmost spot, Picnic Point, views open to

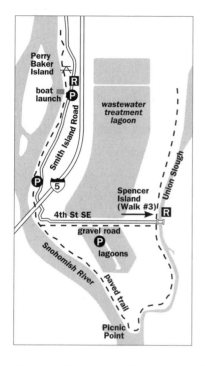

grasslands, the Cascades, and, on clear days, Mount Rainier.

From Picnic Point the trail heads north along Union Slough, where a variety of deciduous trees line the pathway on a dike above the tidal trough. Across the water (if it's high tide) or mud (if it's low tide) lie the marshes, ponds, and dikes of Spencer Island, a nature preserve (Walk #3). Jackknife Bridge ahead spans Union Slough, serving as an entrance to the preserve. From the bridge, you can retrace your route to stay on the paved trail, or complete the loop by walking west on the gravel maintenance road (4th Street SE) back to the river. Along the road you walk between waste treatment ponds, where waterfowl abound. With binoculars you can see a palette of colors: the distinct black-and-white plumage of the hooded merganser, the orange bill of the scoter, or the blue bill of the male ruddy duck in late spring.

**GETTING THERE:** From I-5 north of Everett, southbound, take exit 198 (SR 529 south, N Broadway). Go south on N Broadway (SR 529) over two bridges. Look for a brown sign for Langus Riverfront Park, and turn right onto the frontage road. Follow the road left under SR 529 and at another sign for the park turn right. Stay to the right for Smith Island Road, which leads to the park.

From I-5 in Everett, northbound, take exit 195 (Port of Everett, Marine View Drive). Turn left, then merge to the right onto SR 529 north (Pacific Hwy). After crossing the Snohomish River, take the first road to the right (signposted Smith Island Road) and follow it (staying right) to the park.

**ADDRESS:** 400 Smith Road, Everett

**CONTACT:** City of Everett (425) 257-8300; www.everettwa.org/parks

**3**

# SPENCER ISLAND

**6.5 miles east of downtown Everett**

*Union and Steamboat Sloughs surround this bird-watchers'
wetland paradise.*

| | |
|---|---|
| **TRAIL** | 3.5-mile loops, 0.5 mile cross-trail; natural surface |
| **STEEPNESS** | Level |
| **OTHER USERS** | Pedestrians only; hunters; no pets |
| **DOGS** | Not allowed |
| **CONNECTING TRAILS** | Langus Riverfront Park (Walk #2) |
| **PARK AMENITIES** | Restrooms, bike rack near footbridge |
| **DISABLED ACCESS** | None |

Spencer Island is a birder's
paradise, and a frequent destination for Audubon Society
field trips. On bright days the
ruddy ducks and American
wigeons appear to be floating
on top of their upside-down
twins as they waft across the
mirrorlike surface of the pond.
Northern harriers and red-
tailed hawks hunt overhead.
In the still waters by the marsh

grasses, you might see river otters flipping and diving for fish. Nesting boxes
for wood ducks and swallows dot numerous islets in the marsh, and on the
southern loop bat boxes make welcome homes for these flying mammals.

But even without binoculars and a passion for birds, the miles of trail
along dikes above the estuary are inviting for their hours of strolling and
scenery-gazing. After entering the preserve over Jackknife Bridge, turn either
north or south on the wide, wood chip–lined paths. To the east, Mount
Pilchuck dominates the skyline, and to the north, Mount Baker stands clear
and proud.

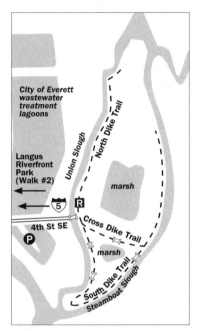

City of Everett
wastewater
treatment
lagoons

Langus
Riverfront
Park
(Walk #2)

Union Slough

North Dike Trail

marsh

4th St SE

Cross Dike Trail

marsh

South Dike Trail

Steamboat Slough

Early settlers created dikes and sloughs to remove the tidal influx of salt water and to protect their farmlands. When Washington State, Snohomish County, and the City of Everett joined forces in the early 1990s to return this area to its natural state, they breached the dike wall with culverts and bridges. Now the wetland is an estuary again, responding to the ebb and flow of the tides from Puget Sound. This combination of salt water and fresh water from the Snohomish River provides a habitat for hundreds of species of birds and mammals.

From mid-October to mid-January the northern trails (administered by the state Department of Fish and Wildlife) are open to hunting, so most walkers go south during those months. Interpretive signs give both history and natural history information. Benches and viewing platforms add a human touch to this otherwise wild and beautiful estuary.

**GETTING THERE:** From I-5 north of Everett, southbound, take exit 198 (SR 529 south, N Broadway). Go south on N Broadway (SR 529) and turn right onto the frontage road. Follow the road left under SR 529, and at another sign for Spencer Island turn right. Stay to the right for Smith Island Road, which leads to Langus Riverfront Park. Park at the southern end of Langus (near the I-5 overpass) or turn left on 4th St SE (gravel road) and go a few hundred yards to a small parking lot on the right. Continue walking east on 4th St SE to the Jackknife Bridge, which leads to Spencer Island.

From I-5 in Everett, northbound, take exit 195 (Port of Everett, Marine View Drive). Turn left, then merge to the right onto SR 529 north (Pacific Hwy). After crossing the Snohomish River, take the first road to the right (signposted Smith Island Road) and follow it (staying right) through Langus Riverfront Park. Proceed as above.

**ADDRESS:** East end of Fourth Street SE, Everett

**CONTACT:** Snohomish County Parks (425) 388-6616; www1.co.snohomish .wa.us/departments/parks

# 4 CENTENNIAL TRAIL

**Lake Stevens (8 miles northeast of Everett) through Machias (8 miles east of Everett) to Snohomish (8 miles southeast of Everett)**

*Walk along the Pilchuck River for Cascades views in pastoral Snohomish Valley.*

| | |
|---|---|
| **TRAIL** | 17.5 miles one way; paved rails-to-trails conversion |
| **STEEPNESS** | Level |
| **OTHER USERS** | Bicycles; horses on separate equestrian trail |
| **DOGS** | Leash and scoop |
| **CONNECTING TRAILS** | None |
| **PARK AMENITIES** | Restrooms, picnic tables |
| **DISABLED ACCESS** | Trail access, restrooms at Pilchuck trailhead on Machias Road and in Machias |

Just minutes east of the I-5 corridor lies the fertile Snohomish Valley with its pastures, dairy farms, and picturesque barns. You've probably driven through it countless times en route to the Cascades or Eastern Washington. Now, the Centennial Trail lets you slow the pace and walk this valley, breathing the clear, fresh air (and, yes, sometimes the aroma of fertilizer). Views are expansive from the dairy-farm pastures to the peaks of the Cascades.

Like other paved, converted railroad grades, this trail is great for distance walking, stroller pushing, or bicycling. There are four trailheads, so you can choose to walk either north or south.

From historic downtown Snohomish, the trail parallels Maple Street and the Pilchuck River. Soon, vistas open to embrace the pastures and farms. In the 1880s settlers cleared trees and drained the swampy land to leave rich, fertile soil. Now, as then, it is prime dairy land. Cows and horses graze in the lush fields.

In the small town of Machias, a replica of the old railroad station now serves as a rest area. Near the trail's northern end, on the outskirts of Lake Stevens, you'll cross several country roads and driveways, so be sure to keep kids in close check.

**GETTING THERE:** To reach the southern end (Snohomish): From I-5 in Everett, north- or southbound, take exit 194 (US 2 east, Wenatchee, Everett Ave). Head east on US 2, bearing right (south) at the end of the trestle, then go about 2.5 miles to SR 9. Head south on SR 9 to the Snohomish/Riverview Road/2nd St exit. Turn left on 2nd St. Go about 12 blocks and turn left (north) on Maple Ave. Park at the junction of Maple Ave and Pine Ave. More parking is found 1.5 miles north on Maple Ave (it becomes S Machias Road) at the Pilchuck trailhead, just south of the US 2 underpass.

To reach the northern end (Lake Stevens): From I-5 in Everett, north- or southbound, take exit 194 (US 2, Wenatchee, Everett Ave). Head east on US 2, bearing left (north) at the end of the trestle onto SR 204. Go north 2.3 miles, following signs to Lake Stevens. Turn left (north) on SR 9, then right (east) on Lundeen Park Way. Continue 0.4 miles to a roundabout. Continue straight. Go 0.5 miles to the next roundabout and take the 2nd exit onto 20th Street NE/Lake View Drive. Go 1.8 miles to parking.

**ADDRESS: SNOHOMISH TRAILHEAD:** 1103 Maple Avenue, Snohomish
**PILCHUCK TRAILHEAD:** 5801 S Machias Road, Snohomish
**MACHIAS TRAILHEAD:** 1624 Virginia Street, Machias
**LAKE STEVENS TRAILHEAD:** 13205 20th Street NE, Lake Stevens
For other trailheads, refer to the website.
**CONTACT:** Snohomish County Parks (425) 388-6600; www1.co.snohomish
.wa.us/departments/parks

# HOWARTH PARK

**2 miles southwest of downtown Everett**

*A forested ravine leads to beaches, views, and an off-leash area on Possession Sound.*

| | |
|---|---|
| **TRAIL** | 0.5 mile; boardwalk, natural surface |
| **STEEPNESS** | Level to steep |
| **OTHER USERS** | Pedestrians only |
| **DOGS** | Leash and scoop on trails; designated off-leash area on beach |
| **CONNECTING TRAILS** | None |
| **PARK AMENITIES** | Restrooms, bridge over railroad tracks, picnic/BBQ area, playground, tennis courts |
| **DISABLED ACCESS** | Restrooms |

Beachcomb, swim, or cavort with your dog—free of its leash!—while harbor seals frolic in the waters of Possession Sound and drift logs entice children to clamber. Howarth Park offers one of the few beach access trails in the City of Everett. Nestled almost secretly behind suburban lawns and homes, this community park welcomes forest walkers, beach explorers, or just casual strollers.

Near the tennis courts at the western end of the park you'll find restrooms, picnic areas, and a playground. Dropping steeply from the lawn to the ravine below, a staircase trail ends at a boardwalk, which meanders above a stream. Following this trail does not lead to the beach, however, but to a T-junction with a narrow, steep trail bordering the railroad tracks. In dry weather, you can ascend this natural-surface path back to the playground and parking, or return along the ravine walk. Unauthorized trails lead onto the railroad tracks, but crossing is illegal and, given the frequent passage of trains, extremely dangerous.

To reach the beach safely, either walk or drive to the eastern end of the park. From the eastern parking area you'll find a trail that follows Pigeon Creek in a young scrub forest, and another that traverses a small wetland, then climbs to a pedestrian overpass above the railroad tracks. This is a favorite place to stand when the train whistle shrills and the locomotive and

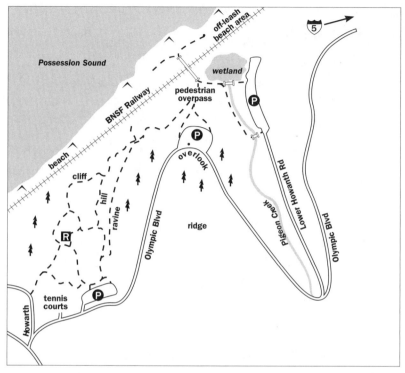

cars rumble beneath you. At the beach end is a tower and lookout with panoramic views of Port Gardner Bay and the navy ships. Just north of the tower is the off-leash area where dogs are free to romp in the sand and saltwater, or play tag with their human companions among the drift logs and boulders. A short walk south takes you to the public beach.

**GETTING THERE:** From I-5 in Everett, southbound, take exit 192 (Broadway, Naval Station). Turn right on 41st St and continue through two traffic lights. The road turns up a hillside and becomes Mukilteo Blvd. Go west on Mukilteo Blvd past the traffic light at Dogwood Drive and around the first curve of the road after the intersection. Just after the intersection with Seahurst Ave, enter the park by turning right on Olympic Blvd.

From I-5 south of Everett, northbound, take exit 192 (41st St). Turn left onto 41st St and continue as above.

**ADDRESS:** 1127 Olympic Boulevard, Everett

**CONTACT:** City of Everett (425) 257-8300; www.everettwa.org/parks

# FOREST PARK

1 mile south of downtown Everett

*Explore playgrounds, forest, and a petting farm in this large city park.*

| TRAIL | 1.5 miles; natural surface, paved utility road |
|---|---|
| STEEPNESS | Moderate to steep |
| OTHER USERS | Pedestrians only |
| DOGS | Leash and scoop |
| CONNECTING TRAILS | None |
| PARK AMENITIES | Restrooms, animal farm, picnic shelters, playground, pool, sports fields, water playground |
| DISABLED ACCESS | Restrooms, animal farm, picnic shelters, pool |

When you've hauled the kids off the massive playground (which is fully fenced to keep them from wandering into the steep forest), look for the wooden gate and trailhead between Cedar House and the picnic shelter. Here, in the largest of Everett's city parks, forest tranquility beckons to a trail that heads north along a ridge above a ravine. Wide, wood-chipped paths lined with logs welcome you into the bigleaf maple and cedar forest high on a ridge. Look for old snags decorated with fungus and old-growth stumps with springboard notches still visible, like eyes peering out from the sometimes-charred wood. You can stroll the ridge awhile, then rest on a bench overlooking the fern-filled ravine and out to the sunny baseball diamond beyond. Though the forest looks wild, an occasional rhododendron bush and a proliferation of English ivy tell of a more cultivated past when the park housed a full-fledged zoo. The trail begins just north of the playground.

If you want heart-pumping exercise, head east on the staircase trails that lead down to the East Entrance Road and back up again. For a more gentle stroll, follow the contoured trails that wind through open forest to the old utility road to the west. Next to a lawn, the road, lined with rock walls—and, in summer, the bright colors of foxglove in bloom—makes its way toward Mukilteo Boulevard. You can climb back to the main park grounds through the forest or on the ridges on either side of the ravine. If you choose the ridge west of the utility road, you'll find fern- and cedar-filled forest, with dozens of

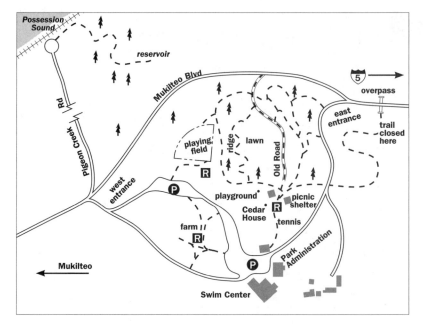

old-growth stumps. Just below the playground fence are open cedar groves, perfect for warm-weather picnics. Be sure to pack out all that you pack in, as there are no trash receptacles on the trails.

Another forest walk begins at the end of Pigeon Creek Road (just across Mukilteo Boulevard from the west entrance). Drive about 0.5 mile north to the parking lot by the railroad tracks. There is no beach access, and crossing the tracks is prohibited. The wooded trail that begins here climbs the hill toward a reservoir in about 0.5 mile. Eagles nest high in the branches of the 80-year-old fir trees.

For those with kids, don't miss the animal farm and a chance to pet, and maybe feed, the resident rabbits, ducks, pigs, goats, ponies, and llamas. The farm is open late spring through September.

**GETTING THERE:** From I-5 in Everett, southbound, take exit 192 (41st St). Turn left (east) onto 41st St. Turn right immediately onto S 3rd Ave and continue about 1 mile. This road becomes Junction Ave, which becomes S 2nd Ave. Turn left (east) onto Lenora St/Lowell Snohomish River Road. The entrance to the park is on the left at the top of the curves.

From I-5 south of Everett, northbound, take exit 192 (41st St). Turn right (east) onto 41st St. Turn right again immediately onto S 3rd Ave and continue as above.

**ADDRESS:** 802 Mukilteo Boulevard, Everett

**CONTACT:** City of Everett (425) 257-8300; www.everettwa.org/parks

# 7

# LOWELL RIVERFRONT TRAIL

**2.5 miles southeast of downtown Everett**

*Snohomish River wetlands and meadows yield views of birds and the Cascades.*

| | |
|---|---|
| **TRAIL** | 1.75 miles one way; paved |
| **STEEPNESS** | Level |
| **OTHER USERS** | Bicycles |
| **DOGS** | Leash and scoop |
| **CONNECTING TRAILS** | None |
| **PARK AMENITIES** | Restrooms, picnic tables, viewpoint |
| **DISABLED ACCESS** | Trail, restrooms |

This strip of manicured trail on the banks of the Snohomish River offers intimate river-edge walking and dramatic views of the Cascades. A late-afternoon visit reveals the Cascades set in bright relief to the east and a sheen of slate blue and mauve on the glassy Snohomish River. In contrast to the manicured park, the river is lined with old tumbledown shacks and craggy remains of piers. Pilings bound by cable still stand, resisting the unrelenting push of the water.

A bustling private industrial site for the past century, this area is now being restored to its natural state of meadow and wetland. From the parking lot, head either north or south. The walk to the south is more sylvan, with cottonwoods, alders, and blackberry thickets by the river. Across the water a barn, now softened by weathering, winds, and climbing vines, squats on its old foundation. It was here that E. D. Smith ran a sawmill and a logging camp, with a store, a post office, and

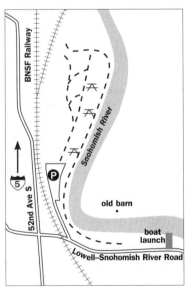

a blacksmith shop, from the 1860s to the 1880s. For decades, the river was active with boats and log barges making their way to the Everett mills.

If you walk north from the parking lot you'll find a more parklike setting, with lawns, benches, and picnic tables. When the trail turns west into a sandy meadow, you can loop back to the parking lot on one of the myriad access roads or return on the pavement by the river's edge, completing a 3-mile walk.

**GETTING THERE:** From I-5 in Everett, southbound, take exit 192 (41st St, Evergreen Way). Turn left (east) on 41st St over the freeway. Go right (south) on Junction Ave. Go 6 or 7 blocks. Bear left on 47th St SE, then right onto S 2nd Ave. At the 4-way stop at Lenora, turn left on Lowell–Snohomish River Road. The park is on the left just past the railroad tracks.

From I-5 in Everett, northbound, take exit 192 (Broadway, Naval Station) on the left side of the freeway. Stay in the right-hand lane. Go under two overpasses. Take the cloverleaf to the right to 41st St. (This merges with the southbound exit from I-5 at 41st St.) At the stop sign on 41st St, turn left (east). Stay in the right-hand lane to go over the freeway. Turn right immediately on Junction Ave and proceed as above.

**ADDRESS:** 3505 Lowell–Snohomish River Road (off S 2nd Avenue)

**CONTACT:** City of Everett (425) 257-8300; www.everettwa.org/parks

# 8  MEADOWDALE BEACH PARK

**Lynnwood, 14.5 miles southwest of Everett**

*Follow Lund's Gulch Creek through forest to reach a Puget Sound beach.*

| | |
|---|---|
| **TRAIL** | 2.5-mile round trip; natural surface, paved (in lower meadow) |
| **STEEPNESS** | Moderate to steep |
| **OTHER USERS** | Bicycles |
| **DOGS** | Leash and scoop |
| **CONNECTING TRAILS** | None |
| **PARK AMENITIES** | Restrooms, picnic tables |
| **DISABLED ACCESS** | Paved trail, restrooms, picnic area; call (206) 339-1208 to request disabled parking pass to beach and picnic area |

A gracefully curved descent on a wide, graveled trail brings you into the aromatic forest. By keeping your eyes low on the huge bases of the Douglas fir and cedar stumps, you can envision these giants as they were a hundred years ago before they were cut for the mills. Robins and rufous-sided towhees hop slowly from the trail.

This upland-to-beach park was created with walkers in mind. Although the beach is car-accessible to those who need to drive, the layout forces all others to take the 1.25-mile walk from the upper parking lot to the beach. Allow walking time (about 30 minutes) to return to the parking lot from the beach in daylight.

Small mileposts help you keep track of the distance traveled. At 0.5 mile a washout shows the power of water and the need to preserve soil-retaining plants on steep hillsides. Beside the trail, Lund's Gulch Creek cuts a swath in the forest and whispers its wet sounds on its way to

> **Bring a Bucket and Shovel**
> Many Puget Sound beaches are open for clamming. Some are seasonally closed; others are permanently closed due to pollution or natural marine toxins. For information, call the individual park or the Washington State Marine Biotoxin Hotline, (800) 562-5632.

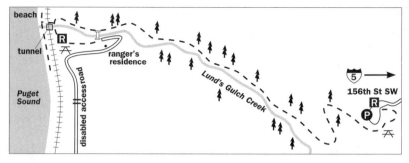

Puget Sound. At the footbridge, you can choose to cross to the picnic area, lawns, and lower parking lot or continue straight, still in the woods, to arrive at the tunnel to the beach. You may hear a train whistle blow, then watch a long freight chug past on the tracks that separate the forest from the sand.

To reach the water, pass beneath the tracks through the echo-filled tunnel. After the narrow ravine, the view feels exceptionally expansive. The snowy, hazy forms of the Olympics rise in the west, ferries from Mukilteo and Edmonds ply the Sound, and at low tide the beach beckons you to explore its rippled sand.

**GETTING THERE:** From I-5 south of Everett, north- or southbound, take exit 183 (164th St SW). Turn west (right if southbound, left if northbound) on 164th St SW and go 1.7 miles to the intersection of 168th St SW and SR 99. Cross SR 99 and continue west. Go 2 blocks and turn right on 52nd Ave W. Turn left on 160th St SW, then right onto 56th Ave W. Turn left onto 156th

St SW to the park entrance at the end of the road.

**ADDRESS:** 6026 156th Street SW, Edmonds; disabled access with card gate: 15433 75th Place W, Edmonds

**CONTACT:** Snohomish County Parks (425) 388-6600; www.1co.snohomish.wa.us /departments/parks

# LYNNDALE PARK

Lynnwood, 15 miles southwest of Everett

*A quiet, second-growth forest invites year-round exploration.*

| | |
|---|---|
| **TRAIL** | 1.5 miles total; natural surface, paved |
| **STEEPNESS** | Level to steep |
| **OTHER USERS** | Bicycles on paved trails |
| **DOGS** | Leash and scoop |
| **CONNECTING TRAILS** | None |
| **PARK AMENITIES** | Restrooms, amphitheater, basketball courts, ball fields, picnic shelter, playground, tennis courts, skate park |
| **DISABLED ACCESS** | Paved trail, restrooms, picnic shelter |

Like many other community parks, this one hides its best features behind sports courts and picnic shelters. Very accessible to wheelchairs, strollers, and little feet in skates, a half mile of paved trails lead from the easternmost parking lot west past an amphitheater, and from there another mile of trail winds through the quiet, second-growth forest. Here bigleaf maples form a cool canopy in summer or create graceful frames around a pale winter sky. Autumn paints the forest orange, red, yellow, and brown.

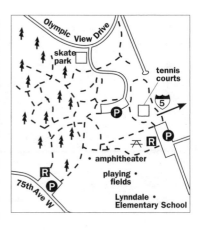

The paved trail crosses wide gravel trails and narrow natural trails, all hinting at the possibilities for exploration. Venture onto the natural trails and find the ravine (an old gravel pit, long ago reclaimed by nature) and the new wooden steps, the latter courtesy of the local Boy Scouts. The park boundaries are clear, so wander at will.

**GETTING THERE:** From I-5 south of Everett, southbound, take exit 181 (SR 524, Lynnwood). Turn right (west) on 196th St SW/SR 524. Go west about

2.2 miles and turn right (north) on 68th Ave W at the light. Turn left on 189th Pl SW to reach the easternmost parking lot. A northern parking lot is reached via Olympic View Drive; a southern parking lot is reached via 75th Ave W.

From I-5 south of Everett, northbound, take exit 181 (SR 524, Lynnwood, 44th Ave W). Turn left (north) on 44th Ave W and go under the freeway. Go 2 blocks and turn left onto 196th St SW/SR 524. Go west about 2.5 miles and turn right (north) on 68th Ave W at the light. Proceed as above.

**ADDRESS:** 18927 72nd Avenue W, Lynnwood

**CONTACT:** Lynnwood Parks (425) 771-4030; www.ci.lynnwood.wa.us

# 10 SCRIBER LAKE PARK

Lynnwood, 15 miles southwest of Everett

*Observe birds and the work of beavers by wetlands and a peat bog.*

| | |
|---|---|
| **TRAIL** | 1.5-mile loop and spurs; natural surface, paved |
| **STEEPNESS** | Level |
| **OTHER USERS** | Bicycles, except on soft-surface trails, where they are discouraged |
| **DOGS** | Leash and scoop |
| **CONNECTING TRAILS** | Scriber Creek Trail to Interurban Trail |
| **PARK AMENITIES** | Restrooms, dock, interpretive signs, picnic tables |
| **DISABLED ACCESS** | Paved trail, restrooms |

This lush pocket of wetlands beauty is so central to downtown Lynnwood that it was proposed as the site of the Civic Center in the 1960s. Luckily, sanity prevailed, leaving this magical landscape of stream, lake, ponds, peat bogs, and wildlife undisturbed.

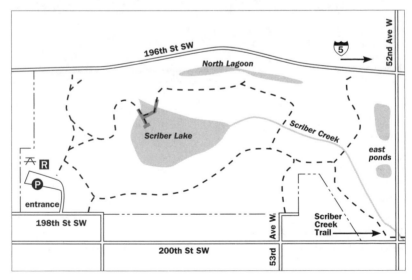

Follow a bark-chip trail across the top of 50-foot-deep peat, where yellow iris, Labrador tea, and cattails harbor salamanders, frogs, migrant waterfowl, and nesting birds. Interpretive signs explain the vital role of the marsh in purifying water and providing essential habitat to Northwest species. Side trails lead to homes or other small parks.

From the paved trail on the south side of the lake, follow the short, steep natural trail to the south to see a strange example of a western red cedar, with 19 trunks rising from a central core like a giant candelabra.

You can follow the stream trail clear to 200th Street SW, turn left, and, after a block of sidewalk, cross 52nd Avenue W/Cedar Valley Road. There, enter Scriber Creek Park with a pond and wetlands. A footpath, Scriber Creek Trail, leads east all the way to the Park and Ride near I-5 and the Interurban Trail.

When wet weather or winter storms flood the chipped path, stick to the paved walkway on the south side of the lake. Even in dry weather, though, the lake may rise above portions of the walkway. That's due to a family of beavers that has its own ideas about how to use the water in Scriber Lake.

**GETTING THERE:** From I-5 south of Everett, southbound, take exit 181A (SR 524, Lynnwood). Turn right (west) on 196th St SW. Go about 1.5 miles and turn left on Scriber Lake Road (across from 58th Ave W). Take the first left on 198th St SW. Park entrance is on the left.

From I-5 south of Everett, northbound, take exit 181A (SR 524, Lynnwood, 44th Ave W). Turn left (north) on 44th Ave W and go under the freeway. Go 2 blocks and turn left onto 196th St SW. Go about 1 mile and turn left on Scriber Lake Road (across from 58th Ave W). Proceed as above.

**ADDRESS:** 5322 198th Street SW, Lynnwood

**CONTACT:** Lynnwood Parks (425) 771-4030; www.ci.lynnwood.wa.us

### But They're Such Fun to Feed!

Most park authorities prohibit the feeding of waterfowl. Here's why: Human food is junk food to waterfowl, with none of the nutrients they need. Undernourished birds are more susceptible to disease. Feeding entices waterfowl to overwinter, which means more breeding pairs and an ever-increasing number of ducks and geese in our lakes. Waterfowl waste contains parasites that cause swimmer's itch, an allergic rash you wouldn't wish on anyone. Clean water means more swimming beaches. Waterfowl waste not only pollutes, it also fertilizes aquatic weeds that choke out other plants and animals. You can't swim or fish in a choked lake.

# YOST PARK

Edmonds, 17 miles southwest of Everett

*Explore interpretive trails through Shell Creek's forested ravine and wetlands.*

| | |
|---|---|
| **TRAIL** | About 1.5 mile total; natural surface, paved |
| **STEEPNESS** | Gentle to steep |
| **OTHER USERS** | Pedestrians only |
| **DOGS** | Leash and scoop |
| **CONNECTING TRAILS** | None |
| **PARK AMENITIES** | Playground, interpretive trail<br>Summer only: restrooms, picnic tables, pool |
| **DISABLED ACCESS** | Ridge Trail, restrooms, pool area |

Despite its well-trodden trails, this ravine of wooded wildness in a neat residential area of Edmonds may be unknown to folks who come for the more obvious pleasures: swimming and picnicking. Deep in the greenery below the pool, Shell Creek cuts a path through a second-growth red-alder forest.

To walk in this sylvan wonderland, leave the parking lot by the yellow maintenance gate and stroll Ridge Trail (the paved maintenance road) east along the rim of the gulch. From here you can look into the upper branches of alders, maples, and firs as though you were an owl perched nearby, surveying all your domain. There are several places where you can descend to the natural trail, letting the shouts of playing children fade above you. Listen instead for the high, tinkling warble of the winter wren or the *dee-dee-dee* of the black-capped chickadee.

Wooden bridges and walkways cross Shell Creek and its tributaries (some dry by late summer). The eroded banks of these streams show evidence of winter flooding. To prevent erosion, stay on the trails in this steep forest. Old stumps, long dead themselves, now provide life to saplings of cedar and red huckleberry. Numbered posts correspond to notes on an informal nature guide that is available at the pool or the city parks office at 700 Main Street.

A loop trail encircles the base of the ravine. Feeder trails branch off, some rising steeply up the hillside and then petering out, others emerging on Main Street to the north. To the west, the trail crosses bogs and ends at the remains

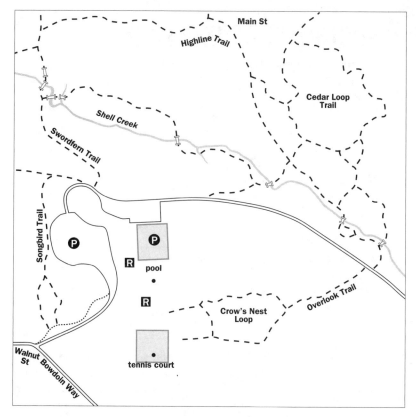

Main St

Highline Trail

Cedar Loop Trail

Shell Creek

Swordfern Trail

Songbird Trail

P

R

pool

R

Crow's Nest Loop

Overlook Trail

Walnut St

Bowdoin Way

tennis court

of an old concrete dam. Backtrack a short way to where the trail climbs again to rejoin the Ridge Trail near the parking area.

**GETTING THERE:** From I-5 south of Everett, southbound, take exit 181 (SR 524, Lynnwood). Turn right on 196th St SW. Go about 4.25 miles and turn left on 9th Ave S. Go 1 mile and turn left on Walnut St, which becomes Bowdoin Way. The park entrance is on the corner of Bowdoin Way and 96th Ave W.

From I-5 south of Everett, northbound, take exit 177 (SR 104, Edmonds). Turn left and go under the freeway. Go about 2.8 miles and turn right on 100th Ave W. Go about 1 mile and turn right on Walnut St (which becomes Bowdoin Way) and proceed as above.

**ADDRESS:** 9535 Bowdoin Way, Edmonds

**CONTACT:** Edmonds Parks (425) 771-0230; www.ci.edmonds.wa.us or www.ci.edmonds.wa.us/discovery_programs_website/yost_park.html

# SOUTHWEST COUNTY PARK

**Edmonds, 16 miles south of Everett**

*Inviting trails meander through the mature forest that borders Perrinville Creek as it makes its way to Brown's Bay on Puget Sound.*

| | |
|---|---|
| **TRAIL** | 1 mile total; natural surface |
| **STEEPNESS** | Gentle to steep |
| **OTHER USERS** | Bicycles |
| **DOGS** | Leash and scoop |
| **CONNECTING TRAILS** | None |
| **PARK AMENITIES** | Interpretive trail |
| **DISABLED ACCESS** | None |

Immerse yourself in the natural sounds of bickering squirrels and cheerful birdsong just minutes from the Edmonds/Kingston ferry and the I-5 corridor. This park, also known as Olympic View Park (because of its location, not for views!) is the largest tract of forest within Edmonds city limits and a haven for wildlife, and with a mile of trail, it is an inviting respite from the bustle of traffic and commerce. While touted to have two nature trails, at present only the walk to the south of Olympic View Drive is fully developed as an Interpretive Trail. For those with little time, or a desire for an easy, wide trail, the south side is where you'll find a mini-arboretum with trees bearing Latin and local names, benches for resting weary feet, and an easy gradient for walking.

Across the road, to the north, the park is less developed but entices with steeper hills and numerous less-defined neighborhood trails. Here you can wander amongst remnants of old-growth forest where five-foot-wide stumps now nurture young saplings, and small trails

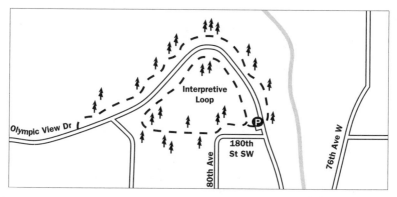

lead to children's forts and rope swings. For a good workout, head down the hill to the west and back up, but be careful with your footing!

Like most of the land bordering Puget Sound, this parcel was logged more than 100 years ago, and evidence of the old-growth forest remains today in the form springboard notches cut in the sides of huge stumps. These 120 acres were later donated to the University of Washington and, when the land was transferred to Snohomish County in 1971, it came with the condition that the parcel be forever managed as a passive woodland open space.

**GETTING THERE:** From I-5 south of Everett, southbound, take exit 181 (196th St SW SR 524) and keep right to merge on 196th St SW. Turn right at 76th Ave W. Turn left at Olympic View Drive. The parking lot is on your left after you pass 180th St SW.

From I-5 north of Seattle, northbound, take exit 179 (220th St SW). Turn left onto 220th St SW. Turn right at 76th Ave W then left onto Olympic View Drive. The parking lot is on your left after you pass 180th St SW.

**ADDRESS:** Olympic View Drive near the intersection with 180th Street SW, Edmonds 98026

**CONTACT:** Snohomish County Parks (425) 388-6600; www.snocoparks.org

# 13

# TERRACE CREEK PARK

**Mountlake Terrace, 16 miles south of Everett**

*A streamside trail wanders through a quiet forested ravine.*

| | |
|---|---|
| **TRAIL** | 1.5 miles one way, plus spurs; gravel, paved |
| **STEEPNESS** | Gentle to steep |
| **OTHER USERS** | Bicycles |
| **DOGS** | Leash and scoop |
| **CONNECTING TRAILS** | None |
| **PARK AMENITIES** | Restrooms, disc golf course, picnic shelter, playground, playing fields |
| **DISABLED ACCESS** | Paved trail, restrooms |

In this small neighborhood park, the trail gently ascends a peaceful strip of forest in a ravine below suburban Mountlake Terrace. Beginning as a paved walkway by the playground lawn, the trail soon changes to more rugged gravel and climbs moderately into the stately second-growth forest. Deep in the wooded ravine, the air is still and quiet. Winter wrens hop from bush to bush and woodpeckers tap old snags for their beetles and bugs.

Terrace Creek murmurs softly alongside the trail. Side trails lead to ridgetop homes invisible behind summer growth. The main trail ends when it reaches 221st Street SW, but additional walking can be had up the side trails and back down.

The strange, open, metal "trash containers" throughout the park are in fact holes for disc golf, a game of skill for those adept at tossing Frisbee-like discs long distances. Most of the disc course is along spur trails on the sides of the steep ravine. It's interesting to imagine the contortions necessary to retrieve stray discs from the thickets of blackberry and nettle.

**GETTING THERE:** From I-5 south of Everett, southbound, take exit 179 (220th St SW, Mountlake Terrace). Turn left (east) onto 220th St SW. Turn right (south) on 56th Ave W, then left (east) on 236th St SW. Go about 0.8 mile and turn left (north) on 48th Ave W. The park is on the left at the corner of 48th Ave W and 233rd St SW.

From I-5 south of Everett, northbound, take exit 178 (236th St SW, Mountlake Terrace). Turn right (east) on 236th St SW and proceed as above.

**ADDRESS:** 23200 48th Avenue W, Mountlake Terrace

**CONTACT:** Mountlake Terrace Parks (425) 776-9173; www.ci.mountlake -terrace.wa.us

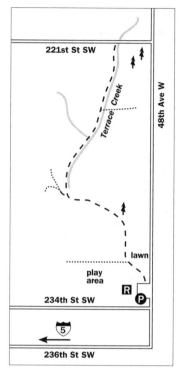

# NORTH CREEK PARK

**14**

**Mill Creek, 12 miles south of Everett**

*Interpretive boardwalks through wetlands of Mukilteo muck feature bird-watching and nature study.*

| | |
|---|---|
| **TRAIL** | About 1.5 miles round-trip; boardwalk |
| **STEEPNESS** | Level |
| **OTHER USERS** | Pedestrians only |
| **DOGS** | Leash and scoop |
| **CONNECTING TRAILS** | None |
| **PARK AMENITIES** | Restrooms, interpretive signs, picnic tables, viewpoint |
| **DISABLED ACCESS** | Restrooms |

Step from the pavement to a sturdy boardwalk rimmed by waving cattails. Overhead, red-tailed hawks may soar, and in the hardhack Virginia rails may cackle. This enclave of open wetlands is excellent for bird-watching or studying the wetland habitat. Although surrounded by suburban homes, the reed canarygrass and beaked sedge grow tall enough to give you a sense of solitude. But you are most definitely not alone: not only is the wetland home to dozens of species of birds, including great blue herons, song sparrows, common snipes, marsh wrens, and many species of ducks, but beaver dwell here as well.

This level, boardwalk trail meanders north for more than a half mile over what is technically called Mukilteo muck (really!), which refers to the waterlogged soil

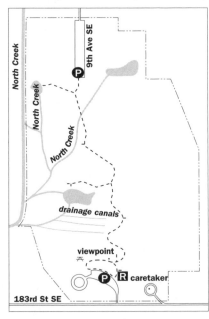

of the wetland. Interpretive signs and benches border the trail; two spurs lead west to ponds and viewpoints near the creek.

Nestled between rolling hills, this 80-acre park was once owned by the Bailey family of Mill Creek. When the county purchased it, they recognized its value as a natural storm-water retention area. Luckily, they also saw its value as a natural classroom and park.

**GETTING THERE:** From I-5, north- or southbound, take exit 183 (164th St SW). Turn east (left if southbound, right if northbound) on 164th and go 1.8 miles. Turn right (south) on the Bothell-Everett Hwy (SR 527) and go 1.3 miles. Turn right on 183rd St SE and go 0.2 mile. The park is on the right.

**ADDRESS:** 1011 183rd Street SE, Mill Creek

**CONTACT:** Snohomish County Parks (425) 744-0847; www1.co.snohomish .wa.us/departments/parks

# PARADISE VALLEY CONSERVATION AREA

**Woodinville, 20 miles southeast of Everett**

*In a fern-filled forest, follow miles of well-signed trails up to a ridge for Cascade views and back down into lush wetlands.*

| | |
|---|---|
| **TRAIL** | 13 miles; natural surface |
| **STEEPNESS** | Gentle to moderate |
| **OTHER USERS** | Bicycles, horses |
| **DOGS** | Leash and scoop |
| **CONNECTING TRAILS** | None |
| **PARK AMENITIES** | Restrooms, interpretive trail, map sign |
| **DISABLED ACCESS** | Restrooms |

Step back in time to a land bedecked in soft and rustling sword ferns, a land green with salal and Oregon grape undergrowth, shaded by young deciduous trees. Imagine small dinosaurs lurking about in the brush. Such is the luxuriant beauty of Paradise Valley Conservation Area. This almost 800-acre park was part of the 1887 homestead of the Lloyd family and remained in the family until its purchase by Snohomish County in 2000. Logging roads crisscrossed the land, and form the basis for some of today's trails through this almost 100-year-old secondary forest. The ridge trails remain green throughout the year under their canopy of Douglas fir and western hemlock, while the valleys' cottonwoods, willows, and dogwoods glow with color in autumn. The park's extensive wetlands are home to beaver, frogs, and salamanders, while the forest provides habitat for coyote, bear, and cougar. Just outside the current park boundary (but part of the next phase of development) Cottage Lake Creek abounds in resident trout and is graced by migrating salmon in spawning season.

Well-developed and maintained multiuse trails testify to the park's appeal to a variety of users, and its strong support in the hiking, mountain biking, and equestrian communities. There are miles of hiking-only trails, and with extensive signage, walkers can choose to avoid the popular (and sometimes

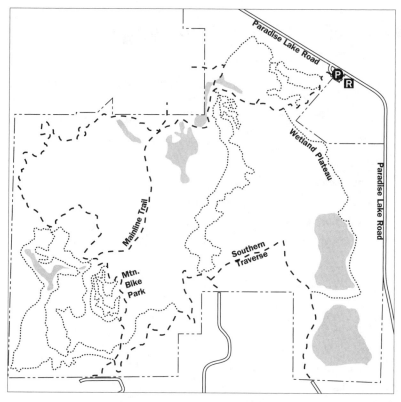

muddy) biking trails if they wish. The gentle Whispering Firs Interpretive Trail is a great "starter hike" for young families.

**GETTING THERE:** From I-5 south of Everett, southbound, take exit 182 merging onto I-405 S (Renton-Bellevue). Take exit 23A SR 522 east. Take the left fork merging onto SR 522 east. Turn right at Paradise Lake Road. Go 1.7 miles to the parking lot, which is just north of the Lloyd family farm on the west side of the road.

From I-405 north of Bellevue, northbound, take exit 23 (US2) toward Woodinville/Wenatchee then merge onto SR 522 east. Go 5 miles and turn right at Paradise Lake Road. The parking lot is 1.7 miles on the right, just north of the Lloyd family farm.

**ADDRESS:** 23120 Paradise Lake Road, Woodinville

**CONTACT:** Snohomish County Parks (425) 388-6616; www.snocoparks.org

# LORD HILL REGIONAL PARK

**15 miles southeast of Everett**

*Ponds, Snohomish River beaches, and mountain views highlight this multiaged forest/wetland habitat.*

| | |
|---|---|
| **TRAIL** | More than 6 miles total; gravel, natural surface |
| **STEEPNESS** | Gentle to moderate |
| **OTHER USERS** | Bicycles, horses |
| **DOGS** | Leash and scoop |
| **CONNECTING TRAILS** | None |
| **PARK AMENITIES** | Restrooms, interpretive signs, picnic areas, playground, viewpoints |
| **DISABLED ACCESS** | None |

In the middle of the Snohomish River valley, a single hill rises 600 feet above the floodplain, welcoming walkers and horses to its wild and shaded forest paths. A remnant of long-ago volcanic outcroppings, Lord Hill derives its name from homesteader Mitchell Lord, who dairy-farmed the flat land below the hill in the 1880s. By the 1930s the last old-growth timber had been cut, and in the 1980s the Department of Natural Resources cut patches of second-growth forest, producing today's multiaged forest/wetland habitat.

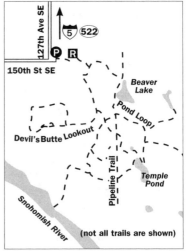

From the parking lot, head down the fragrant wood-chip path deep into the fir, hemlock, and maple forest. Where the trail levels, you'll be glad of sturdy puncheon bridges that span the miniature wetlands along the horse-trodden trail. Soon the wood chips and puncheons give way to a wide, graveled path leading to a T junction. To the left you reach one of the

park's nine ponds. Turning right takes you up a rise in dense forest from which several trails branch off.

The map at the parking lot can be confusing and until the signage and trails are completed, keep your internal compass working and ask equestrians the way out if you're not sure. With luck, you'll find one of the ponds with active beavers, or evidence of the resident deer or occasional bear or bobcat. A trek to the pipeline trail or Devil's Butte Lookout affords grand views of Mount Baker to the north and the Olympics to the west.

**GETTING THERE:** From I-5 in Everett, north- or southbound, take exit 194 (US 2, Wenatchee). Head east on US 2, bearing south at the end of the trestle. Go about 2.5 miles to SR 9 and turn right (south). At the Snohomish/Riverview Road/2nd St exit, turn left on 2nd St, then right onto Lincoln Ave S (which becomes the Old Snohomish–Monroe Hwy). Go 2.7 miles and turn right (south) on 127th Ave SE. Go 2 miles to 150th St SE. Turn left into the parking lot.

**ADDRESS:** 12921 150th Street SE, Snohomish

**CONTACT:** Snohomish County Parks (425) 388-6600; www1.co.snohomish .wa.us/departments/parks

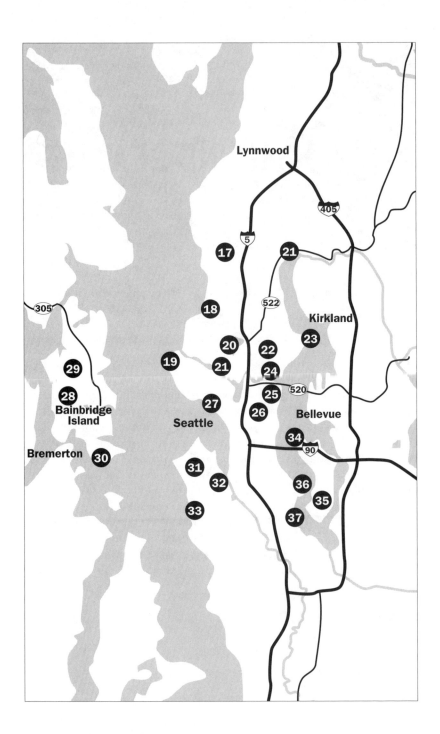

# IN AND AROUND **SEATTLE**

# 17 BOEING CREEK PARK

**Shoreline, 17 miles north of Seattle**

*A clear stream fills a hidden lake in this pristine urban forest, which is home to some unusual native flora and fauna.*

| TRAIL | 2–4 miles; natural surface |
| --- | --- |
| STEEPNESS | Moderate to steep |
| OTHER USERS | Pedestrians only |
| DOGS | Leash and scoop |
| CONNECTING TRAILS | Shoreview Park |
| PARK AMENITIES | Benches, picnic area |
| DISABLED ACCESS | None |

Follow serpentine trails deep into the ravine and then up onto the ridge of this green gem of forest in the heart of Shoreline. Watch for pileated woodpeckers on the snags and cedar waxwings in the meadows in summer. Rated one of Puget Sound's finest urban forests by the scientists at Earthcorps/Seattle Urban Nature Association, this park has a corps of volunteers who have put in many hours rejuvenating the trails and removing invasive plants from the waterway. The park is home to mountain beaver, raccoon, and red fox, as well as a number of unusual trees such as a 200-year-old western yew. Both eastern grey squirrels and Douglas squirrels frolic among the branches.

From the northern parking lot, you can walk around the detention pond, or dive straight into the forest. Going southwest (right), into the forest, the trail follows the streambed, crossing over a bridge of concrete steps placed there by a Girl Scout troop, and replaced each year when the stream floods. The sandy soil is especially vulnerable to erosion, so it's important to stay on the trail, and not be

### Trees Wanted—Dead or Alive

When you see a downed log or an old snag or stump, think of all the years the tree lived before it fell or burned. And look at all the life it supports now that it's dead. Old logs (usually Douglas fir) with young trees growing out of them are called "nurse logs." Stumps can also host the new growth of other plant species. As the late Californian biologist Tony Hacking used to say, "A tree is arguably more alive after it's dead."

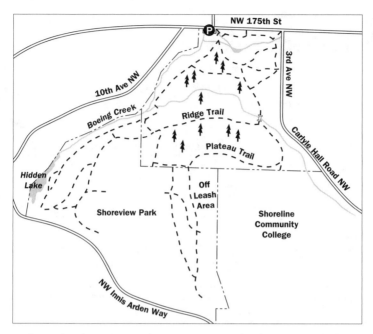

10th Ave NW

Boeing Creek

Ridge Trail

Plateau Trail

3rd Ave NW

Carlyle Hall Road NW

Hidden Lake

Off Leash Area

Shoreview Park

Shoreline Community College

NW Innis Arden Way

Seattle

tempted to take shortcuts up the steep ravine sides. Coming round a corner brings you to Hidden Lake with its glass-clear water and usually a family or two of ducks. If you're lucky you may see them dive and skim the algae off the bottom.

From Hidden Lake, the trail climbs through the forest to emerge in an open space of broom and berries, madrona, and cottonwood. Although the boundary isn't marked, you've now crossed into adjoining Shoreview Park, an active recreation area with tennis courts, sports fields, restrooms, playground, and ADA-accessible walkways. Above the tennis courts is a large off-leash area with a track for running your canine friend through his or her paces. Back to the north, into the forest again, the trail stays high on a traverse above the creek and then angles down to meet the streambed once again.

**GETTING THERE:** From I-5 north of Seattle, northbound, take exit 176 (NE 175th St). Turn left (west) on 175th St. Go 1 mile and turn left on Fremont Ave N. Take the 2nd right onto N 172nd St. Turn right on Dayton Ave N. Take the 1st left onto St Luke Pl N. Turn right on N 175th St. Parking lot is on the left.

From I-5 north of Seattle, southbound, take exit 176 (NE 175th St). Turn right (west) on NE 175th St and proceed as above.

**ADDRESS:** 601 NW 175th Street, Shoreline

**CONTACT:** City of Shoreline Parks (206) 801-2600; www.shorelinewa.gov

## 18

# CARKEEK PARK

**North Seattle, 8 miles north of downtown**

*Piper's Creek winds through forest to Puget Sound and Olympic Mountain views.*

| | |
|---|---|
| **TRAIL** | 6.1 miles; natural surface, paved |
| **STEEPNESS** | Gentle to moderate |
| **OTHER USERS** | Bicycles |
| **DOGS** | Leash and scoop |
| **CONNECTING TRAILS** | None |
| **PARK AMENITIES** | Restrooms, Environmental Learning Center, model airplane field, picnic shelters, playgrounds |
| **DISABLED ACCESS** | Salmon to Sound Trail, Wetland Trail, part of Piper's Creek Trail, restrooms |

Leave commercial Seattle behind as you wind down either a road or a footpath into this verdant ravine, where moss clings to the bigleaf maples and old logs straddle Piper's Creek. Like other ravines along Puget Sound, this one enchants with the steady downward flow of several small streams, the surprising gurgles of miniature waterfalls, and the profuse undergrowth of the forest. Salmon still spawn in this urban stream.

In spring the trailside is lush with salmonberry bushes, the fruit still yel-

### Safe Walks with Kids

Establish clear rules for on-the-trail-behavior: stay in sight, no running on forest paths, walk on the right side on multiuse trails, stand still to let horses pass, and always ask to pet horses or dogs. Beware of poison oak (usually signposted because it's rare), devil's club, and stinging nettle. Don't eat wild berries unless you're 100 percent sure what they are.

low and orange, awaiting the summer sun. Incredibly large stumps, too big to hug, provide nutrients for young salal bushes and Douglas firs. But all is not wild here. The old orchard remains as testimony to the early settlers, A.W. Piper and his wife, Minna, who supplied produce to downtown Seattle from this homestead in the late 1800s.

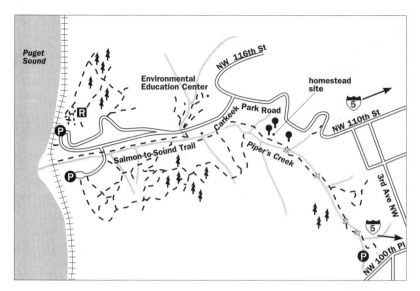

In the lower parking area, look for the footbridge leading over the train tracks to the watery world of Puget Sound. The sound of whinnying robins is replaced by the call of gulls, and your eyes are no longer drawn to branches overhead but farther away to the lofty Olympics in the west, or to your feet where the beach sand ripples under the retreating tide.

**GETTING THERE:** From I-5 in Seattle, north- or southbound, take exit 173 (Northgate Way, 1st Ave NE). If southbound, go right on N Northgate Way (which becomes N 105th St). If northbound, turn left on 1st Ave NE, then left on N Northgate Way and go under the freeway. Go west 8 or 9 blocks and turn right on Greenwood Ave N. Go 2 blocks and turn left on NW 110th St (which becomes Carkeek Park Road and winds down to the lower parking lot). Gates close at 9 pm.

To access the trail at the southeast end of the park, stay on N 105th St as it veers left to become Holman Road NW. Go 2 blocks and turn right on 3rd Ave NW. Go 1 block and turn left on NW 100th Pl to the small picnic/parking area.

**ADDRESS:** 950 NW Carkeek Park Road, Seattle

**CONTACT:** Seattle Parks (206) 684-4075; www.seattle.gov/parks

# DISCOVERY PARK

**Magnolia, 6 miles northwest of downtown Seattle**

*Visit meadows, wetlands, forest, and beaches for views, bird-watching, art, and a historical site.*

| | |
|---|---|
| **TRAIL** | 11.8 miles (including 0.5-mile Nature Trail and 2.8-mile Loop Trail) plus 2 miles of beach; gravel, natural surface, paved |
| **STEEPNESS** | Gentle to steep |
| **OTHER USERS** | Bicycles on paved roadways; pedestrians only on Loop Trail, Wolf Tree Nature Trail |
| **DOGS** | Leash and scoop; no dogs on Wolf Tree Nature Trail |
| **CONNECTING TRAILS** | None |
| **PARK AMENITIES** | Restrooms, brochures, classes, courts, interpretive center, picnic tables, playgrounds, maps; Daybreak Star Cultural Center (206) 285-4425 |
| **DISABLED ACCESS** | Restrooms, buildings; pass available to drive to beach |

Walk a windswept bluff by a grassy meadow, hunt ghost shrimp on the Puget Sound beach, or search the treetops for an eagle's nest. With 7 miles of trails to tread, Seattle's largest park (more than 500 acres) presents a variety of urban wilderness habitats to explore.

Start at the visitor center (east gate) for maps, then set off on the Loop Trail to the west. Crossing the flower-strewn meadow, watch for violet-green swallows in summer, or listen for the screech of hawks in winter. The old buildings are what remain of Fort Lawton, and they're worth exploring when you're in the mood for local history.

From the sandy bluff, listen for foghorns and the barks of sea lions, and watch the vessels ply the Sound far below. If the wind is from the south, head down the forested trail to South Beach (the goal being to stay upwind of the Metro sewage treatment plant on the headland). The trail is steep, with steps and observation platforms. Geology buffs can study the 300-foot cliffs for clues to our region's glaciated past.

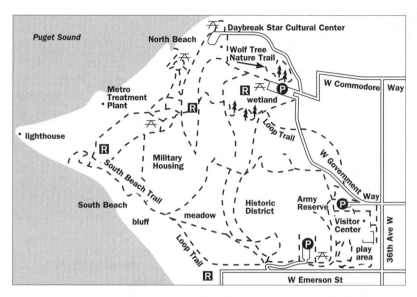

Back on the Loop Trail, stick to the larger, marked trails. Later, as you become familiar with the large park's layout, you can explore the shortcuts and side trails with confidence. The Loop Trail takes you past the south entrance's picnic area and playground before returning to the visitor center. At the north parking lot, leave time for the half-mile Wolf Tree Nature Trail, which features interpretive signs and peaceful walking.

**GETTING THERE:** From I-5 north of downtown Seattle, southbound, take exit 169 (NE 50th St, NE 45th St). Turn right on NE 50th St and go about 1.7 miles (past the zoo) until it merges (to the right) onto NW Market St; continue west. Turn left on 15th Ave NW, cross the Ballard Bridge and take the first exit on the right (Fisherman's Terminal/Emerson). Emerson merges to the right onto Gilman Ave W; continue west. At W Fort St, bear left; it becomes W Government Way and leads to the park's east entrance.

From I-5 in downtown Seattle, northbound, take the left-lane exit 167 (Mercer St, Seattle Center) and follow signs for Seattle Center. At the Pacific Science Center, turn right on Denny Way, which veers right to become Elliott Ave at the waterfront. From here go north 1.2 miles to the W Garfield St bridge to Magnolia, where Elliott Ave becomes 15th Ave W. Continue north on 15th Ave W 1 mile, then exit right for Dravus St and turn left (west). Immediately after crossing the railroad yards, turn right on 20th Ave W, which merges into Gilman Ave W. Proceed as above.

Organized groups and cars with children under 5 or people over 62 can drive to the beach on the park's access road; inquire at the visitor center.

**ADDRESS:** 3801 W Government Way, Seattle

**CONTACT:** Seattle Parks (206) 684-4075; www.seattle.gov/parks

# GREEN LAKE

### North Seattle, 4.5 miles north of downtown

*Lawns and landscaping border the paved trail that circumnavigates placid Green Lake.*

| | |
|---|---|
| **TRAIL** | 2.8-mile loop; paved |
| **STEEPNESS** | Level |
| **OTHER USERS** | Bicycles, in-line skaters (in designated lane) |
| **DOGS** | Leash and scoop |
| **CONNECTING TRAILS** | Woodland Park trails (south of lake) |
| **PARK AMENITIES** | Restrooms, beach, boating (nonmotorized), community center, concessions, fishing piers, playing fields, theater, wading pool |
| **DISABLED ACCESS** | Trail, restrooms, buildings, playground |

Circle this peaceful urban lake on a defined 2.8-mile paved trail and meet a cross section of Seattle life. Year-round, Green Lake attracts families, dog-walkers, joggers, bicyclists, the old and the young—all out to enjoy this strip of greenery in the 260-acre park. In spring, walk beneath flowering cherry and dogwood trees. In fall, look for the red berries on the hawthorns.

No matter the time of year, there is activity on the lake: in summer the paddleboaters, small sailboats, and wind surfers; in winter the wind kicking up whitecaps. Two nature-preserve islands provide shelter for many birds, but are inaccessible to walkers except through the magic of binoculars. Fall, winter, and spring are the best times to see the migratory birds such as buffleheads and white-fronted geese. Throughout the year, the omnipresent mallards and Canada geese forage in the reeds by the lake's edge, and red-winged blackbirds add a splash of color to the scene.

Because of the paved trail's popularity, traffic flow on it is regulated: walkers (including those with baby strollers) take the inside half and can travel either direction, while those on wheels must stick to a counterclockwise direction on the outer half. A new crushed-gravel trail parallel to the paved path allows joggers and walkers to circle without encountering bicyclists.

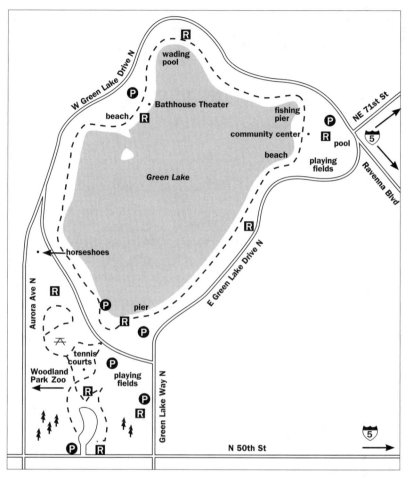

**GETTING THERE:** From I-5 in Seattle, north- or southbound, take exit 169 (NE 45th St, NE 50th St) and head west on NE 50th St. Go about 0.8 mile to Green Lake Way N, turn right, and park along the street by the lake or in lots farther north. Alternatively, continue west on NE 50th St to park near the tennis courts (on the right). This also allows easy access to the wooded trails and hillsides of Woodland Park.

**ADDRESS:** 7201 E Green Lake Drive N, Seattle

**CONTACT:** Seattle Parks (206) 684-4075; www.seattle.gov/parks

**21**

# BURKE-GILMAN TRAIL

Seattle (Ballard district, 4 miles north of downtown) to Kenmore, 12 miles north of Seattle

*Visit parks along Lakes Union and Washington via an old railroad grade.*

| TRAIL | 16.5 miles one way; paved |
|---|---|
| STEEPNESS | Level to gentle |
| OTHER USERS | Bicycles, in-line skaters |
| DOGS | Leash and scoop |
| CONNECTING TRAILS | Magnuson Park and NOAA Art Walk (Walk #23), Sammamish River Trail (Walk #38) |
| PARK AMENITIES | Restrooms, beaches, picnic shelters |
| DISABLED ACCESS | Trail, restrooms, picnic areas |

Beginning in the Ballard district of Seattle, and snaking along the shore of Lake Washington, this 16.5-mile, paved corridor of off-road walking meets the needs of those who seek the freedom of the trail just blocks from home.

From its beginning at the east edge of Seattle's Ballard district at 8th Avenue NW, the trail follows the original grade of the Seattle, Lake Shore & Eastern Railroad, which, after almost a century, was abandoned in 1971 under the ownership of Burlington Northern. Seven years later, Seattle opened the Burke-Gilman (named in honor of the original railroad's founders) as an off-road, multiuse trail. Near the western end, the trail passes Gas Works Park, a mini-walk in itself, with views of Lake Union and downtown Seattle, then continues east through the University of Washington campus and north past Warren G. Magnuson Park (Walk #23). Enjoy the fall colors of the hazelnut trees and bigleaf maples along this stretch.

North from here, increasing greenery lines the trail, which often runs between backyards, well landscaped with both native and exotic trees and shrubs. You get peekaboo views of Lake Washington, but the best is saved for the far north. Blackberries line the trail, providing spring color and fragrance and summer snacking. Two miles east of Tracy Owen Station in Kenmore, the trail changes to the Sammamish River Trail (Walk #38). Here you can enjoy a beach, a green lawn, and views south across Lake Washington.

One warning: the trail is heavily used by bicyclists and in-line skaters. Always walk on the right—in single file if it's a busy weekend. Toddlers and impatient children might do better on a quieter trail.

**GETTING THERE:** The best access points with parking are: Gas Works Park, Warren G. Magnuson Park (see Walk #23), or Tracy Owen Station (Log Boom Park). Trail brochure shows other access points.

To reach Gas Works Park: From I-5 in Seattle, north- or southbound, take exit 169 (NE 45th St, NE 50th St). Go west on NE 45th St and turn left (south) on Stone Way N. Follow Stone Way N to Lake Union and turn left on N Northlake Way. Parking is on the right.

To reach Tracy Owen Station: From I-5 in Seattle, northbound, take exit 171 (SR 522, Bothell, Lake City Way). Go north 6.5 miles and in Kenmore turn right on 61st Ave NE into the park.

From I-405 north of Bellevue, northbound, take exit 23 (SR 522 west, Bothell, Seattle); southbound, take exit 23B (SR 522 west, Bothell). Go west on SR 522 about 4.4 miles and turn left on 61st Ave NE into the park.

**ADDRESS:** No street address

**CONTACT:** Seattle Parks (206) 684-4075; www.seattle.gov/parks

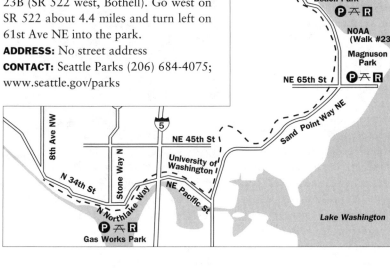

# 22

# RAVENNA PARK

**North Seattle, 5 miles northeast of downtown**

*Tranquil forest trails explore a ravine and stream hidden from urban bustle.*

| | |
|---|---|
| **TRAIL** | 4.5 miles total; natural surface |
| **STEEPNESS** | Level to steep |
| **OTHER USERS** | Bicyclers on 5-foot-wide paths only |
| **DOGS** | Leash and scoop |
| **CONNECTING TRAILS** | None |
| **PARK AMENITIES** | Restrooms, picnic tables, play area, tennis courts, wading pool |
| **DISABLED ACCESS** | Restrooms, playground at Cowen Park |

This secret cleft of choice greenery in the midst of urban Seattle offers some of the quietest, most treasured walking in the city. In fair weather, the steep side trails, the paths along the rims, and the wide trail in the ravine are filled with hikers, joggers, and dogwalkers. Even in winter, when a dusting of snow coats the trail, footprints still tell of dedicated Ravenna-lovers out to enjoy their park despite slippery trails and a partially frozen stream.

One of Seattle's oldest parks—acquired before the 1909 Alaska-Yukon-Pacific Exposition—Ravenna has seen bad years and good. Known at midcentury as a squatter's haven, it was later cleaned up and has now become a magnet park for Seattleites.

From the massive footbridge (at 20th Avenue NE) over the ravine and the rim trails where wild roses and berry bushes bloom, you look out into the canopy of immense red alder and maple. As you descend the angled

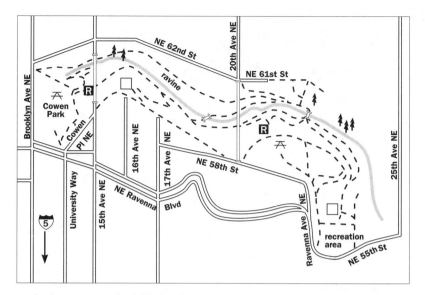

trails that traverse the hillside, the vegetation changes to a mix of native and ornamental trees (yew, redwood, Pacific dogwood, Douglas fir) sheltering an undergrowth of fern and salal. Leaning madrona trees form intricate patterns with their peeling bark branches.

Once in the ravine, you have no sense of city, no sight of houses. The stream flows from west to east, heading for Lake Washington. Working its way around boulders and logs, it brings nutrients to the skunk cabbages and stream creatures that live in its water and along its banks.

**GETTING THERE:** From I-5 in Seattle, south- or northbound, take exit 169 (NE 50th St, NE 45th St) and head east on NE 50th St. Turn left (north) onto 11th Ave NE, then, in 4 blocks, turn right onto (divided) Ravenna Blvd. Go 3 blocks to Brooklyn Ave NE and park on the street near Cowen Park; walk up Cowen Pl NE to the western edge of Ravenna Park. You can also continue east on NE Ravenna Blvd to the recreational end of Ravenna Park.

Alternatively, from I-5 northbound only, take exit 170 (Ravenna Blvd, NE 65th St) and go right on Ravenna Blvd to Cowen Park.

**ADDRESS:** 5520 Ravenna Avenue NE, Seattle

**CONTACT:** Seattle Parks (206) 684-4075; www.seattle.gov/parks

# 23

# WARREN G. MAGNUSON PARK AND NOAA ART WALK

**North Seattle, 8 miles northeast of downtown**

*Enjoy beaches, meadows, Cascades views, art, and an off-leash area along Lake Washington.*

| | |
|---|---|
| **TRAIL** | About 3 miles total; gravel, natural surface, paved |
| **STEEPNESS** | Level |
| **OTHER USERS** | Bicycles (NOAA trail pedestrians only) |
| **DOGS** | Off-leash in designated area; otherwise, leash and scoop |
| **CONNECTING TRAILS** | Burke-Gilman Trail (Walk #21), via streets |
| **PARK AMENITIES** | Restrooms, art, boat launch, picnic areas, playground, playing fields, tennis courts, wading pool |
| **DISABLED ACCESS** | Shoreline trail in Magnuson Park, restrooms, picnic areas |

Still called Sand Point from its former days as a naval station, Magnuson Park is one of the brightest parks in the Seattle area, with 200 acres of open meadows and lakeshore walking. Purchased from the Navy in 1975, the park has

seen years of improvement since the bleak days when it smelled of aviation fuel. To increase the greenery, the city originally planted trees, many of which died from lack of water. Now the park's pastoral setting is part of its allure, and any future plantings call for native shrubs, not trees. Only the southern end has a forested hillside with dirt

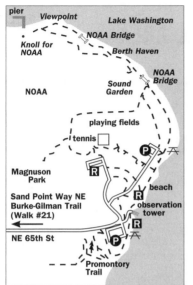

trails; elsewhere, be prepared for sun and wind.

Blustery days offer entertainment as you walk the wide aggregate trail from south to north. Windsurfers and wake-boarders race from the headland onto the wind-whipped lake, and kite-flying aficionados wrestle with their colorful winged creatures from the hillock.

If you come with a dog, or want to walk in seclusion, follow signs to the western border of the park, where the designated off-leash area is rimmed by luscious summer blackberry thickets. This trail meanders past the playing fields and rejoins the paved, aggregate walkway at the NOAA gate.

At the end of the pavement, a gated fence marks the boundary of the grounds of the National Oceanic and Atmospheric Administration (NOAA), which, due to heightened security, are open to the public 11:30 to 1:30 M-F only. Visitors with valid ID can access the grounds via the main NOAA gate by passing on foot through security check 9-5 M-F. Backpacks will be searched, and no picnic baskets or large containers are allowed. Five art-in-the-parks projects here enhance the waterside graveled walk. Stroll across two bridges inscribed with quotes from Moby Dick, enjoy views over the lake at Berth Haven and Viewpoint, guess the artist's intentions for the conical Knoll for NOAA, and walk through a haunting, moaning, otherworldly symphony of wind in the Sound Garden.

**GETTING THERE:** From I-5 north of downtown Seattle, north- or southbound, take exit 169 (NE 45th St, NE 50th St). Turn east on NE 45th St and go past the University of Washington, down the viaduct, and another 0.5 mile. Bear left onto Sand Point Way NE. Turn right on NE 65th St into Magnuson Park; the southern parking lot is straight ahead. Other lots, near the playing fields and beaches, are to the left. The NOAA Art Walk extends north from Magnuson Park.

**ADDRESS:** 7400 Sand Point Way NE, Seattle

**CONTACT FOR WARREN G. MAGNUSON PARK:** Seattle Parks (206) 684-4075; www.seattle.gov/parks

**CONTACT FOR NOAA ART WALK:** www.wrc.noaa.gov

# 24

# UNION BAY NATURAL AREA

**North Seattle, 5 miles northeast of downtown**

*Resident and migrating birds abound among meadows, wetlands, and ponds near Lake Washington.*

| | |
|---|---|
| **TRAIL** | 1.5 miles total with loops north and south; gravel, natural surface |
| **STEEPNESS** | Level |
| **OTHER USERS** | Bicycles |
| **DOGS** | Leash and scoop |
| **CONNECTING TRAILS** | None |
| **PARK AMENITIES** | Restrooms (weekday only), picnic tables |
| **DISABLED ACCESS** | Trails, restrooms (weekday only) |

This swath of untamed greenery between the University of Washington's Husky Stadium and the Center for Urban Horticulture is a stopover for thousands of migrating waterfowl and other birds on the Pacific Flyway. Come during fall, winter, or spring, when the ponds may host ruddy ducks, hooded

mergansers, and green- or blue-winged teals. The trees and bushes may be dotted with goldfinches, vireos, and waxwings. In summer the meadows are bright with yellow Scotch broom and blue chicory. All year long, mute swans glide on the calm waters of Union Bay, while Swainson's hawks hunt overhead, and muskrats make their homes in Shoveler's Pond.

Before 1916 this was another cove of Lake Washington, but when the Ship Canal was built the water receded and the land slowly adapted to its dry status. It's now an ecological research area, and walkers are welcome provided they keep pets on a leash and walk only on established paths.

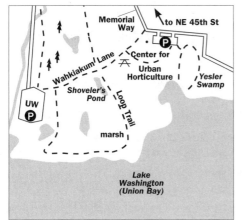

From Wahkiakum Lane, take the first left onto a woodchip trail, which passes the seasonal Shoveler's Pond (dry in summer) and then crosses the meadow to the lakeshore. Stay alert for ring-tailed pheasants in the grass and the shadow of eagles overhead. Several small paths weave through the cattails at the water's edge. In summer these are practically impassable due to blackberry invasion, but in winter you can find tiny clearings from which you can watch the lake-loving waterfowl.

Continue on the paths around the other ponds, where you may see plovers and bitterns. New plantings of dogwood and other trees enhance the seclusion and help ensure the repeated return of the seasonal migrants. A new trail called "Yesler Swamp" has been created to the east of the parking area. Boardwalks lead you to two different viewpoints in the wetlands by he lake. Union Bay is a walk for nature observers and for those who find pleasure in the wildlife surprises that each day brings.

**GETTING THERE:** From I-5 north of downtown Seattle, north- or southbound, take exit 169 (NE 45th St, NE 50th St). Turn east on NE 45th St and go past the University of Washington and down the viaduct, staying on NE 45th St. Take the first right after University Village on Mary Gates Memorial Way where signs point to the Center for Urban Horticulture (CUH). Park along the road and walk from the west end of the CUH parking lot onto Wahkiakum Lane into the preserve.

From the Eastside, cross Lake Washington on the SR 520 bridge. Take the Montlake exit (north) and turn right on Montlake Blvd NE. Stay to the right, passing Husky Stadium and merging with NE 45th St heading east. Turn right on Mary Gates Memorial Way and proceed as above.

**ADDRESS:** 3501 NE 41st Street, Seattle

**CONTACT:** University of Washington, Center for Urban Horticulture (206) 543-8616; www.uwbotanicalgardens.org

# 25 WASHINGTON PARK ARBORETUM

**4 miles east of downtown Seattle**

*Birds and botanical treasures abound in gardens and wetlands along Lake Washington.*

| | |
|---|---|
| **TRAIL** | Waterfront 0.5 mile one way; garden paths at least 4 miles; natural surface |
| **STEEPNESS** | Level to gentle |
| **OTHER USERS** | Bicycles on paved roads only |
| **DOGS** | Leash and scoop |
| **CONNECTING TRAILS** | None |
| **PARK AMENITIES** | Restrooms, classes, flower shows, gift shop, interpretive trail, Japanese Garden (admission fee), playground, visitor center |
| **DISABLED ACCESS** | Azalea Way (when dry), restrooms, visitor center |

With each season, color lures you deeper into the graceful elegance of the arboretum. Spring and summer bring an explosion of pink and white cherry blossoms; red, purple, and yellow rhododendrons; pink and white camellias; and an artist's palette of other perennials; fall's warm tones of orange and yellow brighten the trails. Even in winter, the myriad colors of bark, foliage, and winter berries contrast cheerfully with the drab days; as you walk, look for the striped-bark maples, the tiger bark of the cherries, and the sinewy shapes of trees and shrubs.

First-time visitors may want to get a free map of this 200-acre park from the Graham Visitor Center and then set off on Azalea Way, taking small side trips into specialized gardens such as the Winter Garden, the Rhododendron Glen, and the Woodland Trail. Meander paths on hillsides planted with

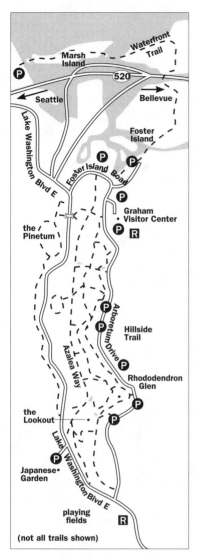

**Marsh Island**

**Waterfront Trail**

520

Seattle ← → Bellevue

**Foster Island**

P P

Foster Island Road

P

Graham Visitor Center

the Pinetum

P R

Hillside Trail

P P

Arboretum Drive

Azalea Way

Rhododendron Glen

P

the Lookout

P

Lake Washington Blvd E

Japanese Garden

P

Lake Washington Blvd E

playing fields

R

(not all trails shown)

exotic trees and shrubs. Cross the old stone bridge to the Pinetum for the pungent scent of fir and pine.

Along the Waterfront Trail bordering Lake Washington, wildlife abounds. Here you'll find mallards, coots, and grebes. In spring the tree swallows swoop and dive for insects above the marsh and in the evenings return to their nesting boxes along the trail. Canada geese nest on the hummocks beneath the reeds and cattails. Test your knowledge of marsh plants with the self-guiding tour booklet that illustrates many of the common plants seen here. Whatever your reason for walking, this mature and well-loved park, dating back to 1934, provides constantly changing botanical treasures on its interlacing trails.

**GETTING THERE:** From I-5 in Seattle, north- or southbound, take exit 168B (SR 520, Bellevue). Take the first exit (Montlake) from SR 520. Cross Montlake Blvd NE and wind down the hill to the junction with Lake Washington Blvd E. Turn right onto the boulevard and then left into the arboretum onto Foster Island Road. As you wind past several parking areas, Graham Visitor Center is on your left; free park maps available.

From the Eastside, take the SR 520 bridge over Lake Washington. Take the first Seattle exit (Lake Washington Blvd). The ramp turns left over the freeway; at the junction with Lake Washington Blvd E, turn left. Take the next left into the arboretum onto Foster Island Road and proceed as above.

**ADDRESS:** 2300 Arboretum Drive E, Seattle

**CONTACT:** The Graham Visitor Center (206) 543-8800; www.uwbotanic gardens.org

# 26

# INTERLAKEN TRAIL

**4.5 miles east of downtown Seattle**

*Forested ravines teem with birds; astounding views from Lake View Cemetery.*

| | |
|---|---|
| **TRAIL** | About 1 mile round-trip, 2 miles in cemetery; natural surface, paved |
| **STEEPNESS** | Gentle (paved trail) to steep (natural trails) |
| **OTHER USERS** | Bicycles |
| **DOGS** | Leash and scoop |
| **CONNECTING TRAILS** | None |
| **PARK AMENITIES** | Benches, some trash containers |
| **DISABLED ACCESS** | Paved road (closed to vehicles) |

Listen for the drumming of pileated woodpeckers or the chatter of squirrels as you stroll a historical green-belt in the heart of Seattle. Interlaken is a birding hot spot hosting robins, bald eagles, osprey, juncos, pine siskins, flickers, owls, hummingbirds, and more. A bird list is posted at the trailhead.

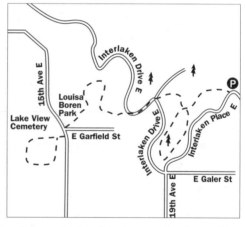

Recommended by the Olmsted Brothers for preservation in 1903, Interlaken's forest and ravines boast remains of the region's original evergreen forest. You can walk the gently inclined paved road, or climb one of several steep forested ravines on renovated footpaths. Crossing streams and ravines and climbing the hillsides, these steep paths with an occasional bench for resting offer good exercise and reward hikers with expansive city views. One side trail joins the road at the corner of 19th Avenue and Interlaken Drive E, another at Boren Park.

The Friends of Interlaken have been working to restore the trails and remove invasive plants such as English ivy, blackberry, and clematis. They request that hikers stick to the main trails and avoid the shortcuts. Separated by lush forest from the traffic of Interlaken Drive E, this hillside greenbelt offers silence and nature study with views over Husky Stadium and Montlake Cut.

Although maps show a continuous greenbelt running west from the arboretum (Walk #25) to Volunteer Park, the best walking is from the trailhead at the corner of Interlaken Place E and 21st Avenue E to the junction with Interlaken Drive E. Turn left on the drive and follow the road for 0.1 mile to the historical marker and trailhead for Boren Park. Leave the road and switchback up a shrub- and forest-covered hill to tiny Boren Park with its tall sculpture, benches, and great views.

If you want to extend your walk, cross 15th Avenue E and enter serene Lake View Cemetery. Perched atop Capitol Hill, with views in all directions, this pioneer cemetery welcomes the public during daylight hours.

**GETTING THERE:** From I-5 in Seattle, north- or southbound, take exit 168 (SR 520). Take the Montlake Blvd exit off SR 520 before crossing Lake Washington. Turn right onto Montlake Blvd and go south. It becomes 24th Ave E. Go 0.5 mile and turn right on Interlaken Pl E. The trailhead is on the right in about 3 blocks where the road turns sharply left at 21st Ave E.

**ADDRESS:** 2100 E Interlaken Place, Seattle

**CONTACT:** Seattle Parks (206) 684-4075; www.seattle.gov/parks

### Thank the Visionaries

"We want a ground to which people may easily go after their day's work is done, where they may stroll for an hour, seeing, hearing, and feeling nothing of the bustle and jar of the streets...." Building upon the words uttered by their father, Frederick Olmstead, Sr., in 1870, Frederick Jr. and John Olmsted created public parks and boulevards in Seattle at the dawn of the 20th century. Many of the parks you walk today, including the Washington Park Arboretum, and Interlaken, Ravenna, Lincoln, Myrtle Edwards, Discovery, Schmitz, and Seward Parks, owe their existence to the vision and energy of the Olmsted brothers.

Seattle

_In and Around Seattle_ | 55

# 27

# MYRTLE EDWARDS AND ELLIOTT BAY PARKS

**1 mile north of downtown Seattle**

*Walk along Elliott Bay for views of mountains, downtown, wildlife, and artwork.*

| | |
|---|---|
| **TRAIL** | 1.25 miles one way; paved |
| **STEEPNESS** | Level |
| **OTHER USERS** | Bicycles |
| **DOGS** | Leash and scoop |
| **CONNECTING TRAILS** | Elliott Bay Bikeway (via north end of Elliott Bay Park) |
| **PARK AMENITIES** | Restrooms, concessions, fishing pier |
| **DISABLED ACCESS** | Trail, restrooms, concessions, fishing pier |

This necklace of green so close to downtown Seattle offers fresh salt air, an ever-changing view of vessels on Puget Sound, and peaceful walking since wheels and feet are segregated on separate trails. Landscaped with roses, lawns, and low shrubs, this strip of garden park attracts walkers for sunrise glow on the Olympics, fresh air at midday, and sunset views of the last golden light on Mount Rainier. After dark, the lighted pier attracts fishing and crabbing aficionados.

Offshore you may see sea lions, harbor seals, and numerous waterfowl, especially in the fall and winter. Occasionally, too, a river otter pads along a tiny beach, clambers over rocks, then slithers back to do rolls and otter-wheelies in the cold salt water of the Sound.

Here nature and industry blend in a fine harmony: The setting sun puts the gigantic grain terminal in silhouette against the Olympics. The cacophony of seagulls resounds above the drone of a foghorn and Mount Rainier asserts its majesty over the city's skyline.

Stroll the whole length of the two parks or a bit from either end. The grass is interrupted by a carefully laid out gravel canvas upon which artist Michael Heizer created his immense rock and concrete sculpture, *Adjacent, Against,*

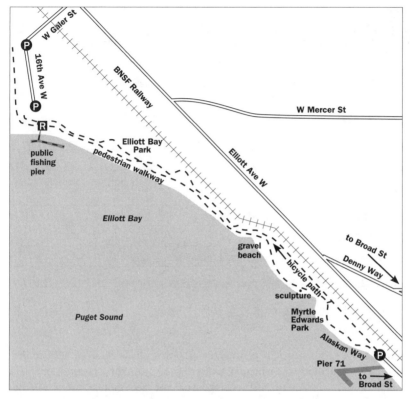

*Upon.* Just north of the boundary between Myrtle Edwards and Elliott Bay Parks, Shipmate's Light stands in honor and memory of those lost at sea.

**GETTING THERE:** For Myrtle Edwards Park, from I-5 in Seattle, north- or southbound, take exit 167 (Mercer St, Seattle Center). Follow signs for Seattle Center, staying on Broad St past the center, which takes you to the waterfront. Turn right onto Alaskan Way and drive to its north end near Pier 70 and park.

For Elliott Bay Park, from Broad St, turn right on Elliott Ave. Go about 1.5 miles and turn left on W Galer St. Cross the railroad tracks and proceed straight to the water for free parking. (Alternatively, after crossing the tracks, follow trail signs to the left, which puts you near the fishing pier, open dawn to 10 or 11 pm for night fishing.)

**ADDRESS:** 3130 Alaska Way W, Seattle

**CONTACT FOR MYRTLE EDWARDS PARK:** Seattle Parks (206) 684-4075; www.seattle.gov/parks

**CONTACT FOR ELLIOTT BAY PARK:** Port of Seattle (206) 728-3000; www.portseattle.org/community/resources/publicaccess.shtml

# 28

# GAZZAM LAKE NATURE PRESERVE

**Bainbridge Island, 14 miles west of Seattle (including a ferry ride)**

*A towering mature forest surrounds placid Gazzam Lake, and trails lead to beaches on Puget Sound.*

| | |
|---|---|
| **TRAIL** | 4 miles total; natural surface |
| **STEEPNESS** | Gentle to steep |
| **OTHER USERS** | Bicycles, horses; pedestrians only on Peters & Close Property |
| **DOGS** | Leash and scoop |
| **CONNECTING TRAILS** | None |
| **PARK AMENITIES** | Two small parking areas |
| **DISABLED ACCESS** | None |

More than 440 acres of near-pristine upland forest shields you from the sound of vehicles, and allow the chirping, twittering, and chattering sounds of small forest animals to resound. The logging history of the region is revealed in the immense, moss-softened stumps, still scarred with axe-cuts. The quiet, cushioned earth yields beneath your feet, like walking on the soft belly of Mother Earth. Sword ferns create a green and bushy understory. From either of the two trailheads, the path undulates gently, staying wide, and welcoming you near the edge of Gazzam Lake where a few spur trails lead you to the water's edge. Swallows dive and swoop for mosquito meals and in summer the native yellow water lilies burst forth. Closed to swimming, boating, and fishing, the lake remains an unspoiled habitat for beaver, muskrat, and river otter.

South of Deerpath Lane parking, the trail enters an extension of Gazzam Lake Trail on Peters Property, heading south and downhill toward Rich Passage. North of Marshall Road the trail joins the recently purchased Close Property, a 49-acre addition to the Preserve.

Well-engineered switch-backs lead down to a secluded beach on Puget Sound. Before the water comes into view, the forest's scent changes from sweet, fresh water to the bite of salt air.

**GETTING THERE:** From Seattle, take the ferry to Bainbridge Island. Follow Winslow Way E for 0.3 mile and turn right on Madison Ave N. Take the first left onto Wyatt Way NW. Go 1 mile and turn left on Eagle Harbor Drive NE. Go 0.2 mile and take a slight right onto Bucklin Hill Road NE. This

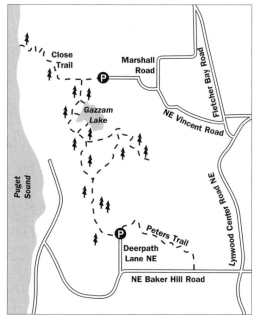

becomes Blakely Ave NE. Go 1 mile and turn right at NE Baker Hill Road. Go 1.2 miles and turn right on Deer Path Lane. Continue to the end and the parking lot/trailhead on left. No facilities.

To reach the Marshall Road Trailhead, proceed as above, but after turning onto Bucklin Hill Road, take the first right, which is the continuation of Bucklin Hill Road. Go 1 mile and turn left at Fletcher Bay Road, then immediately right onto NE Vincent Road. Go 0.5 mile and turn left on NE Marshall Road. Limited parking.

**ADDRESS:** Deerpath Lane NE or 6105 Marshall Road, Bainbridge

**CONTACT:** Bainbridge Island Metro Park and Recreation District (206) 842-9929; www.biparks.org

**Eagle Food, Not Dog Food!**

Dead salmon make a tasty meal for hawks and eagles, but before you let your dog near that carcass, realize this: dead salmon can carry a poison called Rickettsia which is not harmful to birds, but can be deadly to your dog.

# 29

# THE GRAND FOREST

### Bainbridge Island, 12.5 miles west of Seattle (including ferry)

*A maze of quiet forest trails offers bird-watching and streamside solitude.*

| | |
|---|---|
| **TRAIL** | 12 miles; natural surface |
| **STEEPNESS** | Gentle to steep |
| **OTHER USERS** | Bicycles, horses |
| **DOGS** | Leash and scoop |
| **CONNECTING TRAILS** | Forest-to-Sky Trail to Battle Point Park |
| **PARK AMENITIES** | Picnic area |
| **DISABLED ACCESS** | None |

Soft dirt trails quilt this open forest of Douglas fir in large, easy loops. Silence is broken by the sudden bird-like chatter of the tawny Douglas squirrels that patrol the tree trunks and branches like overzealous guardians of the woods. Three separate areas comprise Bainbridge's Grand Forest, acquired from the Department of Natural Resources in 1990.

In the Mandus Olson block, called Grand Forest East, map signs along the trail with "You are here" dots help steer you around the loops. If your sense of direction is anything less than that of a migrating bird, you'll be glad they're there. So uniform is this forest that without the guidance of low, slanted sunshine it is easy to get turned around. In the

southeastern corner a shallow ravine, a deep cradle of fern and shrub, extends to the east. Elsewhere, the understory shrubbery is low enough to give a clear

view of the middle layer of polelike trunks, characteristic of a farmed forest. Above it all spreads the upper story of Douglas fir boughs. With the openness comes great bird-watching possibilities: easy viewing to the tops of shrubs, and a chance to see woodpeckers, nuthatches, and brown creepers on the trunks.

In the more recently developed trail system of the Grand Forest West section off Miller Road, you can explore a spider web of loops in a denser, more varied forest. Bigleaf maple and red alder mix with Douglas fir and western red cedar, and the eastern part is highlighted by a small stream and surrounding wetland. Two parallel trails lead north and south, with tributary paths joining them. Next to the westernmost one is a picnic table. Huge stumps border the trail, doing their work as nurseries for saplings.

The third section, known as the Grand Forest North, is the most recently opened and has the newest trails.

**GETTING THERE:** From downtown Seattle, take the ferry to Bainbridge Island. Head north out of Winslow on SR 305. To reach the Mandus Olson section, go 1.6 miles north and turn left on Sportsman Club Road. After the school, turn right on New Brooklyn Road. Go 1.3 miles and turn right on Mandus Olson Road. Park (limited parking) where the road makes a sharp left turn.

To reach the Miller Road section, return to New Brooklyn Road and turn right (west). Go 0.75 mile and turn right on Miller Road. Just past the Bainbridge Gardens Nursery (on the left), at the top of a rise look on the right for a sign for the Grand Forest. Two pullouts provide limited parking.

For the North section, there are several trailheads without parking. Head north on Miller Road; the first trailhead is just north of the northern parking area for Grand Forest West. Continue north to Koura Road, where there are a couple more trailheads. Turn right (east) on Koura Road to Hart Lane and turn right (south) to reach two more trailheads.

**ADDRESS:** Mandus Olson Road and Miller Road, Bainbridge Island

**CONTACT:** Bainbridge Island Parks (206) 842-9929; www.biparks.org

# 30

# FORT WARD STATE PARK

**Bainbridge Island, 16 miles west of Seattle (including ferry)**

*Beaches and forest trails provide historic sites, bird-watching, and Olympic views.*

| | |
|---|---|
| **TRAIL** | 2 miles; natural surface, paved |
| **STEEPNESS** | Level to steep |
| **OTHER USERS** | Bicycles (on paved shoreline path only) |
| **DOGS** | Leash and scoop |
| **CONNECTING TRAILS** | None |
| **PARK AMENITIES** | Restrooms, boat launch, campground, gun battery ruins, interpretive signs, picnic tables, underwater park, viewing blinds |
| **DISABLED ACCESS** | Paved shore trail (Pleasant Beach Drive), restrooms, picnic area, upper parking lot |

Although it was an extensive military holding near the turn of the century, not much remains of the original Fort Ward. Today, the appeal of this state park lies in its sylvan tranquillity and water's-edge walking, rather than its military history. In the dense second-growth Northwest forest, the ferns and towering bigleaf maples enclose walkers in a green cocoon.

If you park at the boat launch at the northern end of the gated Pleasant Beach Drive, you can warm up with a stroll along the 4,300-foot paved trail bordering Rich Passage. To one side, sword ferns and horsetail vie for space beneath the hulking limbs of bigleaf maples and western red cedars. By the water, delicate white snowberries and wild roses line the path in late summer. Short spur trails lead to the water's edge and blinds for observing

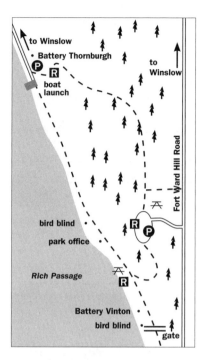

herons, cormorants, loons, and maybe harbor seals.

At high or low tide, the best walking may be along the almost-mile-long beach, from which you can more easily smell the fresh salt air, watch ferries negotiate the narrow Rich Passage, and observe the antics of the double-crested cormorants as they stretch and preen on the offshore pilings.

At the southern end of the road, past the bird blind, you can ascend the steep paved trail to the upper picnic area. From here, if the ground is not too muddy, head down the half-mile natural-surface trail back to the lower parking lot where you started. Along the way, you can search the forest trees for Steller's jays and winter wrens. Don't leave the trail, though; poison oak, an uncommon plant in the Northwest, lurks in the undergrowth—green in summer, red in fall.

**GETTING THERE:** From downtown Seattle, take the ferry to Bainbridge Island. Head north out of Winslow on SR 305. Go 1 mile and turn left on High School Road. Follow the brown state park signs south. In summer, you can enter the upland picnic area (Fort Ward Hill Road) or the boat launch area (Pleasant Beach Drive). In winter, only the boat launch area is open for parking.

From Bremerton, take SR 3 north to Poulsbo. Turn south on SR 305 to Bainbridge Island. Follow the brown state park signs south to Fort Ward, and park as described above.

**ADDRESS:** 2241 Pleasant Beach Drive NE, Bainbridge Island

**CONTACT:** Washington State Parks (206) 842-4041; www.parks.wa.gov

# 31

# SCHMITZ PRESERVE

West Seattle, 4 miles southwest of downtown

*An old-growth forest reveals Seattle's roots amid birdlife and a small stream.*

| | |
|---|---|
| **TRAIL** | 1.7 miles; natural surface |
| **STEEPNESS** | Gentle |
| **OTHER USERS** | Pedestrians only |
| **DOGS** | Leash and scoop |
| **CONNECTING TRAILS** | None |
| **PARK AMENITIES** | None |
| **DISABLED ACCESS** | None |

To stroll in Schmitz Preserve is to sense how the Puget Sound region looked before the arrival of the logging mills. Towering, massive western red cedar, western hemlock, and Douglas fir create an ancient ambience all around. Although it is not pristine—non-native English ivy invades from the neighborhoods, and a few old stumps reveal the ravages of the logger's saw—most of the forest remains untouched.

Walking the fir needle–lined path, you can hear birds singing, calling, moving about, and seeking food. Listen for the tapping of the pileated

woodpecker, the largest North American woodpecker, with its bright red crown, black-and-white neck, and black body. Nuthatches and brown creepers reside here, as does the less frequently seen or heard western screech owl.

As you meander along a small stream, notice the amount and variety of life that comes from fallen trees. Saplings of alder, hemlock, and Douglas fir send fine roots into the decaying

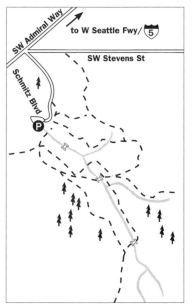

wood of ancient logs. Shrubs, too, such as red huckleberry and salal, find nutrients and moisture in these downed giants. Tall-standing snags house myriad insects that help supply the avian feeders. Removal of this downed wood and stumps would quickly destroy much of the life of the old forest, where the floor is often too thickly covered by needles and leaves to allow young saplings to grow.

For a more extended walk, stroll Schmitz Boulevard (closed to vehicles) north out of the parking lot. This old paved road leads through a deep ravine under Admiral Way, ending at a neighborhood park and playground.

**GETTING THERE:** From I-5 south of downtown Seattle, southbound, take exit 163A (W Seattle Fwy, Columbian Way) and stay right to get on the West Seattle Freeway. Exit onto SW Admiral Way, following it uphill past a commercial district, then down a hill to SW Stevens St. Look on the left for the park sign just before crossing a ravine. Turn left on SW Stevens St, then bear right into the parking lot.

From I-5 south of downtown Seattle, northbound, take exit 163 (W Seattle Fwy, Columbian Way), staying left to get on the West Seattle Freeway, and proceed as above.

**ADDRESS:** 5551 SW Admiral Way, Seattle

**CONTACT:** Seattle Parks (206) 684-4075; www.seattle.gov/parks

> **Forest Playgrounds?**
> Downed logs, stumps, and spring-board holes are not gymnastic equipment. These dead trees might look big and tough, but they're not. Scrambling feet and grabbing hands break off the moss and bark, which harbor the insects that birds eat. Many young saplings can grow only on nurse logs. Teach your children to respect what has taken a long time to grow but takes only a moment to kill.

# 32

# CAMP LONG

West Seattle, 5 miles southwest of downtown

*Interpretive trails explore wild forest and ponds; a rock-climbing wall invites challenge.*

| | |
|---|---|
| **TRAIL** | 3.2 miles; natural surface, paved |
| **STEEPNESS** | Gentle to moderate |
| **OTHER USERS** | Pedestrians only |
| **DOGS** | Leash and scoop |
| **CONNECTING TRAILS** | None |
| **PARK AMENITIES** | Restrooms, brochure, camping, classes, maps, picnic shelters, rock climbing, rustic cabins to rent |
| **DISABLED ACCESS** | Rolling Hill Trail, restrooms, cabins, rock climbing wall |

Walking in Camp Long is like finding wildlands in West Seattle. The air is fragrant with earth and greenery and sweet forest smells. Although this city park offers overnight camping (the only public camping in Seattle), these 68 acres hold more than cabins and a lodge. They are, for the day hiker, a place of tranquility and adventure. Beginning at the rustic 1940s lodge, walk left past the cabins to the beginning of the Animal Tracks Nature Trail. This half-mile loop leads past ancient cedar stumps to a newer forest of alder and willow. Plaster casts of raccoon, heron, skunk, coyote, red fox, and squirrel tracks are displayed at the trailhead.

The longer Midwood Loop trail veers off from the nature walk, leading downhill through second-growth forest to the boundary near the golf course. This is a wet trail in winter, but board walkways provide some relief from the mud. Due east of the lodge, you come to Polliwog Pond, where turtles bask, salamanders slither, and water insects hatch. If you're lucky you may see hawks, owls, or great blue herons.

The park offers classes on wetlands ecology, forest and pond ecology, and forest dwellers. Special park features include a climbing rock (on which instruction is given by prearrangement) and the "glacier," a concrete/stone structure with handholds and toeholds for climbing and rappelling.

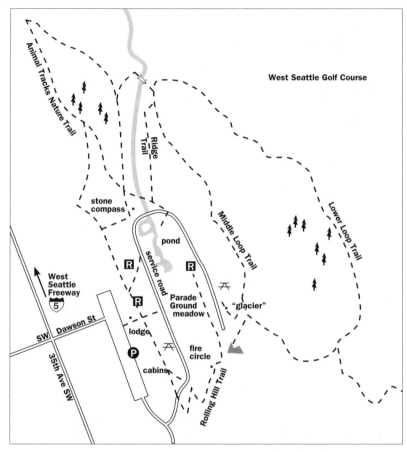

**GETTING THERE:** From I-5 south of downtown Seattle, southbound, take exit 163A (W Seattle Fwy, Columbian Way) and stay right to get on the West Seattle Freeway. Follow it to its end, staying left. At the first light off the freeway, turn left onto 35th Ave SW. Go 1 mile and turn left on SW Dawson St to enter the park.

From I-5 south of downtown Seattle, northbound, take exit 163 (W Seattle Fwy, Columbian Way), staying left to get on the West Seattle Freeway, and proceed as above. Closed Mondays and holidays year-round, and Sundays in January.

**ADDRESS:** 5200 35th Avenue SW, Seattle

**CONTACT:** Seattle Parks (206) 684-7434; www.seattle.gov/parks

# 33

# LINCOLN PARK

West Seattle, 8 miles southwest of downtown

*Bluffs and beaches along Puget Sound offer views of the Olympic Mountains.*

| | |
|---|---|
| **TRAIL** | 5.3 miles, including 1 mile on beach; gravel, paved |
| **STEEPNESS** | Level to steep |
| **OTHER USERS** | Bicycles |
| **DOGS** | Leash and scoop |
| **CONNECTING TRAILS** | None |
| **PARK AMENITIES** | Restrooms, picnic shelters, playgrounds, sports fields, wading pool<br>Summer only: swimming pool |
| **DISABLED ACCESS** | Paved beach walk, restrooms, picnic areas |

From high on the bluff at Lincoln Park, the barges and ferries look like large bathtub toys on the smooth water below. Madrona trees arch their vibrant red-barked limbs over the trail, and offshore an eagle may glide. Located on a bluff in West Seattle, these 130 acres of parkland offer lawns, views, beach, and water's-edge walking.

From the parking lots along Fauntleroy Way SW, choose any of the wide, smooth, and graveled paths and walk west to wander between large old western hemlock and Douglas fir trees. Open lawns and picnic shelters with playgrounds attract many of the park's users, but for a walk, continue west to the bluff. Sloping gently to the south, the now-paved trail gives views out onto Puget Sound and Vashon Island. Curve around and down to the shore, where fresh breezes from the south stir the water and create waves that clatter the pebbles on the beach.

Wide, paved, and level, the mile of beach walk invites either a slow stroll or a heart-pumping power walk. Winter storms bring waves that crash against the seawall and throw mighty drift logs high on the beach. In milder weather, the shoreline begs for exploration. At the northern end, past the swimming pool, the walkway narrows to a seawall under the branches of a slope of mixed conifers, maples, and red alder. Choose a nonthreatening path up (one that slopes rather than climbs) to return to the upper park.

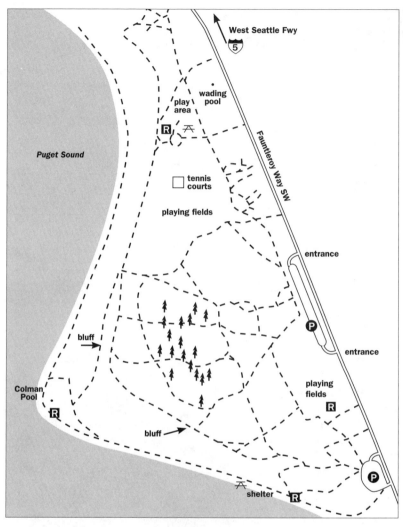

**GETTING THERE:** From I-5 south of downtown Seattle, southbound, take exit 163A (W Seattle Fwy, Columbian Way) and stay right to get on the West Seattle Fwy. Follow it to the end and continue straight as it becomes Fauntleroy Way SW and curves left. In about 2 miles, the park is on the right.

From I-5 south of downtown Seattle, northbound, take exit 163 (W Seattle Fwy, Columbian Way), staying left for the West Seattle Freeway, and proceed as above.

**ADDRESS:** 8011 Fauntleroy Way SW, Seattle
**CONTACT:** Seattle Parks (206) 684-4075; www.seattle.gov/parks

# 34 LUTHER BURBANK PARK

Mercer Island, 6 miles southeast of Seattle

*A historical setting on Lake Washington offers wetlands, meadows, and unusual art.*

| | |
|---|---|
| **TRAIL** | 3 miles; natural surface, paved |
| **STEEPNESS** | Level to gentle; some steps to lake |
| **OTHER USERS** | Bicycles |
| **DOGS** | Leash and scoop; off-leash area |
| **CONNECTING TRAILS** | None |
| **PARK AMENITIES** | Restrooms, boat docks, playground, swimming beach, tennis courts |
| **DISABLED ACCESS** | Paved trails, restrooms, picnic areas |

You can almost imagine the vast hand of the Lake Washington spirit reaching over this northeastern corner of Mercer Island, holding back the surrounding suburbia to preserve this stretch of land. With its grassy meadows and neatly tended lawns, pockets of berries and bogs, Luther Burbank Park offers breathing space and expansive views across the lake to Bellevue and Seattle.

Once the grounds of a home for wayward Seattle boys, these 77 acres retain a few reminders of days past. Two sturdy brick buildings are all that remain intact of the Boys Parental Home (later Luther Burbank School). When you walk north from the building past the elegant poplar and cottonwood trees, stop and explore the ruins of the old barn. For more than 50 years, Holstein cows grazed where boatwatchers sit today on the gentle hills of Luther Burbank Park.

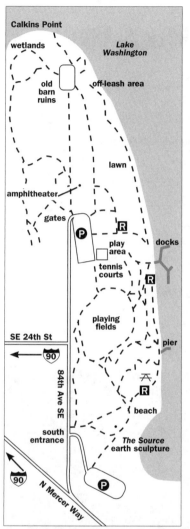

At Calkins Point on the northern tip, a marshland harbors frogs and ducks as well as red-winged blackbirds. Bear right and walk south along the waterfront, past the buildings to the docks, tennis courts, and picnic areas. If you've come with kids, plan on a long pause at the playground. This one was created by someone with a fertile imagination: brick hills to climb, endless slides, and swings—all cushioned with tire chips for safe landings.

When you can lure the kids off the brick mountains, head south across the meadow to explore the earth sculpture with its furrows and hills. What a great landscape for make-believe forts or wild games of tag. In summer, the grassy bumps and the nearby beach ring out with the calls of children. Complete the loop with a stroll north again along the water's edge, past secret hideouts for the lake's feathered inhabitants, ending at the docks.

**GETTING THERE:** From I-90 on Mercer Island, eastbound, take exit 7A (77th Ave SE). Turn left at the stop sign, go across the freeway, then turn right. Continue straight at the stop light near the Park and Ride and turn left onto 81st Ave SE. Go to the stop and turn right on SE 24th St. When the road curves right, go left into the park.

From I-90 on Mercer Island, westbound, take exit 7 (Island Crest Way). At the top of the ramp, veer right, following signs. Turn left on 84th Ave SE to enter the park.

**ADDRESS:** 2040 84th Avenue SE, Mercer Island

**CONTACT:** Mercer Island Parks (206) 275-7609; www.mercergov.org

# PIONEER PARK (MERCER ISLAND)

**Mercer Island, 8 miles southeast of Seattle**

*Explore sound-blanketing forest in a labyrinth of trails in the island's center.*

| | |
|---|---|
| **TRAIL** | 5 miles total; natural surface, paved |
| **STEEPNESS** | Gentle to moderate |
| **OTHER USERS** | Bicycles; horses in SE section and Fire Station Trail in NW section |
| **DOGS** | Leash and scoop |
| **CONNECTING TRAILS** | None |
| **PARK AMENITIES** | None; guidebook available at Mercer Island Parks office |
| **DISABLED ACCESS** | Much of perimeter trail of NW section |

Wander a labyrinth of trails through sound-blanketing forest in this touch of wildness in the center of Mercer Island. Raccoons leave footprints on the dirt trails and squirrels chatter from the branches.

Logged about 75 years ago, the forest now supports a variety of second-growth trees, including alder, maple, madrona, western hemlock,

and Douglas fir. Many have English ivy (an unwanted volunteer from nearby homes) clinging to their trunks like shaggy blankets or display a fine coating of blue-green lichen on their northern sides.

Park on Island Crest Way near SE 68th Street and dive in. Trails meander through each of the three sections of the park, which intersect at SE 68th St and Island Crest Way. You can choose the company of horses (in the northwest and southeast sections) or not, and choose level (northeast section) or sloping (southeast section) land. With many kid-created side trails, you could

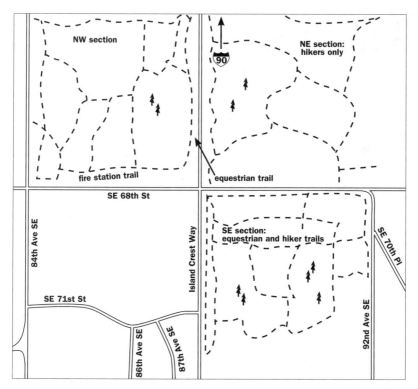

possibly get lost, or at least end up in someone's backyard. To maintain your bearings, listen for the traffic on Island Crest Way, and in the southeast section remember that uphill leads to the west and Island Crest.

Try a winter walk here, when the cold has hardened the dirt trails. With the leaves gone, you can look out through the sinewy forms of naked branches to Lake Washington. Oregon grape, sword ferns, cedars, and hemlocks all shimmer in vibrant green against the browns and grays of winter bark.

**GETTING THERE:** From I-90 on Mercer Island, eastbound, take exit 7B (Island Crest Way). The ramp leads directly onto Island Crest Way southbound. Go about 3 miles and park at the ball fields on the west side of Island Crest Way at about SE 63rd St. Limited, on-road parking only.

From I-90 on Mercer Island, westbound, take exit 7 (Island Crest Way). Turn left at the top of the ramp and cross the freeway. Go straight onto Island Crest Way southbound, and proceed as above.

**ADDRESS:** SE 68th Street and Island Crest Way, Mercer Island

**CONTACT:** Mercer Island Parks (206) 275-7609; www.mercergov.org

# 36

# SEWARD PARK

**6 miles southeast of downtown Seattle**

*Old-growth forest abounds with birds; beaches along
Lake Washington's shoreline offer views of Puget Sound.*

| | |
|---|---|
| **TRAIL** | 5.7 miles; natural surface, paved |
| **STEEPNESS** | Level to gentle |
| **OTHER USERS** | Bicycles on paved loop only |
| **DOGS** | Leash and scoop |
| **CONNECTING TRAILS** | Lake Washington Boulevard |
| **PARK AMENITIES** | Restrooms, amphitheater, art studio, fishing pier, interpretive center, picnic shelters |
| **DISABLED ACCESS** | Paved trail, restrooms, picnic shelter |

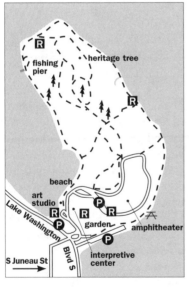

Seattle's largest tract of old-growth forest crowns thumb-shaped Bailey Peninsula, jutting into Lake Washington. Acquired by the city in 1911 as an island, Seward Park was transformed into a peninsula when the lake receded as a result of the building of the Ship Canal in 1916.

Deep in this forest of immense, precolonial western red cedar, western hemlock, and Douglas fir, varied thrushes call in winter, and in spring the forest comes alive with mating songs and calls of the migrant warblers and kinglets. No city sounds impinge on this woodland with its varied undergrowth of sword fern, Oregon grape, thimbleberry, salal, and twinberry. The main trail follows the spine of the gentle ridge, with numerous side trails leading out of the forest to the lake-shore loop walk.

The forest trail and the shore are so different that it's hard to believe they're part of the same park. From the quiet tranquility of the old forest, you emerge to a faster-moving world. On the paved 2.5-mile shore loop, bicycles zoom by and the in-line skaters skate-dance to music in their headphones. But with grassy stretches on either side of the trail, there is plenty of room for everyone.

Seattle

In fall, the southern part of the shore trail is lined in orange and red feathery sumac, salal, and hedges of snowberries, and the maples flash warm orange and yellow colors against the blue of the lake. Poison oak lurks among the shrubbery; look for its distinctive leaves in sets of three, shiny green in summer and turning red in fall. Tall madrona trees with their beautiful peeling bark accent the trail edges. Standing on the lakeshore in winter, you may see a variety of wintering waterfowl such as mergansers, grebes, and wigeons.

**GETTING THERE:** From I-5 south of downtown Seattle, southbound, take exit 163A (Columbian Way). Stay left to cross the freeway onto Columbian Way. Go southeast 1.4 miles and turn right on Beacon Ave S. Go about 0.5 mile and turn left on S Orcas St. Head east and at the T junction at Lake Washington Blvd S, turn right, then immediately left into the park.

From I-5 south of downtown Seattle, northbound, take exit 163 (West Seattle Fwy, Columbian Way). Stay right to get on Columbian Way. Proceed as above.

**ADDRESS:** 5898 Lake Washington Boulevard S, Seattle

**CONTACT:** Seattle Parks (206) 684-4075; www.seattle.gov/parks

# 37

# KUBOTA GARDEN

**7 miles southeast of downtown Seattle**

*Japanese gardens feature a stream, ponds, native and ornamental plants, and art.*

| | |
|---|---|
| **TRAIL** | 1.5 miles total; gravel, natural surface |
| **STEEPNESS** | Level to steep |
| **OTHER USERS** | Pedestrians only |
| **DOGS** | Not allowed |
| **CONNECTING TRAILS** | None |
| **PARK AMENITIES** | Restrooms, benches, free guided tours on weekends (except in winter), map, picnic tables |
| **DISABLED ACCESS** | Some paths |

This public garden, featuring exotic plants, walkways wide and narrow, waterfalls, and ponds is a place for meditation and quiet strolls. Pleasure comes not only from the visual, but from the almost tactile sense of shape and design.

Originally a nursery of 20 acres surrounding an ambitious system of streams and waterfalls, and later passed on to Seattle by the Kubota family, the garden continues to provide a place of beauty through form and color, texture and fragrance. Labeling plants was not a priority of the Kubotas, nor is it now. Mature rhododendrons—some 15 feet high and of unknown lineage—bloom in spring, livening the garden with robust color. Migrating songbirds find refuge here, filling the air with their calls. Japanese red and black pines and both yellow and black bamboo grace the paths.

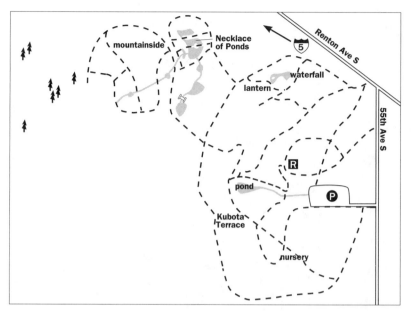

This is a garden for meandering, for viewing from all directions. You may have passed the arched Moon Bridge before, but now you tilt your head another way, the sun has dropped lower, and the garden reveals yet another aspect of color, texture, or shape. Climb the "Mountainside" to enjoy territorial views and perhaps to watch the golden carp in the Necklace of Ponds, 65 feet below.

**GETTING THERE:** From I-5 south of downtown Seattle, southbound, take exit 158 (Boeing Access). Turn left to cross the freeway and head straight up S Ryan Way. At the T junction, turn left on 51st Ave S. Turn right on Renton Ave S, then right on 55th Ave S. The parking entrance is on the right.

From I-5 south of downtown Seattle, northbound, take exit 157 (M. L. King Way). Follow Martin Luther King Way to S Ryan Way and proceed as above.

**ADDRESS:** 9817 55th Avenue S, Seattle

**CONTACT:** Kubota Garden Foundation (206) 725-5060, www.kubota.org; Seattle Parks (206) 684-4584, www.seattle.gov/parks

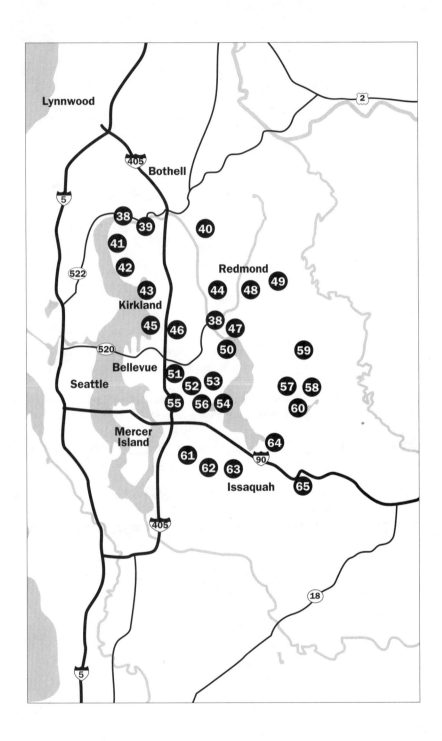

# IN AND AROUND THE **EASTSIDE**

# SAMMAMISH RIVER TRAIL

**Bothell, 13 miles northwest of Bellevue, to Redmond, 6 miles northeast of Bellevue**

*Wind along the Sammamish Slough's meadows and wetlands, with their wood sculptures and Cascades views.*

| | |
|---|---|
| **TRAIL** | 9.4 miles one way; paved |
| **STEEPNESS** | Level |
| **OTHER USERS** | Bicycles, horses |
| **DOGS** | Leash and scoop |
| **CONNECTING TRAILS** | Burke-Gilman Trail (Walk #21), Blythe Park (Walk #39), Powerline Regional Trail (Walk #44), Marymoor Park (Walk #47) |
| **PARK AMENITIES** | Restrooms, picnic shelters, playing fields at various parks |
| **DISABLED ACCESS** | Trail, restrooms |

Along this ribbon of still-rural Washington just minutes off I-405 and SR 520, you'll find miles and miles of walking opportunity. Listen to the soft murmur of water and inhale the clean air of the countryside. In Redmond the trail borders Slough House, the studio of Dudley Carter, late Artist in Residence for King County, whose huge wood sculptures can be seen both there and at nearby Marymoor Park. Farther north, near 124th Street, you pass close to the Chateau Ste. Michelle winery, where a free tour may lure you in from the walk.

The trail follows the grassy banks of the gently flowing Sammamish River, which connects Lake Sammamish to Lake Washington. Although surrounded to the east and west by the creeping spread of suburbia and light industry, parts of the trail still retain a rural feel.

On sunny days, the trail is host to a bevy of bicyclists, joggers, and equestrians, many of whom make the entire 9-mile jaunt between Redmond and Bothell. If the bicycle traffic alarms you, try walking on the soft dirt trail beside the pavement. On the asphalt, stay to the right and be prepared for the call of "Passing" or "On your left" as the bicycles zoom by.

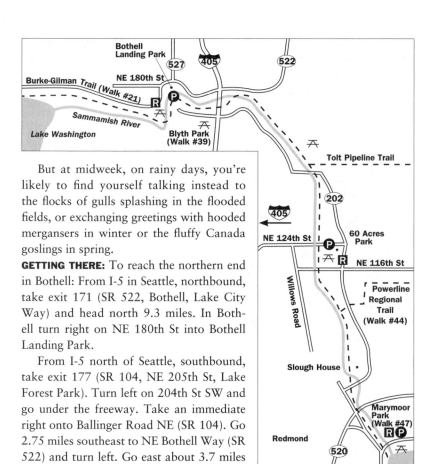

But at midweek, on rainy days, you're likely to find yourself talking instead to the flocks of gulls splashing in the flooded fields, or exchanging greetings with hooded mergansers in winter or the fluffy Canada goslings in spring.

**GETTING THERE:** To reach the northern end in Bothell: From I-5 in Seattle, northbound, take exit 171 (SR 522, Bothell, Lake City Way) and head north 9.3 miles. In Bothell turn right on NE 180th St into Bothell Landing Park.

From I-5 north of Seattle, southbound, take exit 177 (SR 104, NE 205th St, Lake Forest Park). Turn left on 204th St SW and go under the freeway. Take an immediate right onto Ballinger Road NE (SR 104). Go 2.75 miles southeast to NE Bothell Way (SR 522) and turn left. Go east about 3.7 miles and turn right on NE 180th St into Bothell Landing Park.

From I-405 north of Bellevue, northbound, take exit 23 (SR 522 west, Bothell, Seattle). Head west on SR 522 to Bothell/Kenmore. Go about 1.6 miles and turn left on NE 180th St into Bothell Landing Park.

From I-405 north of Bellevue, southbound, take exit 23B (SR 522 west, Bothell) and proceed as above.

To reach the southern end in Redmond: Follow directions for Marymoor Park (Walk #47). Turn into Marymoor Park and you will see the paved trail to your left, before crossing the river. Park near the tennis courts (on the left) and return to the trail by paved walkways.

**ADDRESS:** *Bothell Landing Park:* 9919 NE 180th Street, Bothell
*Marymoor Park:* 6046 W Lake Sammamish Parkway NE, Redmond
**CONTACT:** King County Parks (206) 296-4232; www.kingcounty.gov /recreation/parks

# 39 BLYTH PARK

Bothell, 13 miles northwest of Bellevue

*Trails provide a good dry-weather workout in forest above the Sammamish River.*

| | |
|---|---|
| **TRAIL** | 1 mile total; natural surface |
| **STEEPNESS** | Steep |
| **OTHER USERS** | Pedestrians only |
| **DOGS** | Not allowed on forest trails |
| **CONNECTING TRAILS** | Tolt Pipeline (via unmaintained, rugged trail), Sammamish River Trail (Walk #38, via foot-bridge) |
| **PARK AMENITIES** | Restrooms, picnic shelters, playground, trail-map sign |
| **DISABLED ACCESS** | Restrooms, picnic shelters |

A wooded shoulder of land forces the Sammamish River into its last major turn before it makes a run for Lake Washington. Here, at the head of the lake, just minutes from both north Seattle and Bellevue, you can stroll a lawn above the river or hike the forested hillside.

A great picnic stop for the travel-weary on I-405 or for neighborhood folks wanting an outing, Blyth Park boasts a mile of steep, heart-pumping trails. A trail-map sign, courtesy of an Eagle Scout, shows the possibilities for this wooded walk. From the sign, cross the lawn past the playground to the posted trailhead.

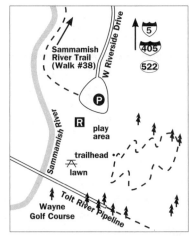

The first right-hand turn puts you on the less-strenuous portion of trail, where you'll pass wooden benches as well as a picnic area nestled in a cedar grove. The trail climbs, passing several small trails made by marauding feet with no regard for potential hillside erosion. Although maintained by the city, this is no wide, gentle path; it is treacherously slippery in rain because of its clay surface and the way it clings to the hillside. On dry days, though, it offers a good workout as you ascend through the forest of conifers and deciduous trees. Two footbridges take you over a small seasonal stream, and a series of tall steps drop you back to the trailhead.

**GETTING THERE:** From I-5 in Seattle, northbound, take exit 171 (SR 522, Bothell, Lake City Way) and head north for 9.8 miles. In Bothell, turn right on 102nd Ave NE. Cross the Sammamish River and take the first right, onto W Riverside Drive. Follow it about 0.5 mile south to the park entrance.

> ### Nasty Nettle or Yummy Veggie?
> Nettles make a tasty vegetable, rich in vitamins, if cut young and steamed up for supper. But most of us meet them on the trail—on a tender bit of leg or arm. When brushed, the plant's little hairs break off, injecting formic acid—the same stuff we hate to get from biting ants. Natural antidotes? Some say rubbing the brown spores of the sword fern on the spot helps. Others say the juice from the stem of wild impatiens (jewelweed) does the trick. If you don't normally have any baking soda with you, try rubbing with one of these plants. It might work. Native Americans used to flail themselves with stinging nettle to stay awake while out fishing all night on the Sound. Ouch!

From I-5 north of Seattle, southbound, take exit 177 (SR 104, Lake Forest Park). Turn left on 204th St SW and go under the freeway. Take an immediate right onto Ballinger Road NE (SR 104) and go southeast 2.5 miles. Turn left on NE Bothell Way and go east about 4 miles. In Bothell, turn right on 102nd Ave NE and proceed as above.

From I-405 north of Bellevue, northbound, take exit 23 (SR 522 west, Bothell, Seattle). Head west on SR 522 to Bothell. Go 1 mile, turn left on 102nd Ave NE, and proceed as above.

From I-405 north of Bellevue, southbound, take exit 23B (SR 522 west, Bothell) and proceed as above.

**ADDRESS:** 16950 W Riverside Drive, Bothell

**CONTACT:** Bothell Parks (425) 486-7430; www.ci.bothell.wa.us

# GOLD CREEK PARK

**Woodinville, 12 miles north of Bellevue**

*Shaded forest trails make a good dry-weather workout above a peaceful creek.*

| TRAIL | 2.8 miles total; natural surface |
|---|---|
| STEEPNESS | Steep |
| OTHER USERS | Horses |
| DOGS | Leash and scoop |
| CONNECTING TRAILS | None |
| PARK AMENITIES | Picnic area, lodge, map sign |
| DISABLED ACCESS | None |

At first glance, this secluded county park with its stream and picnic area appears to offer nothing to a walker. But hidden behind a mantle of blackberries, a well-used trail climbs a forested ravine alongside Gold Creek.

The trail-map sign, drawn by a Boy Scout for his Eagle project, shows two loops, one north and the other south. Both begin with a steep climb up the edge of Gold Creek in quiet woods. The year-round creek gives moisture to the air, increasing the rich scent of humus and greenery. The trails in this park are used equally by walkers and horses, so they tend to be narrow, rough, and in places worn into ruts by hooves.

For the south loop, take the first trail to the right, as it switches back higher on the hillside. Rising to a ridge, you leave the forest cover for a moment to touch the edge of suburbia, and then dive back into the green shelter like that which used to cover most of the Eastside 40 or 50 years ago before the housing developments came. Now on the north loop trail, you descend past Douglas firs and western red cedars up to 2 feet in diameter. Here downed logs and open glens invite a rest or picnic.

Throughout, the trail is steep, rising and falling on the contours of the west-sloping hill. This is a great training walk, or one to challenge your children. A mossy fence marks the northern park boundary. Descend finally to the Gold Creek streambed and return to the trailhead.

In this swatch of wildness there are few landmarks, except your memory of going along the edge of a ravine or a particularly steep hillside. Down, on any trail, should eventually return you to the trailhead.

**GETTING THERE:** From I-405 north of Bellevue, northbound, take exit 20B (NE 124th St). Turn right on NE 124th St. Go 2.5 miles and turn left on Hwy 202 (Woodinville/Redmond Road NE). Go straight for 1.5 miles. At a 4-way stop go straight (the road becomes 148th Ave NE). After 0.5 mile the main road veers left, but continue straight on 148th Ave NE. The park is 0.25 mile ahead on the right.

From I-405 north of Bellevue, southbound, take exit 23A (SR 522 east to SR 202, Woodinville, Monroe), staying left to merge onto SR 522. Take the Woodinville/Redmond exit. At the end of the ramp, turn right. Go straight and turn left on NE 175th St. Turn right on 140th Ave NE and go about 1.5 miles (past the Gold Creek Tennis and Racquet Club) and look for 148th Ave NE merging on the left. Take a sharp (almost U-turn) left onto 148th Ave NE and go 0.25 mile uphill to the park on the right.

**ADDRESS:** 16020 148th Avenue NE, Woodinville

**CONTACT:** King County Parks (206) 296-2964; www.kingcounty.gov /recreation/parks

# 41

# SAINT EDWARD STATE PARK

**Juanita, 12 miles northwest of Bellevue**

*Birds abound in forested ravines near a stream flowing into Lake Washington.*

| | |
|---|---|
| **TRAIL** | 7.5 miles total; natural surface, paved |
| **STEEPNESS** | Moderate to steep |
| **OTHER USERS** | Bicycles prohibited (except on one trail); horses in southeast corner |
| **DOGS** | Leash and scoop |
| **CONNECTING TRAILS** | None |
| **PARK AMENITIES** | Restrooms, picnic areas, playing fields, swimming pool, tennis and racquetball courts, trail-map sign |
| **DISABLED ACCESS** | Paved trail around buildings, restrooms, buildings |

Deep ravines cutting through a forest of mixed conifer, madrona, and bigleaf maple characterize this 316-acre park, the largest piece of undeveloped property on Lake Washington. Coyotes roam the grounds in early evening, and bald eagles often nest along the shoreline. The woodlands provide shelter for many foraging and upper-canopy birds, and red-tailed hawks cruise the open edges of the meadow. Waterfowl on the lakefront include grebes, geese, and all the native ducks.

With the parking lot on a rise high above the lake, the trails in Saint Edward are among the steepest found in the region. If the narrow, leaf-strewn trails on hillsides daunt you, use the wide, gently graded Main Trail to reach the grassy "beach" on the waterfront. For more challenge, try the Gym Trail, which traverses a densely wooded hillside above a stream. Look here for white, three-petalled trillium blooming in the spring. If you want to increase your aerobic exercise, return via the Grotto Trail: it's a strenuous but beautiful climb overlooking the graceful curve of a fern-draped grotto where weddings are often held.

Scattered among the hemlock, cedar, and Oregon ash, you'll see massive stumps with springboard notches cut more than 75 years ago. Look along

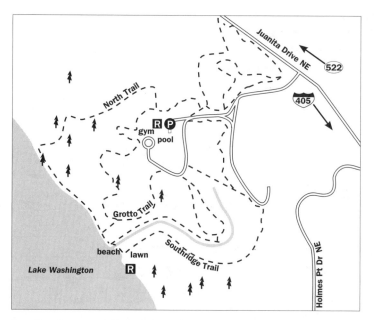

the shoreline for rusted chains entangling many fallen trees. These are all that remain of the log boom once moored offshore.

**GETTING THERE:** From I-405 north of Bellevue, northbound, take exit 20A (NE 116th St). Turn left on NE 116th St and go 1.5 miles to the light at 100th Ave NW. Go straight through the light onto Juanita Drive NE. Go west, then north about 4 miles and, at the top of the hill, look for signs for the park. Turn left into the park. At the Y, bear right and go up the hill to the parking lot.

From I-405 north of Bellevue, southbound, take exit 20 (NE 124th St). Turn right at the end of the ramp and get in the left lane. At the first light, turn left onto 120th Ave NE. Turn right on NE 116th St and proceed as above.

From I-5 in Seattle, northbound, take exit 171 (SR 522, Lake City Way) and head north for 7 miles. In Kenmore turn right on 68th Ave NE, which becomes Juanita Drive NE. Go about 2 miles and look for the park entrance on the right.

From I-5 north of Seattle, southbound, take exit 177 (SR 104, Lake Forest Park). Turn left on 204th St SW and go under the freeway. Take an immediate right onto Ballinger Road NE (SR 104). Go 2.75 miles and turn left on Bothell Way NE. Go 1.3 miles and turn right on 68th Ave NE (which becomes Juanita Drive NE) and proceed as above.

**ADDRESS:** 14445 Juanita Drive NE, Kenmore

**CONTACT:** Washington State Parks (425) 823-2992; www.parks.wa.gov

# 42

# O. O. DENNY PARK

**Juanita, 11 miles northwest of Bellevue**

*Denny Creek flows through mature forest to a popular Lake Washington beach.*

| | |
|---|---|
| **TRAIL** | 1-mile loop; natural surface |
| **STEEPNESS** | Moderate to steep |
| **OTHER USERS** | Pedestrians only |
| **DOGS** | Leash and scoop |
| **CONNECTING TRAILS** | None |
| **PARK AMENITIES** | Restrooms, beach, picnic shelter |
| **DISABLED ACCESS** | Restrooms, beach area |

Follow the contours of a ridge above Denny Creek in dense western red cedar and western hemlock stands. Sword ferns create a tufted carpet of undergrowth to hide mice, voles, and shrews. This forest of century-old trees is much as it might have been when Seattle developer O. O. Denny stepped ashore to survey the land for a homesite in the early 1900s.

On the beach side of the park, the creek has gouged an impressive ravine in its last push to the Sound. Stroll the grassy lawns, and watch for bald eagles overhead.

To reach the forest trailhead, cross the road and start up the forest path to the right of the parking lot. The trail climbs steeply high above the ravine formed by the creek. At the top of the ridge, a graveled road intersects the trail. Turn around here or go left, through a small clearing past a pump house.

In summer you may see berry-rich scat lying on the ground at frequent intervals. Not cat, bear, dog, or deer. Coyote. These carnivores turn into berry eaters when other food is scarce or when berries are easy to forage. In the sunny patches on this western sloping hill, the salal and blackberries are abundant.

To complete the loop, cross the wooden bridge with interpretive signs, and descend into the Denny Creek ravine. Marvelous cedar and Douglas fir stumps hint at the past majesty of this forest. Members of the Denny Creek Association patrol this precious enclave of old forest and ask visiting walkers to respect the land and the trails.

**GETTING THERE:** From I-405 north of Bellevue, northbound, take exit 20A (NE 116th St) and turn left on NE 116th St. Go 1.4 miles to the light at 100th Ave NW. Go straight through the light onto Juanita Drive NE. Go another 2 miles and turn left on 76th Pl NE, which becomes Holmes Point Drive NE. The road goes through the park in about 1 more mile.

From I-405 north of Bellevue, southbound, take exit 20 (NE 124th St). Turn right at the end of the ramp and get in the left lane. Turn left at the first light onto 120th Ave NE. Turn right on NE 116th St and proceed as above.

From I-5 in Seattle, northbound, take exit 171 (SR 522, Bothell, Lake City Way) and head north for 7 miles. In Kenmore, turn right on 68th Ave NE (which becomes Juanita Drive NE). Go about 2 miles and turn right on Holmes Point Drive NE. Go another 2 miles to the park.

From I-5 north of Seattle, southbound, take exit 177 (SR 104, Lake Forest Park). Turn left on 204th St SW and go under the freeway. Take an immediate right onto Ballinger Road NE (SR 104). Go 2.75 miles and turn left on Bothell Way NE. Go 1.3 miles and turn right on 68th Ave NE (which becomes Juanita Drive NE), and proceed as above. Parking lots are on both sides of the road.

**ADDRESS:** 12032 Holmes Point Drive NE, Kirkland

**CONTACT:** Finn Hill Parks and Recreation, www.finnhillparks.net

**43** # JUANITA BAY PARK

### Kirkland, 8 miles north of Bellevue

*Boardwalks traverse wetlands along Lake Washington amid waterfowl and beaver ponds.*

| | |
|---|---|
| **TRAIL** | 1.3 miles; boardwalk, paved |
| **STEEPNESS** | Level to gentle |
| **OTHER USERS** | Bicycles |
| **DOGS** | Leash and scoop |
| **CONNECTING TRAILS** | None |
| **PARK AMENITIES** | Restrooms, interpretive signs, nature tours, picnic tables |
| **DISABLED ACCESS** | All trails, restrooms |

An apron of green lawn spreads out from the streets of suburbia, creating an elegant separation between the manmade and the natural. Below the lawns, hidden from casual view, are boardwalks that meander into natural marshes where blackbirds nest, turtles sun, frogs leap, and cattails sway in lakeside breezes.

This corner of Lake Washington has had a long and active past. Native Americans gathered food here on the shores of the once-higher lake. Later came the frog farmers and the truck gardeners, both working with the land and lake as it was. In 1932 a Kirkland realtor began an onslaught against nature by dumping thousands of truckloads of cedar bark, sawdust, and dirt to fill in the marshes and build a golf course. But the inexorable water won out and, despite berms and pumps, the course was finally closed in 1975.

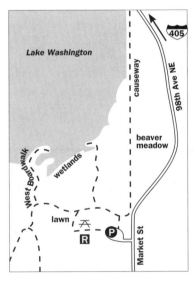

Slowly, now, the lake reclaims its shaggy marsh shoreline. You can observe this wetland either from the broad paved causeway on the eastern edge of the lake or from the boardwalks that wend their way into the thickets of cattails and reeds. Here you may see mallards and teals dabbling, mergansers diving, or beavers gliding across their carefully crafted ponds.

**GETTING THERE:** From I-405 north of Bellevue, northbound, take exit 20A (NE 116th St). Turn left and go about 1.5 miles. Turn left (south) on 98th Ave NE (which becomes Market St), bordering the park. Turn right into the parking lot.

From I-405 north of Bellevue, southbound, take exit 20 (NE 124th St). Turn right at the end of the ramp and get in the left lane. Turn left at the first light, onto 120th Ave NE, which parallels the freeway. Turn right on NE 116th St and proceed as above.

**ADDRESS:** 2201 Market Street, Kirkland

**CONTACT:** Kirkland Parks (425) 587-3300; www.ci.kirkland.wa.us

# 44

# POWERLINE REGIONAL TRAIL

**Redmond, 10 miles northeast of Bellevue**

*Meadows, rolling hills, and Cascades views merge into forest along Bear Creek.*

| | |
|---|---|
| **TRAIL** | 3 miles one way; gravel, natural surface |
| **STEEPNESS** | Gentle to steep |
| **OTHER USERS** | Bicycles, horses |
| **DOGS** | Leash and scoop |
| **CONNECTING TRAILS** | Sammamish River Trail (Walk #38), Farrel-McWhirter Park (Walk #48), Redmond's Watershed Preserve (Walk #49) |
| **PARK AMENITIES** | None |
| **DISABLED ACCESS** | None |

Just north of downtown Redmond, this rugged stretch of green space is appealing for its ups and downs, bushes alive with birds, and striking views of the Cascades.

If walking under power lines is not your idea of fun, forget this trail. But perhaps you can play mental games to imagine these towering structures as some sort of 1950s *War of the Worlds* creatures, or go into engineering bliss imagining the equations necessary to erect them. Or maybe, like the wildlife that frequents these corridors of steel and wire, you can ignore them. As you walk along the trail, look for scat and telltale footprints in mud. As for larger mammals, this corridor that stretches from the Sammamish River to Farrel-McWhirter Park (Walk #48) boasts coyotes, raccoons, possum, deer, and lynx.

At the western end, the trail is accessible only from the Sammamish River Trail (Walk #38), where it meets

### Tree of Life

Native Americans had so many uses for the western red cedar that they called it the "tree of life." The wood made logs for houses, canoes, and household items. From the bark, they wove baskets and clothing. The needles made a natural insect repellent. The shredded bark served as diapers. Many Native Americans believed that leaning your back against the trunk infused strength.

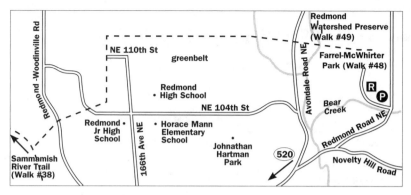

the trail between Sixty Acres Park (off NE 116th Street) and downtown Redmond (off NE 85th Street near the city offices). As it heads east, the trail varies in its surroundings, sometimes following country roads, at other times bordering neighborhoods and backyards. There are several street crossings: be cautious at the Redmond/Woodinville Road, which has a crossing light. For much of the trail, you walk in a narrow greenbelt of Scotch broom, blackberry, salmonberry, and horsetail. (Sometimes real horse tails, too, as you pass the fence of a friendly equine.)

After crossing Avondale Road (use the stoplight), the trail enters quiet second-growth forest, where evidence of long-ago logging shows in spring-board slots on the moss-covered stumps. This is the more peaceful, magical end of the trail, with a soft, fir-needled path underfoot, a bridge over Bear Creek, and in spring, the pinkish floral bells of salal. The trail's east end is currently accessed at Farrel-McWhirter Park (Walk #48).

Where you turn around depends on your time and mood. The trail is great for power walks and training, but also for quiet contemplation. You might decide to set your sights on a certain street crossing. But be warned, there's always the lure of another Cascade view to draw you onward.

**GETTING THERE:** To reach Sixty Acres Park: From I-405 north of Bellevue, northbound, take exit 20 (NE 124th St). If southbound, take exit 20B (NE 124th St). Go east on NE 124th St about 1.5 miles and turn right on Willow Road NE. Go 1.5 miles and turn left on NE 116th St to the Sammamish River Trail. Walk south on the Sammamish River Trail looking for the sign to the Powerline Regional Trail (under the power lines).

**ADDRESS:** No street address

**CONTACT:** Redmond Parks (425) 556-2300; www.ci.redmond.wa.us

# 45

# WATERSHED PARK (KIRKLAND)

**Kirkland, 3.5 miles north of Bellevue**

*A meadow has Mount Rainier views, and the forested ravine hides a stream.*

| | |
|---|---|
| **TRAIL** | 2.8 miles total; natural surface |
| **STEEPNESS** | Gentle to steep |
| **OTHER USERS** | Bicycles (pedestrians-only preferred) |
| **DOGS** | Leash and scoop |
| **CONNECTING TRAILS** | None |
| **PARK AMENITIES** | Interpretive tours |
| **DISABLED ACCESS** | None |

Sunlight traces dancing pictures on the path. Bird calls and songs lilt from one tree to another. Mount Rainier stands tall above a valley of yellow Scotch broom. A clear pool quenches the thirst of a family of coyotes. And all of this is just minutes from both Kirkland and Bellevue.

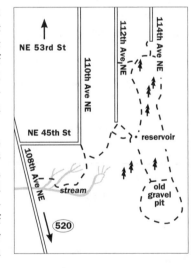

From the 1930s to the late 1960s, a small reservoir in the watershed was built to supply Kirkland's water needs, but the system had too many leaks, and in 1967 Kirkland hooked up with Seattle for water. Today all that remain of this human effort are an empty reservoir and a few pipes partially buried beneath bracken and sword ferns.

For easy walking, follow the chip-lined paths from the 114th Avenue entrance in a long loop at the eastern edge of the forest, where rufous-sided towhees and Bewick's wrens hop about on the forest floor and in the branches of the madrona and maple trees. At the southern end, you come to a ridge above a Scotch broom–filled valley, carved out 35 years ago for

gravel to build I-405. A sandy footpath that dips down into the valley makes another appealing walking loop.

From the 112th Avenue entrance, a steep but well-maintained trail heads west, sloping down and around old stumps and seedling-covered nurse logs. Follow the path into the ravine. Here, less freeway noise intrudes on the forest sounds, and soon the sound of the stream dominates. In the quiet, clear pool, shadows of minnows pattern the sandy bottom.

**GETTING THERE:** From I-405 in Bellevue, north- or southbound, take exit 14 (SR 520) west, and exit immediately onto 108th Ave NE. Go about 1 mile north and turn right on NE 45th St to 110th Ave NE, or continue farther north on 108th Ave NE to NE 53rd St and turn right on 110th Ave NE, 112th Ave NE, or 114th Ave NE; it's on-street parking in any case.

From I-5 in Seattle, north- or southbound, take exit 168B (SR 520, Bellevue) across Lake Washington. Take the Kirkland (Lake Washington Blvd NE) exit. Turn left at the end of the ramp, cross the freeway, and turn right on Northup Way. At the next light, turn left on 108th Ave NE and proceed as above.

**ADDRESS:** 4500 110th Avenue NE, Kirkland

**CONTACT:** Kirkland Parks (425) 587-3300; www.ci.kirkland.wa.us

# 46

# BRIDLE TRAILS STATE PARK

Kirkland, 5.5 miles north of Bellevue

*Hikers and horseback riders wander miles of trails through mature forest.*

| | |
|---|---|
| **TRAIL** | At least 28 miles total; natural surface |
| **STEEPNESS** | Gentle to moderate |
| **OTHER USERS** | Horses |
| **DOGS** | Leash and scoop |
| **CONNECTING TRAILS** | Bridle Crest Trail (many road crossings) |
| **PARK AMENITIES** | Restrooms, arena, brochures, picnic area, posted map, show ring, stands |
| **DISABLED ACCESS** | Restrooms, picnic area |

You may not see the Douglas squirrels chomp on hr cones as though they were corn on the cob, but walking through this almost 100-year-old forest you are likely to see many piles of discarded scales. Though only a mile from the freeway and the urban centers of Kirkland and Bellevue, this enclave of mature forest is a habitat for coyotes, raccoons, possums, native squirrels, and dozens of species of forest-dwelling birds.

It is like home, too, to many horseback riders, who regularly exercise their steeds on the more than 28 miles of natural-surface trails. When the state acquired the land in the 1930s, it soon became overrun by locals who thought of it as their private drag strip for cars and motorcycles. A neighborhood group formed, later becoming the Lake Washington Saddle Club, and took on the role of forest guardian. In the 1940s, members cleared the trails and built the show ring. Today the State and the club cooperate in maintaining the park, and these 480 acres are open to both hikers and horses.

Entering by the big arena on 116th Avenue NE, take the trail heading up the gentle hill to the east, which quickly puts you under canopies of fir and hemlock that soon muffle the freeway noise. After a good rain, you'll find a few deep mudholes, so wear appropriate shoes. If the weather has been dry, you can probably negotiate the edges of the mire without mishap.

Bridle Trails is a great walk for those who know or want to get to know indigenous plants. Here you'll find several varieties of ferns, Oregon grape,

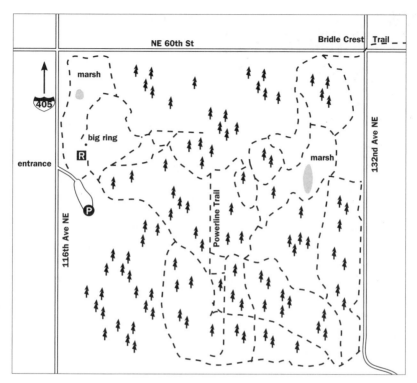

huckleberry, salal, and many species of wild mushrooms, some edible and others poisonous.

With its miles of interweaving trails, the park makes it easy to become disoriented. The western part of the park is the most straightforward. Trails east of the power lines meander like a child's scribbles. If you feel lost, just ask someone. All the riders know their way around, and are receptive to friendly hikers.

**GETTING THERE:** From I-405 north of Bellevue, north- or southbound, take exit 17 (NE 70th Pl). If northbound, turn right at the end of the ramp onto 116th Ave NE and go south about 1 mile to the park entrance on the left. Park at the northeast corner of the parking lot to access trails. If southbound, turn right at the end of the ramp onto NE 72nd Pl, cross the freeway, then turn right again onto 116th Ave NE and proceed as above.

**ADDRESS:** 116th Avenue NE, Kirkland

**CONTACT:** Washington State Parks/Lake Sammamish Office (425) 455-7010; www.parks.wa.gov

# 47 MARYMOOR PARK

**Redmond, 7.5 miles northeast of Bellevue**

*Sammamish—river and lake—wetlands and meadows feature trails and a historical site.*

| | |
|---|---|
| **TRAIL** | 5 miles total; natural surface, paved |
| **STEEPNESS** | Level |
| **OTHER USERS** | Bicycles, horses on equestrian trail only |
| **DOGS** | Leash and scoop; off-leash in designated area |
| **CONNECTING TRAILS** | Sammamish River Trail (Walk #38), East Lake Sammamish Trail (via Marymoor Connector) |
| **PARK AMENITIES** | Restrooms, bicycle velodrome, climbing rock, model airplane field, museum, picnic shelters, playing fields, pea patch, tennis courts |
| **DISABLED ACCESS** | Paved trails (not southern riverside walk), restrooms, picnic areas |

Marymoor's vast open spaces—520 acres of them—give this park a true year-round appeal. Walkers can choose to watch the bicyclists careen around the sloped velodrome or gape at the nonacrophobic attacking tiny handholds on the climbing rock. An undulating whine and hum comes from the eastern edge of the park, where earthbound pilots put their model airplanes through their tricks.

For a more serene walk, take the nature trail south into the alder and oak forest. Interpretive signs guide you along a boardwalk over a peat bog, then out to the northern shore of Lake Sammamish. Completing the loop, the boardwalk leads back along the Sammamish River through a thicket of blackberries and salal and the gentle shade of alders.

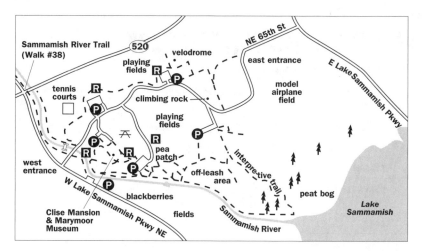

Here songbirds chatter and flit, and on the river you can see the iridescent flash of the mallard drakes or the elegant suits of the Canada geese.

Where the boardwalk ends, be prepared to greet dogs. Hundreds of them. Marymoor's off-leash area is a mecca for dogs, where they can romp and dig on the water's edge and in the fragrant fields adjoining.

Year-round, keep the binoculars handy for a look at the red-tailed hawks circling overhead. On hot summer days, expect a sky alive with hot-air balloons as they glide to rest on Marymoor's fields. Bring a camera, and flex your muscles if you want to help deflate the billowing nylon.

What is now the park was developed in the early 1900s as a family cattle farm. The original Willowmoor farmers used to boat across Lake Washington and then drive buckboards to the stately entrance of the farm. The old farmhouse remains, now a museum, as do the remnants of the drive and the bridge across the river. Inside, the museum takes you back to a time when the Eastside was a wild and rugged place.

**GETTING THERE:** From I-405 in Bellevue, north- or southbound, take exit 14 (SR 520, Redmond) east. Continue east on SR 520 for 4.8 miles to the West Lake Sammamish Pkwy exit (signposted for Marymoor Park). At the end of the ramp, go right on West Lake Sammamish Pkwy, then immediately left at the next light into the park.

From I-5 in Seattle, north- or southbound, take exit 168B (SR 520, Bellevue) across Lake Washington and continue east on SR 520. Proceed as above.

**ADDRESS:** 6046 West Lake Sammamish Pkwy NE, Redmond

**CONTACT:** King County Parks (206) 296-4232; www.kingcounty.gov /recreation/parks

# 48

# FARREL-MCWHIRTER PARK

**Redmond, 10 miles northeast of Bellevue**

*Mackey Creek divides a mature forest from lawns, fields, and farm animals.*

| | |
|---|---|
| **TRAIL** | 2 miles total; natural surface, paved |
| **STEEPNESS** | Level to gentle |
| **OTHER USERS** | Bicycles on paved surfaces, horses on Equestrian Loop Trail |
| **DOGS** | Leash and scoop |
| **CONNECTING TRAILS** | Powerline Regional Trail (Walk #44) |
| **PARK AMENITIES** | Restrooms, classes, horse arena, orienteering course, picnic shelters, playground |
| **DISABLED ACCESS** | Restrooms (via gravel area), buildings, paved trail |

Beyond the seductive green lawn, the picnic area, and the farm animals lies an inviting swath of mature (nearly 100-year-old) forest. Wide, natural trails form a loop inside the park for walkers, while horseback riders are confined to the outer trail and arena area.

Cool, shallow Mackey Creek bisects the park—open spaces to the south, forest to the north. In summer, day campers study the flora and fauna of the forest and stream habitat and learn to care for the rabbits, goats, pigs, ponies, ducks, and chickens.

To explore the forest, bid adieu to the animals and head north on paved Charlotte's Trail, then turn right into the forest on the wide, soft-surfaced Watershed Trail. For a short time, leave civilization behind as you wander under stately Douglas fir and inhale the spicy scent of western red cedar. Let your eyes rove over the lacy green carpet of ladyferns and sword ferns. In spring, orange and yellow salmonberries and white trillium punctuate the lush greenery, and white blackberry flowers promise sweet fruits for summer. Look for evidence of deer, and listen for the shriek of the red-tailed hawk high overhead.

**GETTING THERE:** From I-405 in Bellevue, north- or southbound, take exit 14 (SR 520, Redmond) east and follow SR 520 to its end at Avondale Road.

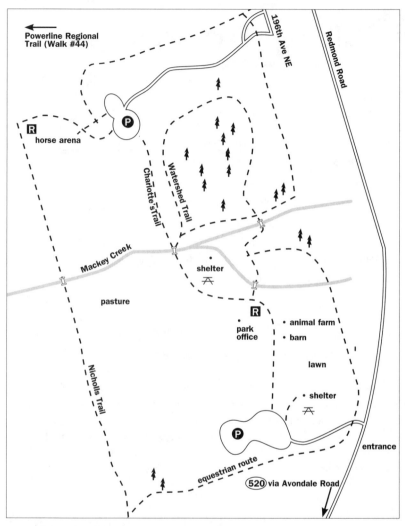

Powerline Regional Trail (Walk #44)

196th Ave NE

Redmond Road

Eastside

R
horse arena

Charlotte's Trail

Watershed Trail

Mackey Creek

shelter

pasture

Nicholls Trail

R
park office

animal farm

barn

lawn

shelter

P

equestrian route

520 via Avondale Road

entrance

Go about 1 mile north on Avondale Road and turn right on Novelty Hill Road. Go 0.25 mile and turn left on Redmond Road (signposted). Go 0.5 mile and turn left into the park.

From I-5 in Seattle, north- or southbound, take exit 168B (SR 520, Bellevue) across Lake Washington, continue east on SR 520 to its end, and proceed as above.

**ADDRESS:** 19545 Redmond Road, Redmond

**CONTACT:** Redmond Parks (425) 556-2300; www.ci.redmond.wa.us

## 49

# WATERSHED PRESERVE (REDMOND)

**Redmond, 11 miles northeast of Bellevue**

*Forest, wetlands, and Seidel Creek hold habitat for many animals and birds.*

| | |
|---|---|
| **TRAIL** | 7.5 miles total; natural surface, paved |
| **STEEPNESS** | Level to moderate |
| **OTHER USERS** | Bicycles on multiuse trail, horses |
| **DOGS** | Not permitted |
| **CONNECTING TRAILS** | Powerline Regional Trail (Walk #44), Tolt Pipeline Regional Trail |
| **PARK AMENITIES** | Restrooms, interpretive trail, maps |
| **DISABLED ACCESS** | Treefrog Loop interpretive trail, restrooms |

Stroll the wetlands and ridges of richly scented forest in one of the Eastside's premier natural preserves. Crossed by streams, highlighted by fir- and maple-covered ridges and fern-filled ravines, this preserve is home to black-tailed deer, beaver, wood ducks, and playful, chattering Douglas squirrels. Close observers may see signs of black bear, and possibly coyote and cougar.

Just minutes from SR 520, you can choose the short (0.3-mile) paved Treefrog Loop Trail with interpretive signs and benches by a beaver pond, or a heartier walk along the Siler's Mill Trail or Trillium Trail above the Seidel Creek ravine for a total of more than 5 miles.

There are two entrances to the park, and two regional trails cross the preserve: the Powerline Regional Trail (Walk #44), running east and west, is accessed at the preserve's southern entrance, and the Tolt Pipeline Regional Trail, running north and south is accessed at either the southern or northern entrance. These two multiuse trails add more than 4 miles of access for cyclists, hikers, and equestrians alike. Trails are clearly signposted for usage: multiuse, equestrian (which also allow hikers), or hikers only.

These rich 800 acres of forest and wetland were purchased from the Weyerhaeuser Corporation in the 1920s and 1940s with the goal of creating a new water supply for the city of Redmond. But water quality never met state standards, and the land came up for use proposals ranging from an airport to a golf course to commercial development. In 1989 the City of Redmond

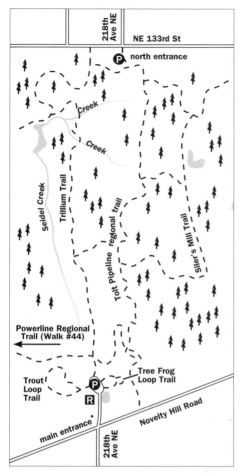

began restoring habitat and establishing a systematic network of trails; in 1997 the preserve was dedicated.

Because of the sensitive nature of the wetlands and almost 100-year-old forest, pets of all kinds are prohibited within the preserve.

**GETTING THERE:** To reach the southern entrance: from I-405 in Bellevue, north- or southbound, take exit 14 (SR 520, Redmond) east and follow SR 520 to its end at Avondale Road. Continue straight on Avondale Road and after 1.25 miles turn right on Novelty Hill Road. Drive 2.4 miles to 218th Ave NE. The Watershed Preserve parking area is on the left.

To reach the northern entrance: From I-405 in Bellevue, north- or southbound, take exit 14 (SR 520, Redmond) east and follow SR 520 to its end at Avondale Road, then continue north on Avondale Road to Bear Creek Road. Turn right, then turn right again onto Seidel Road, which becomes NE 133rd St. The trail gate and parking for a few vehicles are on the right at 218th Ave NE.

To reach either entrance from I-5 in Seattle, north- or southbound, take exit 168B (SR 520, Bellevue) across Lake Washington, continue east on SR 520 to its end at Avondale Road, and proceed as above.

**ADDRESS:** 21760 Novelty Hill Road, Redmond

**CONTACT:** Redmond Parks and Recreation (425) 556-2322; www .ci.redmond.wa.us

# 50

# ARDMORE PARK

**5.5 miles northeast of downtown Bellevue**

*A forest nestled in suburbia hides a small stream and wetland.*

| | |
|---|---|
| **TRAIL** | 1.5 miles total; natural surface |
| **STEEPNESS** | Gentle to moderate |
| **OTHER USERS** | Pedestrians only |
| **DOGS** | Leash and scoop |
| **CONNECTING TRAILS** | None |
| **PARK AMENITIES** | Playground, picnic tables |
| **DISABLED ACCESS** | None |

This compact neighborhood park is a walker's dream, with wide, wood-chip trails through a spacious forest of hemlock, cedar, and Douglas fir. Although it's nestled in the heart of suburbia, its sounds are sylvan, not motorized. In summer, robins hop along the trail, and chickadees and wrens call from the branches.

The trail meanders up and down gentle terrain and along the sides of a ravine cut by a tiny stream, where bare earth on its sides tells of winter flooding. So open is the forest floor, the path gives the impression of even greater length than its true 1.5 miles. The spacious forest and the silence are so compelling that you could wish the trail went on and on through these sword-fern valleys and hills.

Summer visitors are rewarded with a feast of blackberries, red huckleberries, and thimbleberries. Traversing from south to north, you cross a bridge and angle up a short, steep hill some local walkers call "cardiac hill." An untrustworthy-looking rope swing

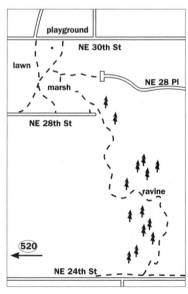

dangles above a ravine, and moss-covered steps are remnants of once-loved tree houses built long ago by neighborhood kids.

The trail leads to a marshy patch of skunk cabbage in a cedar glen, but a sturdy puncheon bridge keeps your feet dry in this dell of old tree stumps. Here signposts point to several different park exits, each only a tenth of a mile away.

On the northwest corner lies the tiny lawn, perfect for picnics (although there are no tables or other services) either before or after this charming walk.

**GETTING THERE:** From I-405 in Bellevue, north- or southbound, take exit 14 (SR 520, Redmond) east. Take the 148th Ave NE exit south. Turn right on 148th Ave NE, then left immediately on NE 24th St. Go east about 1.5 miles and look on the left for the "Nature Trail" sign and entrance. Other entrances are located on suburban streets at NE 28th St, NE 30th St, and NE 28th Pl. The picnic lawn lies along NE 30th St. Parking is on streets and limited.

**ADDRESS:** 16833 NE 30th Street, Bellevue

**CONTACT:** Bellevue Parks (425) 452-6885; www.ci.bellevue.wa.us

# 51

# BELLEVUE BOTANICAL GARDEN AND WILBURTON HILL PARK

**2.5 miles east of downtown Bellevue**

*Trails range from native forest to the botanical garden's wetlands and meadows.*

| | |
|---|---|
| **TRAIL** | 3.4 miles; gravel, natural surface, paved |
| **STEEPNESS** | Gentle |
| **OTHER USERS** | Pedestrians only in garden; bicycles in Wilburton Hill Park |
| **DOGS** | Not allowed in garden; leash and scoop in Wilburton Hill Park |
| **CONNECTING TRAILS** | Kelsey Creek Park (Walk #52), via streets on Lake to Lake Trail |
| **PARK AMENITIES** | Restrooms, concerts, docent-led garden tours, gift shop, horticultural classes, picnic tables, playground, playing fields, tennis courts |
| **DISABLED ACCESS** | Garden Loop Trail, restrooms |

Although Bellevue Botanical Garden is technically within the borders of Wilburton Hill Park, the two are very different places. In Wilburton, beyond the playing fields, you walk through a forest green with salal and Douglas fir; in the garden, you are led along established paths showcasing native and hybrid plants and vibrant floral displays.

For a good warm-up walk, head east from the Wilburton parking lot to the loop trail that borders the playing fields. As you enter the forest, it becomes a richly scented wood-chip trail zigzagging to the eastern boundary. Here, turn left along the quiet residential street for part of a block, then head back into the forest on a smaller, woodsy spur trail. Near the playing fields, you pass an innovative playground, where kids can scramble up and down the spiderweb and frolic in and out of the "town hall."

When you're ready for a quieter, slower stroll, step into the manicured year-round symphony of color in the botanical garden. The original owners, Cal and Harriet Shorts, toiled for many years to transform the heavy clay soil into the rich loam of the garden, and the work continues. Two years after the

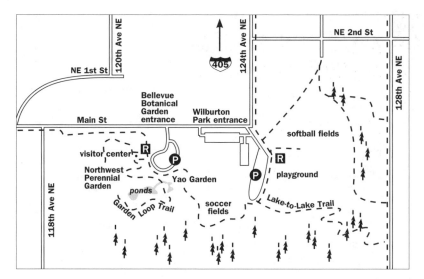

City of Bellevue received the land as a donation, the garden opened with 36 acres of woodlands, gardens, bogs, and meadows. Today it is a showplace for the Northwest Perennial Alliance, the Eastside Fuchsia Society, the King County Herb Society, and the American Rock Garden Society.

Follow the graveled Garden Loop Trail into a glory of huge rhododendrons set in a forest of hemlock and fir. The Yao Garden is a contemporary garden that combines both Japanese and Northwest influences. Along the western slope of the garden, the Perennial Border, already world-famous, is reminiscent of an abstract painting created with plants, each carefully chosen for the hue and shape of both flower and foliage.

**GETTING THERE:** From I-405 in Bellevue, northbound, take exit 13B (NE 8th St). Turn right onto NE 8th St and go about 0.6 mile. Turn right (south) on 124th Ave NE and follow it until it ends at a sharp right with Main St. Wilburton Park is straight ahead. The garden entrance is to the right on Main St.

From I-405 in Bellevue, southbound, take exit 13B (NE 8th St). Turn left onto NE 8th St and proceed as above.

**ADDRESS:** 12001 Main Street, Bellevue

**CONTACT:** Bellevue Parks (425) 452-6885, www.ci.bellevue.wa.us; Botanical Garden Society (425) 451-3755

# 52

# KELSEY CREEK PARK

**3 miles east of downtown Bellevue**

*Forested trails lead to wetlands, pastures, and farm animals beside Kelsey Creek.*

| | |
|---|---|
| **TRAIL** | 2.5 miles total; gravel, natural surface |
| **STEEPNESS** | Gentle to steep |
| **OTHER USERS** | Bicycles on gravel; pedestrians only on forest trail |
| **DOGS** | Leash and scoop; not allowed in farm area |
| **CONNECTING TRAILS** | Lake to Lake Trail (via streets) |
| **PARK AMENITIES** | Restrooms, classes, farm animals, historic cabin, picnic tables |
| **DISABLED ACCESS** | Restrooms, farm |

Tucked neatly into a nook of suburban Bellevue, this well-loved park surprises newcomers with open meadows and fenced pastures, the baa-ing of sheep and the clucking of chickens. This early 1900s-style farm with its white fences, red barns, pens of pigs, and peacocks has long been a favorite with families wanting to show their children how farm animals were raised before the advent of chicken factories.

From the parking lot, cross a tributary of Kelsey Creek south to lawns, picnic areas, and a small marsh with wild ducks. Then climb the hill east to the barnyard. A graveled loop road takes you past the ducks and ponies, then to the south by the old pioneer log cabin, moved here for renovation and preservation.

Most visitors end their tour here, returning to picnic by the stream. But east of the barns

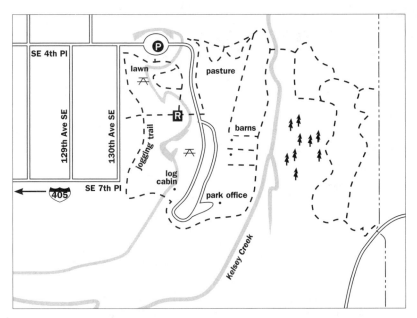

SE 4th Pl

129th Ave SE

130th Ave SE

P

lawn

pasture

R

barns

jogging trail

log cabin

park office

SE 7th Pl

405

Kelsey Creek

and pony fields, another trail follows the pasture edge and then dives into the wooded hillside at the footbridge over Kelsey Creek. Here several adjoining loops take you up soft, needle-padded paths, over footbridges above marshes. Wooden steps take you higher into the deciduous forest where, in fall, the red and yellow leaves of the maples frame the farm buildings below, and in winter the vista opens to show a broad expanse of this farmland park.

### When You Run Out of Breadcrumbs

If a park isn't too big, you can explore it in the same way as a maze, by "keeping one hand on the wall." If a trail map shows there are loops, you can continue taking right turns, thereby making your way back to where you started. In larger parks, such as Bridle Trails Park or on Cougar, Tiger, or Squak Mountain, it's best to develop a good sense of direction, and walk with a friend, a cell phone, and a map. Look for map brochures at trailheads.

In spring look for the white hanging flowers, and in summer the red berries, of the Indian plum.

**GETTING THERE:** From I-405 in Bellevue, north- or southbound, take exit 12 (SE 8th St). Go east on SE 8th St. Go under the railroad trestle to the light at Lake Hills Connector. Go straight onto SE 7th Pl. Go a few blocks and turn left on 130th Ave SE, and then right on SE 4th Pl into the park.

**ADDRESS:** 13204 SE 8th Place, Bellevue

**CONTACT:** Bellevue Parks (425) 452-6885; www.ci.bellevue.wa.us

# 53 LAKE HILLS GREENBELT

**3.5 miles east of downtown Bellevue**

*Farmland and birds abound around Larsen and Phantom Lakes'
meadows and forest.*

| TRAIL | 3 miles total; gravel, paved |
|---|---|
| STEEPNESS | Level |
| OTHER USERS | Bicycles |
| DOGS | Leash and scoop |
| CONNECTING TRAILS | Lake to Lake Trail, Phantom Lake Trail (both via streets) |
| PARK AMENITIES | Restrooms, classes, demonstration gardens, display garden, free nature walks late spring through September, pea patch, ranger station |
| DISABLED ACCESS | Some trail sections, restrooms, ranger station |

If you begin your walk at the Larsen Lake Blueberry Farm, you may see a single great blue heron standing in motionless, graceful posture among the lakeshore reeds, watching for fish, frogs, salamanders, and other aquatic prey. Ripples on the water tell of diving ducks, and between the water-lily pads, iridescent male mallards and their quacking brown mates glide. Both Larsen and Phantom Lakes, at the two ends of the Lake Hills Greenbelt, are important stopovers for waterfowl along the Pacific Flyway. As many as 24 species have been identified, including green-winged teals, northern shovelers, and ruddy ducks. In the twigs of the 40-year-old blueberry bushes, wrens and sparrows flit and twitter. In late summer look for flocks of cedar waxwings feeding on the berries.

Continuing around Larsen Lake, the trail turns east then south along the reed-lined irrigation channel, crosses Lake Hills Boulevard (there's a crosswalk with a flashing light), and then enters an open meadow rimmed by conifers—good hunting grounds for red-tailed, Cooper's, and sharp-shinned hawks. In the forest of Douglas fir and Sitka spruce, watch for signs of squirrels and the more secretive coyotes that travel the game trails through the undergrowth. River otters have been spotted in the lakes and the stream, as well as moles and muskrats along their banks.

110|TAKE A WALK

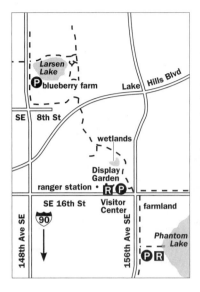

At the corner of SE 16th Street and 156th Avenue SE, a small fruit stand operates through fall, selling fresh produce harvested from the rich peat-bog soils of the neighboring farms. If you turn west here, along SE 16th Street, you come immediately to the Display Garden, where you can pore over informative signs about a variety of herbs, flowers, and produce, and investigate a hands-on display of composting techniques. At the Lake Hills Greenbelt Ranger Station adjoining the garden, you'll find dioramas of the wildlife of the greenbelt, and a three-dimensional display of the Larsen/Phantom Lake drainage. Members of the East Lake Chapter of the Audubon Society often staff a booth to answer questions about the area's birds. Cross 156th Avenue SE diagonally to continue another quarter mile to the dock and boat launch on Phantom Lake.

**GETTING THERE:** To reach Larsen Lake: From I-405 in Bellevue, north- or southbound, take exit 13 (NE 8th St) east and take NE 8th St east. Turn right on 148th Ave NE and go south. At the light at SE 8th St, smaller vehicles can make a U-turn (on the green left turn arrow) and go north 1 block to park in the greenbelt parking lot by the blueberry farm.

To reach the ranger station: Continue south on 148th Ave SE another 0.5 mile and turn left (east) on SE 16th St. Continue for another 0.5 mile and park at the corner of 156th Ave SE.

To reach Phantom Lake: Turn right on 156th Ave SE and go south a few blocks; park on the left.

From I-90 east of Lake Washington, eastbound, take exit 11B (148th Ave SE) and go north on 148th Ave SE to Phantom Lake; or turn right on SE 16th St and look for the ranger station just before 156th Ave SE; or continue north on 148th Ave SE to the blueberry farm parking lot north of SE 8th Ave at Larsen Lake.

**ADDRESS:** 15416 SE 16th Street, Bellevue

**CONTACT:** Greenbelt Ranger Station (425) 452-6885; Bellevue Parks (425) 452-6885, www.ci.bellevue.wa.us

# WEOWNA PARK

**Bellevue, 6 miles east of downtown Bellevue**

*This swath of old forest is vibrantly alive with birdsong and big trees that shade the deep ravines sloping down to Lake Sammamish.*

| | |
|---|---|
| **TRAIL** | 2.5 miles; natural surface |
| **STEEPNESS** | Gentle to steep |
| **OTHER USERS** | Pedestrians only |
| **DOGS** | Leash and scoop |
| **CONNECTING TRAILS** | Bellevue's Lake to Lake Trail |
| **PARK AMENITIES** | Interpretive signs, picnic tables, viewing platforms |
| **DISABLED ACCESS** | None |

Step from the manicured neighborhoods of Bellevue's suburbs into a forest left wild and free for many decades. Here, in this north-south greenbelt above Lake Sammamish, century-old Douglas firs rise above fern-bedecked ravines, and the beautifully maintained trails lead you on a walk in one of the city's finest forests. Huge stumps, softened by years of moss and rain, stand as reminders of the past. Rectangular holes in the tall snags tell of the pile-

ated woodpeckers that call this forest their home. Under the canopy of western red cedar and bigleaf maples, an understory of sword fern, young alders, mahonia, and stinging nettle flourish. Even at the height of summer the undergrowth is low enough to allow peekaboo views of the glistening waters of Lake Sammamish far below to the east.

Weowna Park has long been on the map as a stretch of green between Lake Sammamish and the homes on the plateau above, but not until a few years ago were the random footpaths mapped, sign-posted, and transformed into graceful wood-chip trails. Long ago, Phantom Creek, which originally ran north from Phantom Lake, was re-engineered by an innovative pioneer, who dug a ditch to allow the creek to drain to the east, into Lake Sammamish. Over the years, the creek wore away at the easily eroded glacial till, and the result today is a deep ravine marked by small waterfalls and pools dur-

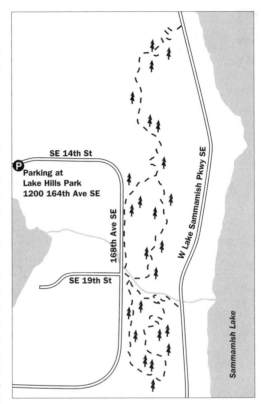

ing the wet months of the year. In summer, all that remains of this creek is a trickle of waterfall visible from a wooden viewing platform about fifty feet above the creek bed. The steep contours of this park offer double bounty: a good workout for those seeking it, and sumptuous views of fern-filled dales studded with the hefty trunks of fir and cedar.

**GETTING THERE:** From I-90 southeast of Bellevue, eastbound, take exit 11B (148th Ave SE). Turn slight right on 148th Ave SE. Go 0.8 mile and turn right onto SE 16th St. Turn slight left onto SE Phantom Way. SE Phantom Way becomes SE 14th St. Stay on SE 14th St as it curves south to become 168th Ave SE. Go 5 blocks to the trailhead on the left. Street parking only.

**ADDRESS:** 1420 168th Avenue SE, Bellevue. Also, 2023 and 529 West Lake Sammamish Parkway SE, Bellevue with very limited parking.

**CONTACT:** City of Bellevue Parks (425) 452-6885; www.ci.bellevue.wa.us /parks-community-services.htm

# 55

# MERCER SLOUGH NATURE PARK

**2.5 miles south of downtown Bellevue**

*Boardwalk and interpretive trails wander through historic
wetlands teeming with birds.*

| | |
|---|---|
| **TRAIL** | 6 miles; boardwalk, natural surface, paved |
| **STEEPNESS** | Level to gentle |
| **OTHER USERS** | Bicycles on paved trails (discouraged on soft-surface trails) |
| **DOGS** | Leash and scoop |
| **CONNECTING TRAIL** | Lake to Lake Trail (via streets), Mountains to Sound Trail |
| **PARK AMENITIES** | Restrooms, brochures, classes, interpretive center, interpretive signs, museum |
| **DISABLED ACCESS** | Paved trail along Bellevue Way, I-90, and 118th Avenue SE, restrooms |

Just minutes from downtown Bellevue, you can stroll miles of secluded trails that surround the Mercer Slough and wetlands, a paradise for birds and bird-watchers alike. Here, in fall and spring, thousands of migrating waterfowl on the Pacific Flyway en route to and from the Arctic find vital haven. Many stay over for the winter, making their nests in the cattails and reeds along the

edges of the slough. Not only a haven for waterfowl, the surrounding iris and cattail marsh, blackberry thickets, and cotton-wood trees provide habitat for more than a hundred other species of birds, including eagles, pheasant, owls, swifts, thrushes, and more.

Long ago the Mercer Slough area was part of the vast marshlands that sur-rounded Lake Washington. Native peo-ples lived here, hunting muskrat and small mammals, fishing for salmon, and gath-ering edible roots and berries. In 1916, when the Ship Canal project lowered Lake Washington by 9 feet, the area could no longer support people whose livelihood depended on the bounty of the marshlands.

Today, 6 miles of trails, both paved and wood-chipped, twist through and around these preserved 320 acres. Overlake Blueberry Farm (open in season) and the historic Winters House add variety to a walk along Mercer Slough.

**GETTING THERE:** From I-90 just east of Mercer Island, east- or westbound, take exit 9 (Bellevue Way SE). Go about 0.25 mile north on Bellevue Way SE and park at the canoe launch, Park and Ride, or Winters House. (Limited parking also along 118th Ave SE on the slough's east side.)

**ADDRESS:** 2102 Bellevue Way SE, Bellevue

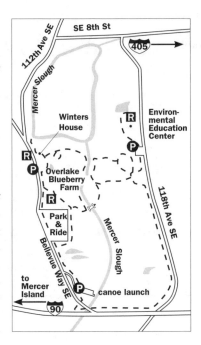

**CONTACT:** Bellevue Parks (425) 452-6885, www.ci.bellevue.wa.us; Mercer Slough Office (425) 462-2752

## 56 ROBINSWOOD PARK

**4 miles southeast of downtown Bellevue**

*Bird-watch in an open forest; stroll past lawns, pond, and an off-leash area.*

| | |
|---|---|
| **TRAIL** | 1 mile total; gravel, natural surface, paved |
| **STEEPNESS** | Level to gentle |
| **OTHER USERS** | Bicycles on paved trails |
| **DOGS** | Leash and scoop; off-leash in designated area |
| **CONNECTING TRAILS** | Lake to Lake Trail (via streets) |
| **PARK AMENITIES** | Restrooms, hospitality/retreat center, picnic shelter, playground, tennis center |
| **DISABLED ACCESS** | Restrooms, buildings, picnic areas, playground |

As though they know the park is named for them, the red-breasted robins whinny and call *tut tut tut* as they hop slowly from the needle-lined path to the salal bushes. This rectangle of green neighborhood park so close to I-90 provides lawns for lazing on, a pond to explore, and a mile of trails through open forest.

If you sometimes feel closed in by the dense Northwest forest, this is a good park to explore, with its more open glades. Begin near Robinswood House on 148th Avenue SE and, if there are no wedding guests milling about, explore the secluded garden

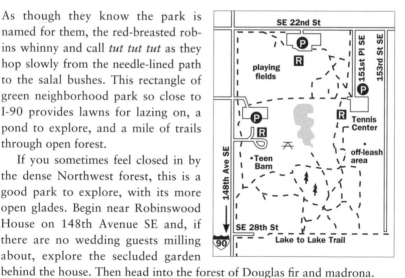

behind the house. Then head into the forest of Douglas fir and madrona.

The trail makes weblike loops, leading finally to steps and the paved Lake to Lake Trail along the southern boundary. Turn east toward 153rd Avenue SE and reenter the forest heading north, where it seems light, even on overcast days. As is characteristic of young Douglas firs, the lower branches have

fallen off as the upper ones seek light. The result: a forest of poles under an umbrella of green. The undergrowth of salal and Oregon grape is clearly visible, as are the robins and wrens that perch in the low shrubs. On this gently padded natural trail, your feet make no sound, so the birds are less quick to take flight.

Soon you emerge at a green, manicured lawn, where a small pond attracts kids with model boats and ducks seeking food. In spring you'll likely see a female mallard with her brood of peeping ducklings. To the east are the tennis center and off-leash area, but heading north returns you to forest and more quiet walking before you emerge at the playing fields.

**GETTING THERE:** To reach the west entrance: From I-90 east of Lake Washington, eastbound, take exit 11B (148th Ave SE) and head north. The park is on the right just after SE 28th St.

From I-90 east of Bellevue, westbound, take exit 11 (161st Ave SE, 156th Ave SE, 150th Ave SE). Turn right on 161st Ave SE, then left on Eastgate Way, and right onto 148th Ave SE; then proceed as above.

The north and east entrances are off SE 22nd St and 151st Pl SE, respectively.

**ADDRESS:** 2430 148th Avenue SE, Bellevue

**CONTACT:** Bellevue Parks (425) 452-6885; www.ci.bellevue.wa.us

> ### Be a VIP
>
> Many city and county parks departments have opportunities for volunteers. In King County, for example, they need people to help with administrative work, data entry, docent programs, fund-raisers, trail restoration, and more. Call your local park authority and ask if they have a VIP (Volunteers in Parks) program. Then get out and help the parks you love.

**57**

# HAZEL WOLF WETLANDS PRESERVE

**Sammamish, 12 miles east of Bellevue**

*A spacious tract of untouched forest and wetlands provides habitat for native species.*

| | |
|---|---|
| **TRAIL** | 1.5 miles total; boardwalk, natural surface |
| **STEEPNESS** | Level to gentle |
| **OTHER USERS** | Pedestrians only; horses on western perimeter trail |
| **DOGS** | Not allowed |
| **CONNECTING TRAILS** | Beaver Lake Preserve (Walk #58) |
| **PARK AMENITIES** | Interpretive signs, maps, viewpoint over wetlands |
| **DISABLED ACCESS** | None |

Walk quietly through one of King County's most diverse and pristine wetland habitats where osprey and bald eagles rest from a day of fishing on nearby Beaver Lake. In summer, salal plants are bedecked with white bellflowers, and yellow, orange, and red salmonberries glisten from their bushes. Slender blue dragonflies with alternating navy- and light-blue bars alight on shrubs by the trail and Douglas squirrels chatter on the trunks of the moss-covered western red cedars. In winter look for wood ducks and hooded mergansers on the pond.

The 116-acre wetlands preserve was named for one of Seattle's most active environmentalists, the late Hazel Wolf, on her 100th birthday. Access to the Preserve passes behind a new housing development, but within a quarter mile you have descended into a forest of bigleaf maples and sword ferns, where the heavy scent

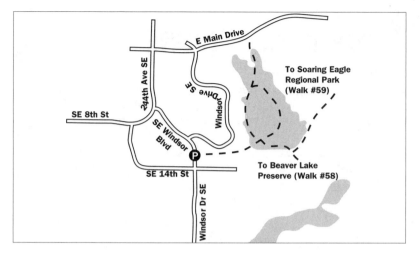

of wet earth and greenery surrounds you. Boardwalks and bridges lead over wetlands water so clear, that it is surprising to hear it in motion. Look for footprints in the mud to see who has been feeding nearby—a muskrat perhaps, or a family of beaver.

A loop trail leads to the viewing platform and interpretive signs over the marshes. Look for coots dabbling in the water, and listen for the deep *thrump* of bullfrogs and the call of red-winged blackbirds. By early summer the native water lilies should be in full bloom, red-rimmed yellow flowers above heart-shaped leaves. In the rainy season the loop trail may not be passable due to high water. If so, you can still enjoy the edge of the wetlands by walking out and back on the one-way trails.

**GETTING THERE:** From I-405 north of Bellevue, north- or southbound, take exit 14 (SR 520 Redmond Seattle). Go east (toward Redmond). Take the SR 202 east exit. Turn right at SR 202/Redmond Way. Go 2.4 miles and turn right at Sahalee Way NE. This becomes 228th Ave NE. Go 2.2 miles and turn left at SE 8th St. Follow this street as it turns north and becomes 244th Ave SE. Go 1.2 miles and turn right at the Windsor Greens entrance onto SE Windsor Blvd. Just after passing Windsor Drive SE, look for the parking lot and trailhead on your left.

**ADDRESS:** Corner of SE Windsor Boulevard and Windsor Drive SE, Sammamish

**CONTACT:** Land Conservancy of Seattle; Phone: (206) 292-5907; www.cascadeland.org

# 58  BEAVER LAKE PRESERVE

**Sammamish, 12 miles east of Bellevue**

*This mature forest, with trees approaching old-growth status, is home to several endangered bird and amphibian species.*

| | |
|---|---|
| **TRAIL** | 1.2 miles total; gravel, natural surface |
| **STEEPNESS** | Level to gentle |
| **OTHER USERS** | Bicycles and horses on connector trail to Soaring Eagle only |
| **DOGS** | Leash and scoop; dogs prohibited in adjoining Hazel Wolf Wetlands Preserve |
| **CONNECTING TRAILS** | Hazel Wolf Wetlands Preserve (Walk #57) and Soaring Eagle Park (Walk #59) |
| **PARK AMENITIES** | Restrooms, interpretive signs, map, picnic area, viewing platforms |
| **DISABLED ACCESS** | Graveled trail, restrooms, parking lot |

Walk a newly protected forest with sword ferns the height of an adult, and towering Douglas firs and western red cedar more than 200 years old. Imagine these trails before the pioneers arrived, when people of the Sammamish

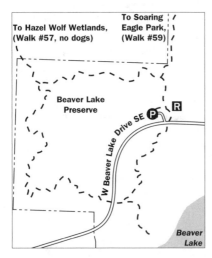

tribe would traverse the forest paths en route to the shores of today's Beaver Lake or stalk black-tailed deer through the understory. This forest and the adjoining Hazel Wolf Wetlands (Walk #57) are some of the least touched wild land in the Puget Sound Region.

Trails loop to the north and south of the parking area (crossing West Beaver Lake Drive, so be wary of traffic). An interpretive trail with nature quiz questions provides entertainment and learning on the northern loop. Bridges cross Laughing Jacobs Creek and other sensitive

wetlands. Spur trails on the south side of Beaver Lake Road lead to a meadow and a shady stand of western red cedars. The city plans to extend the trails all the way to the edge of Beaver Lake, where you may see osprey or bald eagles perched above the water, or flocks of colorful wood ducks or white-headed buffleheads.

If bringing a dog, be vigilant for the boundary signs demarcating Hazel Wolf Wetlands on the northwestern side of the preserve. Dogs are not allowed on the wetland trails, but luckily there are plenty of sights and smells to entertain a canine friend on the Beaver Lake Preserve trails.

**GETTING THERE:** From I-405 north of Bellevue, north- or southbound, take exit 14 (SR 520 Redmond Seattle). Go east (toward Redmond). Take the SR 202 east exit. Turn right at SR 202/Redmond Way. Go 2.4 mile and turn right at Sahalee Way NE. This becomes 228th Ave NE. Go 5.4 miles and turn left at SE 24th St. Go 1.3 miles and turn right to stay on SE 24th. Just after Beaver Lake Park and Lodge, the road curves left to become W Beaver Lake Drive SE. Go about 0.9 mile and look for the parking area on the left.

**ADDRESS:** W Beaver Lake Drive SE, Sammamish (no street address)
**CONTACT:** City of Sammamish (425) 295-0585; www.ci.sammamish.wa.us

Eastside

# 59

# SOARING EAGLE REGIONAL PARK

### Sammamish, 12 miles east of Bellevue

*This 600-acre forest is home to a variety of mammals, including bear and cougar, and more than 40 bird species.*

| | |
|---|---|
| **TRAIL** | 13 miles; natural surface |
| **STEEPNESS** | Gentle to moderate |
| **OTHER USERS** | Bicycles, horses |
| **DOGS** | Leash and scoop |
| **CONNECTING TRAILS** | Connector trail to Beaver Lake Preserve (Walk #58) |
| **PARK AMENITIES** | Restrooms, maps, trail junction markers |
| **DISABLED ACCESS** | None |

In this airy, open forest, ferns bob and nod in the breeze and wren and robin calls surround you. Soft, narrow trails lead you from the main Pipeline Trail into older forest where moss-covered logs play nursery to young ferns and elderberry bushes. Other trails wind and twist through the green understory to a pond and wetlands. Although you are never more than half a mile from development, little to no traffic noise penetrates the woods here, high on the Sammamish Plateau. This is a wild park with relatively young trees. Along the Pipeline Trail, maples and alders dominate, while deeper to the north and south, where the land has not been so recently disturbed, hemlocks, western red cedar, and young Douglas firs are coming to dominate. The forest provides habitat for more than forty bird species, and black bears and cougars have been sighted.

Once a mountain biker's paradise (the trails were created and named by bikers), Soaring Eagle Park has been somewhat gentrified now and the well-signposted trails are shared equally by equestrians, bike riders, and walkers. In summer the salmon berries and thimble berries grow lush and wild by the trail, and in winter, if the muddy trails don't deter you, there are peekaboo views of the Cascade foothills to the east. The best time to enjoy Soaring Eagle Park is in the summer and early fall before the rains. Although the main Pipeline Trail has no intersection maps, all the smaller trails junctions have numbered posts with maps so you always know where you are.

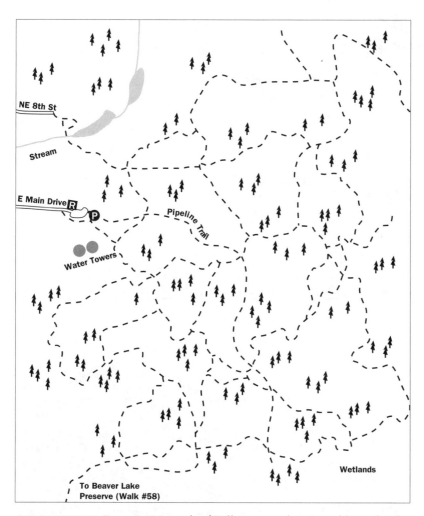

NE 8th St

Stream

E Main Drive R

P

Water Towers

Pipeline Trail

Wetlands

To Beaver Lake
Preserve (Walk #58)

**GETTING THERE:** From I-405 north of Bellevue, north- or southbound, take exit 14 (SR 520 Redmond Seattle). Go east (toward Redmond). Take the SR 202 east exit. Turn right at SR 202/Redmond Way. Go 2.4 miles and turn right at Sahalee Way NE. This becomes 228th Ave NE. Go 2.2 miles and turn left at SE 8th St. Follow this street as it turns north and becomes 244th Ave SE. Turn right on E Main Drive. Go 1.1 miles to the parking lot at the end.

**ADDRESS:** 26015 East Main Drive, Sammamish (for an internet search, better to use intersection of 259th Avenue NE and E Main Drive, Sammamish.)

**CONTACT:** King County Parks (206) 296-2964; www.kingcounty.gov /recreation/parks

# 60

# BEAVER LAKE PARK

### Sammamish Plateau, 15 miles southeast of Bellevue

*Lakeshore totem poles lead to a forest trail crossing Laughing Jacob's Creek.*

| | |
|---|---|
| **TRAIL** | 1-mile loop; natural surface |
| **STEEPNESS** | Level to gentle |
| **OTHER USERS** | Pedestrians only |
| **DOGS** | Leash and scoop |
| **CONNECTING TRAILS** | None |
| **PARK AMENITIES** | Restrooms, conference lodge, fishing area, picnic shelter, playground, playing fields |
| **DISABLED ACCESS** | Restrooms, lodge, picnic shelter |

In this sanctuary from suburbia on the Sammamish Plateau, silence is broken only by the call of birds and the trickle of Laughing Jacob's Creek. Four-hundred-acre Beaver Lake Park is an interesting mix of amenities, art, and nature. The two totem poles, Salmon Pole and Beaver Pole, are examples of British Columbian Tsimshian art by David Boxley, paid for by the King County One Percent for the Arts Fund.

In recent years, toads have been the memorable wildlife attraction of the park, at least during a few weeks twice a year. Each spring, in April or May, hundreds of adult western toads migrate en masse back to their breeding grounds at Beaver Lake. By midsummer, the metamorphosed young toadlets journey through the park and across the road to drier forest where they mature.

From the main parking area near the lake, the 1-mile loop trail begins south of the picnic shelter, in which are displayed three Native American

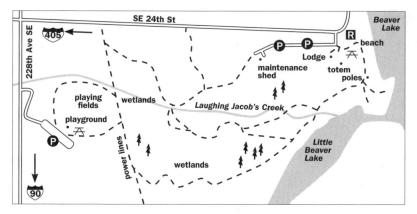

house posts from Upper Skagit tribes carved by David Horsley—again, with King County arts funds. Pass the Beaver Totem Pole and enter the forest. The trail loosely follows the lake edge south and then turns west to cross the creek. Huge snags tell of giant trees felled by wind or fire.

Several narrow trails branch off, but stick to the widest path until it emerges under the power lines. Ahead lie the playing fields, playground, and west parking area. You can retrace your steps from here or take a right under the power lines, then a right again where the trail begins to climb a knoll. Look for a clear path entering the forest; again, follow the widest trail to emerge behind the park maintenance shed near the main parking lot.

**GETTING THERE:** From I-405 in Bellevue, north- or southbound, take exit 14 (SR 520, Redmond) east to Redmond. Turn right onto SR 202 (Redmond–Fall City Road). Go 2.5 miles and turn right on Sahalee Way NE, which becomes 228th Ave SE. Go 5.4 miles and turn left on SE 24th St. Continue 1.5 miles to the park, on the right.

From I-90 east of Bellevue, east- or westbound, take exit 17 (Front St, E Lake Sammamish Pkwy). Turn north on Front St N/E Lake Sammamish Pkwy. Go 2 miles and turn right on SE 43rd Way, which becomes 228th Ave SE. Go 2.5 miles north and turn right on SE 24th St. The park is on the right in 1.5 miles.

**ADDRESS:** 25101 SE 24th Street, Sammamish

**CONTACT:** City of Sammamish (425) 295-0585; www.ci.sammamish.wa.us

> **Wetland Inhabitants**
>
> Amphibians like the Pacific tree frog and the long-toed salamander inhabit the wetlands around Puget Sound. You may see the salamander tadpoles in the water, or hear the song of the tree frogs. Blackbirds and marsh wrens nest in the cattails and reeds. The presence of these creatures indicates the health of the wetland ecosystem. Be sure to stay on boardwalks, and never allow pollutants to reach streams or ponds.

# 61

# COAL CREEK PARK

### 5.5 miles south of downtown Bellevue

*Sylvan wildness offers creekside forest wandering, old mines, and a waterfall.*

| | |
|---|---|
| **TRAIL** | 4.3 miles total; natural surface |
| **STEEPNESS** | Gentle to moderate |
| **OTHER USERS** | Pedestrians only |
| **DOGS** | Leash and scoop |
| **CONNECTING TRAILS** | Cougar Mountain Regional Wildland Park (Walk #62) |
| **PARK AMENITIES** | None |
| **DISABLED ACCESS** | None |

Like a green finger beckoning from the summit of Cougar Mountain toward Lake Washington, Coal Creek Park entices those looking for a low-elevation wildlands walk. Leave your car and let the forest surround you with tangled masses of ferns, blackberries, maples, and cedars. From the western (lower) end, the trail closely parallels Coal Creek. Old fallen trees lie across the sand-and-dirt trail, their mossy coats worn away by countless feet passing over them. In some, notches scar the trunks where volunteers have cut steps for fellow hikers.

Coal Creek Trail climbs steadily for 3 miles to the Red Town trailhead of Cougar Mountain Regional Wildland Park (Walk #62). Although there are a few tangent trails leading up to housing developments on the ridge or to streamside viewpoints, the main trail is fairly clear and often marked with bright plastic tags.

Carved wooden signposts give directions and trail mileages. To make a loop

### Natural or Man-made?

When you see small logs and branches blocking a fork in the trail, they may have been put there on purpose. Trail maintenance crews often close off old trails that are washed out, dangerous, or being replanted or moved. Steep, eroded trails may just be "social trails" that are not part of the trails system plan. Stay off anything that looks like it would be a waterfall in the rainy season, and you'll do your part to help prevent erosion.

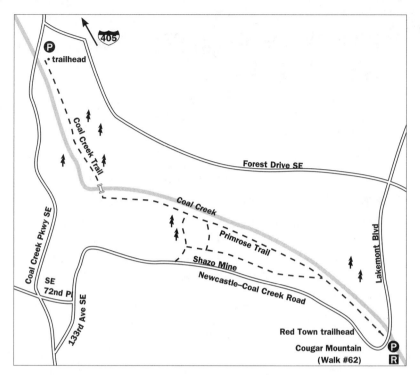

of the walk, after crossing the creek on a footbridge, follow the Primrose Trail off to the left, which passes Sandstone Falls 1.4 miles from the trailhead. Farther along, you pass a side trail to Shazo Mine. This, like other abandoned mines, must be viewed from afar; signs at the Cougar Mountain trailhead just above here warn of odorless, colorless gases that may be present in any mine shaft. The Primrose Trail continues up a steep hillside, then joins the relatively larger, better-maintained Coal Creek Trail. Turn right to complete the loop, or left to meet up with other Cougar Mountain trails at Red Town trailhead (Walk #62).

Not a trail for the timid, this one challenges with narrow ridges, a few steep, slippery stretches, and, after a good rain, the possibility of a washout. If you're equal to it, all of this adds up to the pleasure of a few hours spent in sylvan wildness.

**GETTING THERE:** From I-405 south of downtown Bellevue, north- or south-bound, take exit 10 (Coal Creek Pkwy, Factoria). Turn east onto Coal Creek Pkwy SE. Go about 1.25 miles, past the light at Forest Drive SE. At the low point of the dip in the road, look on the left for a gravel parking lot before crossing the creek.

**ADDRESS:** 5301 Coal Creek Parkway SE, Bellevue

**CONTACT:** King County Parks (206) 296-4232; www.kingcounty.gov /recreation/parks

# 62

# COUGAR MOUNTAIN REGIONAL WILDLAND PARK

**Near Bellevue, 8.5 miles southeast of downtown**

*Groomed trails in untamed forest encourage exploration along Coal Creek and old mining areas.*

| | |
|---|---|
| **TRAIL** | 1 mile to 47 miles; gravel, natural surface |
| **STEEPNESS** | Gentle to steep |
| **OTHER USERS** | Horses on some trails; no bicycles allowed |
| **DOGS** | Leash and scoop |
| **CONNECTING TRAILS** | Coal Creek Park (Walk #61), Squak Mountain State Park (Walk #63) |
| **PARK AMENITIES** | Restrooms, guided walks in summer, maps |
| **DISABLED ACCESS** | None |

The wild Cougar Mountain park is even more inviting now that it's being groomed but not tamed. In its forest you'll find wildlife, streams, cliffs, ravines, and history. Deer, bobcat, porcupine, and black bear roam the 3,000 acres, and many species of forest-dwelling songbirds live in the canopy or in the lush undergrowth. Here, too, you'll see evidence of long-ago logging and mining.

To understand, and come to love, Cougar Mountain, with its 47 miles of trails, you need to start one step at

### How Long Will It Take?

The average adult walks at about 2 to 3 miles per hour; children under age seven, about half that speed; bird-watchers—well, that depends. Variables include age and energy level, activities along the way, and trail conditions. Once you know your own pace and that of your friends or family, you'll know how long to allow for a 2-mile walk on level or hilly terrain.

a time. You may have read about its labyrinth of trails that could foil a maze-trained laboratory rat and given up in despair. Now, thanks to massive efforts by King County Parks and the Issaquah Alps Trails Club (all volunteers), Cougar Mountain is becoming a walker-friendly place. And the Red Town trailhead is the best place from which to take an introductory walk.

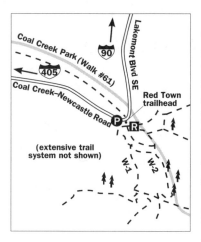

Coal Creek Park (Walk #61)

Coal Creek–Newcastle Road

Lakemont Blvd SE

90

405

Red Town
trailhead

P R

(extensive trail
system not shown)

W-1  W-2

At the parking lot, take a map from the information board; notice that south is at the map's top. Many loop walks are possible, ranging in length from half a mile to many miles. Start small and increase your distances as you become familiar with the trail markings and the map.

For a good introduction, try W-1, the Wildside Trail. Angling due south from the parking lot, it passes a sign warning of danger from gases (mainly $CO_2$) in mines. Believe it, heed it, but don't panic. You will be on well-traveled, open-air trails, not crawling through mine shafts. Wildside is a natural trail that crosses bridges over Coal Creek and threads through a vegetation restoration project, an example of the dedicated care of the Trails Club volunteers. Make a loop back onto W-2, Red Town Trail, for a sampler. On your next visit, branch out. Have fun.

**GETTING THERE:** From I-90 east of Bellevue, east- or westbound, take exit 13 (Newport Way, West Lake Sammamish Pkwy). Eastbound, stay right at the end of the ramp, then turn right onto Newport Way. Westbound, at the end of the ramp turn left onto West Lake Sammamish Pkwy SE, go under the freeway, then turn right on Newport Way. Go 1 mile and turn left (south) on 164th Ave SE. Go 1.3 miles and turn right onto Lakemont Blvd SE. Continue south about 1.5 miles to the trailhead on the left at Coal Creek–Newcastle Road.

From I-405 south of downtown Bellevue, north- or southbound, take exit 10 (Coal Creek Pkwy, Factoria). Turn east onto Coal Creek Pkwy SE. Go about 2.5 miles to the shopping center. Turn left on SE 72nd Pl, then left again on Coal Creek–Newcastle Road. In about 2 miles, look for the trailhead on the right.

**ADDRESS:** 18201 SE Cougar Mountain Drive, Bellevue

**CONTACT:** King County Parks (206) 296-4232, www.kingcounty.gov /recreation/parks; Issaquah Alps Trails Club (206) 328-0480; summer guided walks (206) 296-4171

Eastside

# 63

# SQUAK MOUNTAIN STATE PARK

May Valley, 11 miles southeast of Bellevue

*Stroll a storybook interpretive trail, or walk high into the forested Issaquah Alps.*

| | |
|---|---|
| **TRAIL** | About 10 miles, Equestrian Loop Trail about 2 miles, 0.5-mile Pretzel Tree Trail; gravel, natural surface |
| **STEEPNESS** | Gentle (Pretzel Tree Trail) to steep |
| **OTHER USERS** | Horses in southern part of park |
| **DOGS** | Leash and scoop |
| **CONNECTING TRAILS** | Cougar Mountain Regional Park (Walk #62) |
| **PARK AMENITIES** | Restrooms, interpretive trail, picnic area |
| **DISABLED ACCESS** | Restrooms |

Preserved as a handful of second-growth forest amid the sprawl of suburbia, Squak Mountain State Park's 1,600 acres provide needed wildlife habitat and miles of walking trails. Like its neighboring Issaquah Alps parks—Cougar and Tiger Mountain areas—Squak was pulled from the brink of random off-road destruction, and consequently hosts a spiderweb of paths. To ensure you don't get lost, stick to the signposted, well-maintained trails.

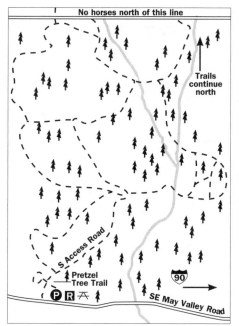

No horses north of this line

Trails continue north

S Access Road

Pretzel Tree Trail

90

SE May Valley Road

Only one official parking area serves the state park, and that lies on the southern boundary, off SE May Valley Road. From there, you can access a half-mile interpretive trail named Pretzel Tree Trail. This level and easy walk caters to the young hiker with many color-illustrated signs, telling the story of fictitious Mr. Mouse and his journey into the forest. Along the way he (and the young hikers) learn about the plants and animals and are encouraged to find the "pretzel tree" (not a species, but a tree twisted like a pretzel).

Climbing the gravel access road (used only by park vehicles) about 0.4 mile leads you to the cutoff for the Equestrian Loop Trail (S4). Step from the gravel to the quiet, soft duff under large Douglas firs and bigleaf maples. This narrow, well-worn path twists its way around old snags that stand like apartment buildings for bugs and birds alike. Sword ferns grace the slopes of the ravines above Phil's Creek, and the light plays on the leaves of the elderberry and salal.

Forks in the path are clearly marked with directions and distances, so you can choose to extend your walk, take a more strenuous cutoff, or, later, head up Phil's Creek Trail (S3) to the Central Peak. On this densely forested mountain, views are limited to the immediately surrounding hillsides, and even at the highest point the trees prohibit distance viewing. But the forest itself delights with its fragrance and terrain—and the chance of seeing the spoor of raccoon, mountain beaver, or even cougar or bear.

**GETTING THERE:** From I-90 west of Issaquah, east- or westbound, take exit 15 (SR 900, Renton). Go south on SR 900 (Renton-Issaquah Road SE) through the stoplight on SE Newport Way. Drive south another 3.5 miles to the next stoplight, at SE May Valley Road. Turn left on SE May Valley Road. Drive 4.25 miles, through a 3-way stop, and in 0.5 mile look for the state park sign on the right and the parking lot on the left.

**ADDRESS:** 21430 SE May Valley Road, Issaquah

**CONTACT:** Washington State Parks, Lake Sammamish Office (425) 455-7010; www.parks.wa.gov

Eastside

# 64

# LAKE SAMMAMISH STATE PARK

8 miles southeast of Bellevue

*Meadows and wetlands provide bird-watching and other lakeside pursuits.*

| | |
|---|---|
| **TRAIL** | 5.2 miles; natural surface, paved |
| **STEEPNESS** | Level |
| **OTHER USERS** | Bicycles |
| **DOGS** | Leash and scoop |
| **CONNECTING TRAILS** | East Lake Sammamish Trail |
| **PARK AMENITIES** | Restrooms, freshwater beaches, picnic shelters |
| **DISABLED ACCESS** | Paved trails, restrooms, picnic areas |

An immense (509-acre) lakeside park, Lake Sammamish State Park attracts hordes of beach-goers, sunbathers, and picnickers in the warm summer months. But beyond the crowds of summer, or on most days the rest of the year, you'll have miles of walking in relative solitude. For power walkers on a wet day, try the paved trails around the parking areas that lead through lawns and fields, past picnic shelters and restrooms.

**Art Along the Trails**

Public art works along these trails range in sophistication and variety from Native American carvings to children's mosaics, from a towering Sound Garden to wrought iron bench backs. These projects add variety and interest to the walks. Have you found the park with totem poles? Cast figures? An eagle? A sound garden? How about an earth sculpture?

The best walking, though, lies farther north at the end of the parking. Here a small footbridge spans quiet Issaquah Creek, and interpretive signs tell about the watershed. Once across the creek, follow the wood-chip trail left under the shade of cottonwoods and firs to a point of land by the mouth of the creek. In summer this is a favorite spot for more remote picnics, sunbathing, and swimming.

If you want summer solitude, once you cross the creek turn right and follow hedgerows of blackberry brambles, which have fragrant blooms in July and succulent fruit in late summer. This natural trail winds its way along the

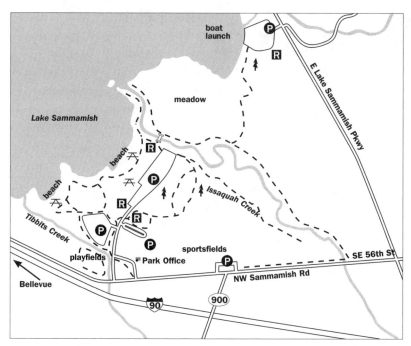

creek and north through meadows (great for bird-watching) and scrub forest to the boat-launch parking area accessible off E Lake Sammamish Parkway.

**GETTING THERE:** To reach the southern entrance: From I-405 in Bellevue, south- or northbound, take exit 11 (I-90) onto I-90 eastbound. Then take exit 15 (Renton, SR 900, Lake Sammamish State Park) and turn left on 17th Ave NW, crossing over the freeway. At the T junction, turn left onto NW Sammamish Road, and in 0.4 mile turn right into the park. Brown state park signs help guide you from the freeway.

To reach the eastern entrance: From the T junction at NW Sammamish Road, turn right (east) and then left onto E Lake Sammamish Pkwy; the boat launch and trailhead are across from 4460 E Lake Sammamish Pkwy.

**ADDRESS:** 2000 NW Sammamish State Park

**CONTACT:** Washington State Parks, Lake Sammamish Office (425) 455-7010; www.parks.wa.gov

# 65

# TIGER MOUNTAIN

**Tradition Lake Plateau, 14 miles southeast of Bellevue**

*Explore Tradition Lake and its wetlands, then branch out for more adventure.*

| | |
|---|---|
| **TRAIL** | 1 to many miles; gravel, natural surface |
| **STEEPNESS** | Gentle to steep |
| **OTHER USERS** | Horses, bicycles on designated trails |
| **DOGS** | Leash and scoop |
| **CONNECTING TRAILS** | Many Tiger Mountain trails |
| **PARK AMENITIES** | Restrooms, picnic shelters |
| **DISABLED ACCESS** | Around the Lake Trail, restrooms |

To choose one walk on Tiger Mountain is like being led to a smorgasbord and then told to taste only one dish. Tiger Mountain, like its neighbor Cougar Mountain, must be sampled on many repeat trips. Both areas, because they are wildlands, challenge the timid walker with their numerous side trails and their sometimes-unmarked intersections. Start with one well-trodden, well-signposted trail. Learn the trailhead area, become familiar with the names of other trails, and then add them, one by one, to your hiking menu.

Tradition Lake Plateau is only a few minutes from Issaquah and has 13 trails to choose from. Many are level or nearly level. Most are signed. From the parking area, pass through the gate and follow the road as it gradually climbs to the power lines. Turn left to find the restrooms, interpretive signs, and map. If you don't have a map in hand (available at the Chamber of Commerce in Issaquah for $2.50), choose either the Around the Lake Trail or the Bus Road Trail for starters; both are clearly signed.

**We're in Their Home**

Cougars and bears still roam the forests bordering our eastern suburbs, but they usually stay far from people. To be safe, always keep children close. Never run from these large animals. For a bear, make noise, and back away. If you happen upon a cougar, pick up children. Act tall and big. In either case, report the sighting to a park authority as soon as possible.

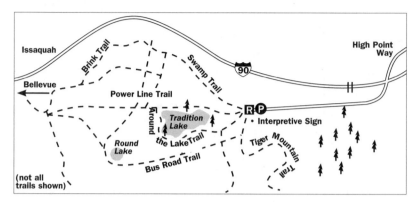

The Around the Lake Trail is graded for wheelchair accessibility. Follow its level wanderings on a hillside in lush forest. In spring, wildflowers such as western trillium and vanilla leaf brighten the shadows under the Douglas fir and western red cedar. Pale green new growth on the lady ferns uncurls like sleeping caterpillars. Down to your right, you'll see glimpses of Tradition Lake—in winter a full body of water, in summer half mint fields and marsh and half water. There are no trails close to the water's edge, in order to protect the fragile habitat of the many woodland animals that live there, but the distance only adds to the lake's charm: a tantalizing glimpse of gentle reflections on pristine water.

After the second interpretive sign along the trail, wheelchairs must turn back. At this point, the crunching gravel gives way to a soft trail crossed by many roots. From here, you can continue on around Tradition Lake to a junction with the Power Line Trail, turning right to return to the trailhead on it; or from the point where gravel turns to natural surface, you can take a small trail to the left to emerge on the wide, smooth Bus Road Trail. To the right, this trail takes you deeper onto the plateau to other trails and Round Lake; to the left it returns you, past the old Scenicruiser bus wreck, to the trailhead.

**GETTING THERE:** From I-90 east of Bellevue, eastbound, take exit 20 (High Point Way). At the end of the exit ramp, turn right and then right again onto the SE 79th St (the frontage road). Park along the roadside.

**ADDRESS:** High Point Way, Issaquah

**CONTACT:** Department of Natural Resources (360) 825-1631; www.dnr .wa.gov

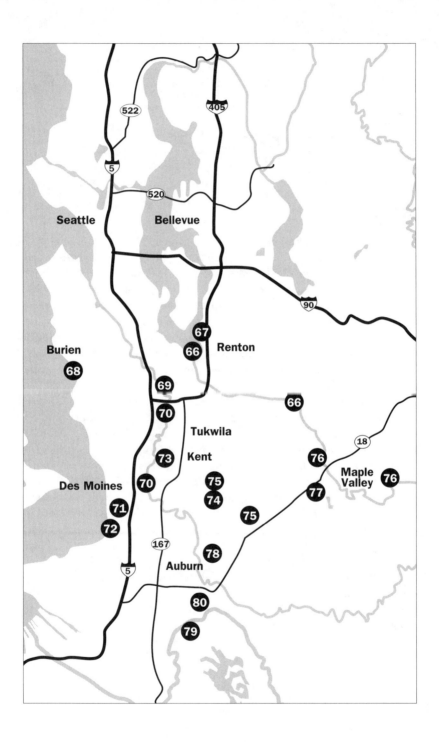

# IN AND AROUND **RENTON, KENT,** AND **DES MOINES'**

# 66

# GENE COULON
# MEMORIAL BEACH PARK

**Renton, 7 miles north of Kent**

*The trail and facilities on this cozy corner of Lake Washington attract bird-watchers, beachgoers, and boaters.*

| | |
|---|---|
| **TRAIL** | 1.5 miles one way; paved |
| **STEEPNESS** | Level |
| **OTHER USERS** | Pedestrians only |
| **DOGS** | Not allowed |
| **CONNECTING TRAILS** | None |
| **PARK AMENITIES** | Restrooms, fishing pier, horseshoe pits, picnic shelters, playground, swimming beach, two restaurants, sports courts |
| **DISABLED ACCESS** | Trail, restrooms, buildings |

Hundreds of coots, their white bills poking the grass for food, waddle awkwardly over the lawn. On the water, dozens of mallards, Canada geese, and gulls cavort and swim. Lining the log booms like sentries, the gulls declare their territory with raucous calls.

Gene Coulon is a long sliver of a park—in places, less than 100 feet wide—sandwiched between Lake Washington and the Burlington Northern & Santa Fe Railway. Yet it's so carefully designed that its broad, level shore walk, equipped with interpretive signs and landscaped with native plants, attracts walkers year-round. In summer you share it with boisterous children and quiet sun-worshippers; in fall, winter, and spring you share it with waterfowl and fellow walkers.

Though the park is most heavily used in summer for its beach and boat launch, the lakeside walk has unexpected beauty in winter. Grasses are tawny yellow against the dark blue of the lake, and among the bare-stemmed bushes hang winter's boldest ornaments: white snowberries and red rose hips. As the trail traces the contours of the lake, it crosses marshes and miniature gardens of native plantings. Look for Trestle Marsh, where old pilings mark the former railroad, cedar mill, and log-dumping site. In spring on Nature Island Bird Sanctuary, you may see nesting mallards and Canada geese. In any season, you can add distance to your stroll by exploring the boardwalks that surround the floating picnic area.

**GETTING THERE:** From I-405 in Renton, north- or southbound, take exit 5 (SR 900, Issaquah, Sunset Blvd). Turn west and go under the freeway on NE Park Drive. Cross the railroad tracks and take a hard right at the light onto Lake Washington Blvd N. The southern park entrance is on the left in a few hundred yards. Other parking is available if you continue north on Lake Washington Blvd N.

**ADDRESS:** 1201 Lake Washington Boulevard N, Renton

**CONTACT:** Renton Parks (425) 430-6600; www.rentonwa.gov

### All Five Senses

Walking is a sensory experience. Teach kids to look, listen, touch, smell, and taste. Teach them the difference between edible and nonedible berries, and between touchable and untouchable plants. Be sure you know which is which.

# 67

# CEDAR RIVER TRAIL
## (NORTHWEST SECTION)

**Renton, 6 miles north of Kent, to Jones Road bridge, 5 miles east of Renton**

*A salmon-spawning river leads from Lake Washington alongside artwork, parks, and forest.*

| | |
|---|---|
| **TRAIL** | 4.75 miles one way; paved |
| **STEEPNESS** | Level |
| **OTHER USERS** | Bicycles |
| **DOGS** | Leash and scoop |
| **CONNECTING TRAILS** | Cedar River Trail (southeast section) (Walk #76) |
| **PARK AMENITIES** | Restrooms, picnic shelters at parks |
| **DISABLED ACCESS** | Paved trail, restrooms, picnic areas |

To experience one of the best examples of urban greenery by a river's edge, begin at Lake Washington at the mouth of the Cedar River and walk south through a manicured park. After crossing under I-405, the trail changes to a more natural, forested setting.

So close is the clear, shallow Cedar River that when it rises only a foot at flood time, water covers the walkway. (Call the city for conditions after heavy rains.) At the Renton Public Library, which spans the river, continue south, past sculptures and through Liberty Park. Street crossings take you under the I-405 trestle to the Renton Community Center and another trailhead in Cedar River Park.

Access to this section begins with a pedestrian bridge across the Cedar River. From here the trail, still well paved, traverses fields and enters a cool, second-growth forest. Visible through a veil of cottonwoods and alder, the Cedar River parallels the path. In summer, swallows swoop for insects over the water, and year-round, birds forage and sing in the maple and hemlock hillside to the south. Riverview Park on the left provides restrooms and access. The trail closely parallels the highway, becoming more a bicycler's than a walker's trail. Those with a yen for a long walk can carry on the full 12 miles to Maple Valley.

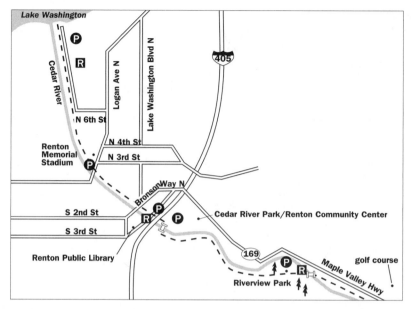

Map showing Lake Washington, Cedar River, Renton Memorial Stadium, Renton Public Library, Cedar River Park/Renton Community Center, Riverview Park, golf course, with streets including Logan Ave N, Lake Washington Blvd N, N 6th St, N 4th St, N 3rd St, Bronson Way N, S 2nd St, S 3rd St, Maple Valley Hwy, I-405, and SR 169.

**GETTING THERE:** To begin at the northern end: From I-405 in Renton, northbound, take exit 4 (SR 169 south, Bronson Way, SR 900 west). Follow signs for SR 900 west. At the end of the ramp turn right. Go under the freeway and cross Sunset Blvd NE. Now on Bronson Way N, cross the Cedar River and turn right (north) on Logan Ave S. Cross the river again and turn left on N 6th St, passing the Boeing buildings. Turn right at the gate and go 0.5 mile to parking.

From I-405 in Renton, southbound, take exit 5 (SR 900 east, NE Park Drive, Sunset Blvd NE) and turn right on NE Park Drive, which merges with Lake Washington Blvd N heading south. Pass the Boeing buildings, turn right on N 6th St, and proceed as above.

For the Renton Community Center trailhead: From I-405 in Renton, northbound, take exit 4A (SR 169 south, Maple Valley Hwy) and go south on Maple Valley Hwy (SR 169). Take the first right into Cedar River Park. The trail is across the river behind the Community Center.

From I-405 in Renton, southbound, take exit 4 and follow signs to SR 169 south (Enumclaw). At the second light, turn left on SR 169, go under the freeway, and take the first right into Cedar River Park.

**ADDRESS:** North end of trail: 1060 N Nishiwaki Lane (previously Riverside Drive), Renton

**RENTON COMMUNITY CENTER:** 1717 Maple Valley Highway, Renton

**CONTACT:** Renton Parks (206) 430-6600; www.rentonwa.gov

# SEAHURST PARK

**Burien, 4 miles north of Des Moines**

*Forest trails and Puget Sound beach provide saltwater exploration and Olympic views.*

| | |
|---|---|
| **TRAIL** | 2 miles; natural surface, paved |
| **STEEPNESS** | Level to steep |
| **OTHER USERS** | Pedestrians only |
| **DOGS** | Leash and scoop |
| **CONNECTING TRAILS** | None |
| **PARK AMENITIES** | Restrooms, Marine Technology Lab (open to the public), picnic shelters, playground |
| **DISABLED ACCESS** | Paved trail, restrooms, picnic areas |

A rugged ravine and a mature forest of bigleaf maples and conifers welcome you to this park-by-the-Sound. Unmapped trails lace the steep, fern-strewn hillsides under moss-draped trees. The beach, at high or low tide, feels wild and open. Views extend west to Vashon Island and the Olympics. Bald eagles may soar above the water, where loons and grebes dive for fish.

Just minutes west of Seattle-Tacoma International Airport, this park is a microcosm of Puget Sound forest and tidal habitat. At low tide, the gently sloping beach invites exploration. Although the Seahurst beach has no rock-lined tide pools, small puddles preserve gallons of the last high tide, and in them often lounge colorful kelp crabs and red rock crabs. Also common are the smaller beach crabs (about 1.5 inches across the body), and the greenish hairy beach crab and its purplish companion.

If the tide is high, or if you prefer dry feet, you can stroll the path above the seawall for almost a mile each way. The steep forest trails are not very well

maintained and are obstructed with blowdowns, but according to park rangers, it's a challenge to get lost: All trails lead to the park boundaries, to the parking lot, or back down to the beach.

**GETTING THERE:** From I-5 just south of Seattle, northbound, take exit 154 (SR 518 west, Burien). Go west on SR 518 until it ends in Burien at 1st Ave S. Continue straight ahead onto 148th St. Turn right on Ambaum Blvd SW, go a few blocks, and turn left onto SW 144th St (marked by a park sign). Go 3 blocks and turn right on 13th Ave SW (another park sign), which becomes SW 140th St as it winds down to the park.

From I-5 just south of Seattle, southbound, take exit 154B (SR 518, Burien, SeaTac Airport) onto SR 518 heading west to Burien. Proceed as above.

**ADDRESS:** 140th Avenue SW and 16th Avenue SW, Burien
**CONTACT:** Burien Parks (206) 988-3700; www.burienwa.gov

# FORT DENT PARK

**Tukwila, 4 miles north of Kent**

*A Green River historical site attracts waterfowl to its pond.*

| | |
|---|---|
| **TRAIL** | 1 mile around open spaces and perimeter; natural surface, paved |
| **STEEPNESS** | Level |
| **OTHER USERS** | Bicycles |
| **DOGS** | Leash and scoop |
| **CONNECTING TRAILS** | Duwamish Green River Trail (Walk #70) |
| **PARK AMENITIES** | Restrooms, picnic tables, playground, playing fields |
| **DISABLED ACCESS** | Section of Duwamish Green River Trail (Walk #70), restrooms |

This large, grassy park offers a pond, open playing fields, and casual walking on the perimeter trail. Located just at the I-405 interchange near South-center, Fort Dent Park has a surprisingly green, rural feel. And the Canada geese, mallards, and other waterfowl that frequent the pond seem content to visit a park, not a wilderness.

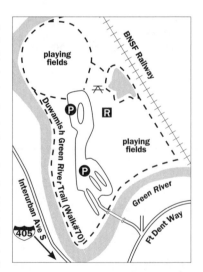

But wilderness it was, a century and a half ago when the U.S. Infantry posted a regiment here to protect the pioneer settlers in the Duwamish, Black, and Green River Valleys. Back then, Fort Dent served not only as an outpost but as a river landing for the passenger- and goods-carrying vessels on the Black River (one of those now-mythical waterways that virtually dried up after 1916 with the building of the Lake Washington Ship Canal).

Today the only reminder of Fort Dent is a monument placed by the Tukwila Historical Society about 250 yards south of the site of the original 1856 stockade. What a shock those infantrymen would have now, coming back to find not one remnant of either the fort or the Black River. However, the Green River is much in evidence near the playing fields.

If you're in the area and want a quick leg stretch, or if you're here to see a cricket or soccer game, this makes a satisfying walk in open air through a landscaped park. It's also a great starting point for the Duwamish Green River Trail (Walk #70).

**GETTING THERE:** From I-5 south of Seattle, northbound, take exit 154 (I-405 north to Renton). From I-405 take exit 1 (SR 181, Tukwila, W Valley Hwy). Turn left off the exit ramp onto Interurban Ave S and go under the freeway. Just after crossing the Green River, turn right on Ft Dent Way into a business park. At the traffic divider, turn left over a small bridge into the park.

From I-5 south of Seattle, southbound, take exit 154B (Southcenter Blvd). At the end of the ramp, go under the freeway and turn right on Southcenter Blvd. Go about 1 mile (through several lights) and turn left on Interurban Ave S. Cross the river and proceed as above.

From I-405 south of Bellevue, southbound, take exit 1 (SR 181 south, Tukwila, W Valley Hwy). Turn right (north) on Interurban Ave S. Take an immediate right on Ft Dent Way and proceed as above.

**ADDRESS:** 6800 Fort Dent Way, Tukwila

**CONTACT:** Tukwila Parks (206) 431-3232; www.ci.tukwila.wa.us

# 70 DUWAMISH GREEN RIVER TRAIL

**Tukwila, 4 miles north of Kent, to Kent**

*A riverside path through varied habitat provides Cascades and Mount Rainier views.*

| | |
|---|---|
| TRAIL | 13.5 miles one way (with breaks and unconnected sections); paved |
| STEEPNESS | Level |
| OTHER USERS | Bicycles along some stretches |
| DOGS | Leash and scoop |
| CONNECTING TRAILS | Fort Dent Park (Walk #69), Interurban Trail |
| PARK AMENITIES | Restrooms, art, picnic shelters, playgrounds |
| DISABLED ACCESS | Trail, restrooms at Bicentennial Park, Briscoe Park, and Van Doren's Landing |

A slice of peace between light industry, shopping malls, and freeways, the Duwamish Green River Trail teases with reminders of a less-industrialized time in the Tukwila/Kent region.

The best starting point is either toward the north end at Fort Dent Park (Walk #69) or Bicentennial Park in Tukwila, or toward the south end at Van Doren's Landing Park in Kent.

From Bicentennial Park the trail goes half a mile north along the river, crosses under I-405, and goes into Fort Dent Park. For the next mile, it skirts the landscaped edge of Fort Dent Park and crosses the footbridge that marks the confluence of the (now mainly dry) Black River and the Green River. The trail follows the Green River north another 3 miles.

Heading south from Bicentennial, the trail hugs the riverbank. Where the river makes a sharp U curve at S 180th Street, a lovely footbridge spans it, offering walks on either side. (If you don't cross, the trail soon peters out into industry.) On the south side, a left turn takes you to a trailhead on West Valley Road S; a right turn takes you south into Kent and, in about a mile or so, to

**Petering Out?**
Keep energy up with water and snacks. Reward kids for reaching landmarks like hilltops or streams. Tell them how far they've walked (in miles!) and congratulate them.

Briscoe Park at S 190th Street. Here you'll find park amenities including disabled access and a launch for hand-carried boats.

If you start at Van Doren's Landing Park and walk south, you can make a side trip east on Puget Power Trail into Green River Natural Resources Area, 304 acres of wetland and bird-watching at its best. South from Van Doren's Landing, a short stretch on Russell Road brings you to another peaceful stretch starting at Russell Woods Park, until you reach the junction with the Interurban Trail near S 259th Street.

**GETTING THERE:** To begin in Fort Dent Park, Tukwila: see directions for Walk #69.

To begin at Bicentennial Park, Tukwila: From I-405 in Tukwila, north- or southbound, take exit 1 (SR 181 south, Tukwila, W Valley Hwy). Turn south on W Valley Hwy (SR 181). Go 0.4 mile and turn right on Strander Blvd. Cross the river and turn right into the park.

To begin at Van Doren's Landing, Kent: Continue south on W Valley Road S (SR 181), which becomes 68th Ave S, and turn right on S 212th St. Go about 1.25 miles and turn left on Russell Road, just before the river. Go 0.5 mile to the parking lot on the right. Alternatively, off I-5 north- or southbound, take exit 152 (S 188th St, Orillia Road). Go south on Orillia Road S about 2 miles as it bends left, becomes S 212th St, and crosses the Green River. Turn right on Russell Road and continue as above.

**ADDRESS: FORT DENT PARK:**
6800 Fort Dent Way, Tukwila
**TUKWILA BICENTENNIAL PARK:**
6000 Christiansen Road, Tukwila
**VAN DOREN'S LANDING PARK:**
21861 Russell Road, Kent

**CONTACT:** Tukwila Parks (206) 433-1800, www.ci.tukwila.wa.us; Kent Parks (253) 856-5100, www.ci.kent.wa.us

Renton & Kent

# 71

# DES MOINES CREEK TRAIL

**SeaTac, 2 miles north of Des Moines, to Des Moines, 1 mile north of downtown**

*A gently sloping trail along the clear Des Moines Creek joins the beach to the forest.*

| | |
|---|---|
| **TRAIL** | About 4 miles; natural surface, paved |
| **STEEPNESS** | Gentle to steep |
| **OTHER USERS** | Bicycles |
| **DOGS** | Leash and scoop |
| **CONNECTING TRAILS** | None |
| **PARK AMENITIES** | Restrooms, fishing pier, picnic area, playground at Des Moines Beach Park; none in north |
| **DISABLED ACCESS** | Paved trail, restrooms at marina |

In a deep green cleft in the suburbs south of Seattle Tacoma International Airport, Des Moines Creek Trail follows the bubbling, salmon-spawning stream toward Puget Sound. Newly extended, and fully paved all the way to Des Moines Beach Park, this forested trail can be walked either downstream or upstream, the grade fairly gentle either way.

From SeaTac the trail leads south between buttresses of blackberries, appearing to be nothing more than a paved right-of-way for the city utility cars. But as it rounds a corner and begins to slope gently downward, the berries give way to ferns, and the alders disappear under the overhanging canopy of bigleaf maples and Douglas firs. After about a quarter mile of walking, the sound of churning water can be heard along with calls of forest birds. And then the stream appears, deep in its own ravine, clear and inviting as it flows over native rocks. Nature is reclaiming the area cleared of houses years ago in anticipation of airport runway expansion.

The paved trail means good walking year-round, but many steep dirt paths entering from the high hillside to the west become impassable in wet weather. No problem, though, for the mountain bikers who careen along the dirt trails in all weather, keen on sliding, jumping, and climbing the convoluted maze of byways. Fortunately, the paved trail by the creek now has a center line so that bicycle and foot traffic is more orderly. Side trails over the creek and up the hillside lead to bordering neighborhoods.

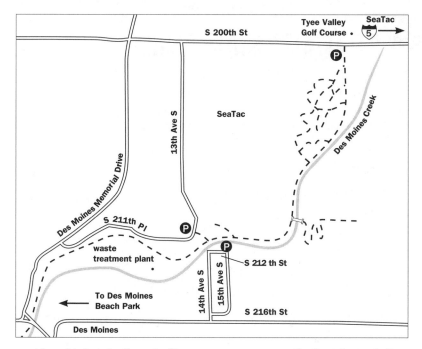

After skirting the fenced-off wastewater treatment facility, the trail dives back into the forest and descends gently, passing under Marine View Drive until it reaches the historical buildings and open lawn of Des Moines Beach Park. Here you leave the scent of wet forest and inhale the rich heady scent of seawater. If the tide is out there are acres of beach to explore and wading birds to watch. Surf scoters, goldeneyes, and grebes dabble, paddle, and muck about in the food-rich soup of salt and fresh water. Gulls call, cheer, and squabble over clams as the creek makes its last burbling yards to the sea.

**GETTING THERE:** SeaTac end: From I-5 south of Seattle, north- or southbound, take exit 151 (S 200th St, Military Road.) Go west on 200th until the road dips sharply. At the bottom of the dip, look on the left for the parking lot and trailhead sign.

For Des Moines end: From I-5 south of Seattle, north- or southbound, take exit 149 (SR 516 west, Kent). Go 2 miles west on the Kent-Des Moines Road (SR 516), and merge right into Marine View Drive S. Go about 5 blocks and turn left on S 223rd St. This drops down the hill becoming Cliff St which enters the park.

**ADDRESS:** 2151 S 200th Street, SeaTac. Or 22030 Cliff Avenue S, Des Moines

**CONTACT:** Des Moines Parks (206) 870-6527, www.desmoineswa.gov/dept /parks_rec/parks_rec.html; SeaTac Parks (206) 973-4780, www.ci.seatac .wa.us

# 72

# SALTWATER STATE PARK

**2 miles south of Des Moines**

*McSorley Creek's forest trails lead to Puget Sound beaches and tide pools.*

| | |
|---|---|
| **TRAIL** | 2 miles total; natural surface |
| **STEEPNESS** | Level to steep |
| **OTHER USERS** | Bicycles |
| **DOGS** | Leash and scoop |
| **CONNECTING TRAILS** | None |
| **PARK AMENITIES** | Restrooms, picnic areas, underwater park<br>Summer only: camping, concession stand |
| **DISABLED ACCESS** | Restrooms, camping, picnic areas |

At low tide, 1,500 feet of rocky beach creates a multitude of tide pools. Here red and yellow starfish cling, crabs scuttle, and snails creep. Inland, cool, shaded forest lets you wander over a hillside to a bluff overlooking Puget Sound and seagoing vessels.

One of the most popular state parks on the Sound, Saltwater sees upward of three-quarters of a million visitors a year. The nice thing is, they come mostly in summer and on warm weekends, and most of them visit the beach. With careful timing, you can be virtually alone on the beach, communing with clams and mussels or watching the antics of the seagulls and crows as they drop the mollusks from the air to the concrete for an instant breakfast. At high tide, walk the several hundred yards of paved walkway next to the seawall.

For a forest stroll, leave from the playground and follow the soft-surfaced path along the hillside under a mix of Douglas fir and bigleaf maple. This forest was last logged more than 70 years ago, and the

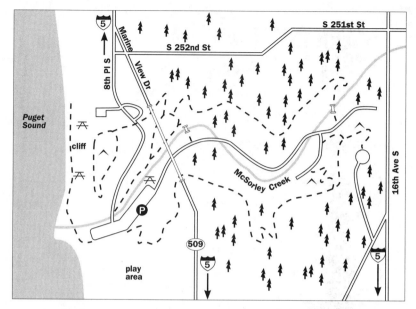

second-growth trees are reaching a hefty size. The lush undergrowth helps to muffle the sounds of visitors and the hum of traffic on the bridge overhead. The trail loops back to the McSorley Creek ravine at the eastern end of the campground. Other trails lead from the valley, make loops, and return. On the north side of the camping area, a footbridge crosses the creek, which once again is seeing a salmon run.

**GETTING THERE:** From I-5 in Des Moines, southbound, take exit 149, go west on SR 516, then turn south on SR 99 (Pacific Hwy). Turn right on S 240th St at the Midway Drive-in, then turn left on Marine View Drive (SR 509); follow the signs and turn right into the park at 8th Pl S, before the bridge over the creek.

From I-5 north of Federal Way, northbound, take exit 147 and turn left on 272nd St S. Follow signs west and turn right on 16th Ave S past the Safeway store. Then follow signs to park: Turn left on Woodmont Drive S, right onto Woodmont Drive S, then right onto Marine View Drive S (SR 509), which runs through the park. After crossing the creek, turn left into the park on S 252nd St and 8th Pl S.

**ADDRESS:** 25205 8th Place S, Des Moines

**CONTACT:** Washington State Parks, Saltwater State Park Office (253) 661-4956; www.parks.wa.gov

# 73

# GREEN RIVER NATURAL RESOURCES AREA

**4 miles northwest of downtown Kent; 7 miles south of Renton**

*Watch for wildlife and birds from a viewing tower in this restored refuge and open space.*

| | |
|---|---|
| **TRAIL** | 1.3 miles; gravel |
| **STEEPNESS** | Level |
| **OTHER USERS** | Pedestrians only; bikes allowed on paved Puget Power Trail |
| **DOGS** | Not allowed |
| **CONNECTING TRAILS** | Puget Power Trail forms the southern boundary, Duwamish Green River Trail (Walk #70) |
| **PARK AMENITIES** | Parking, viewing platforms; picnic area at adjoining Van Doren's Landing Park |
| **DISABLED ACCESS** | Wheelchair-friendly gravel trail |

Let the welcome Seattle sun warm you as you stroll this open space and restored wetlands in western Kent. Listen for the sound of wind in the tall grasses, the call of red-winged blackbirds in the reeds, and keep an eye out for evidence of coyote—fur-filled scat on the pathways. On clear days Mount Rainier forms a dramatic backdrop to the southeast.

Previously a wastewater lagoon system with stormwater detention ponds, the Green River Natural Resources Area (also known as Kent Ponds) is undergoing a face-lift with the addition of thousands of young native shrubs, tree plantings, and wheelchair-friendly paths. The wetlands and surrounding meadows are a natural breeding, brooding, and feeding site for more than 160 bird species, and home to more than 50 mammal species including river otter, beaver, coyote, and deer. At 300 acres, this is one of the largest man-made wildlife refuges in the United States.

For the best bird-watching, fall and winter are good times to visit, when the grasses are low and the pond is more visible. Flocks of migrating birds use the area as a rest and staging place on their way south. On the water you may see ruddy ducks, great blue herons, and American coots; look overhead

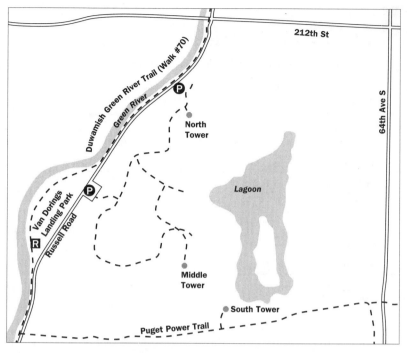

or on the bare tree branches for merlin and bald eagles. Two tall viewing platforms accessible from the GRNRA paths and one accessed from the paved Puget Power Trail on the southern boundary offer birds-eye views over the meadows. Due to the sensitive nature of the GRNRA, dogs are not allowed in the reserve.

**GETTING THERE:** From I-405 in Renton, north- or southbound, take exit 2 (SR 167 Renton Auburn) and head south on SR 167 toward Auburn. Go 4 miles and take the S 212th St exit. Turn right on S 212th St and go 2 miles. Turn left onto Russell Road. A small parking area is on your left, the larger one by Van Doren's Landing Park is in 0.5 mile on your left.

From I-5 south of Seattle, north- or southbound, take exit 152 (Orillia Road). Turn left (if southbound, right if northbound) on Orillia Road. Continue on Orillia down the hill. It becomes S 212th St. Cross the Green River and turn right on Russell Road. Proceed as above.

**ADDRESS:** Van Doren's Landing Park: 21861 Russell Road South, Kent
**CONTACT:** Kent Parks (253) 856-5110; www.ci.kent.wa.us

# CLARK LAKE PARK

**4.5 miles east of downtown Kent; 18 miles south of Renton**

*This 126-acre park has a touch of everything natural: wetlands, lakes, meadows, groves of forest, and great mountain views.*

| | |
|---|---|
| **TRAIL** | 2 miles; boardwalk, natural surface |
| **STEEPNESS** | Level to gentle |
| **OTHER USERS** | Bicycles |
| **DOGS** | Leash and scoop |
| **CONNECTING TRAILS** | None |
| **PARK AMENITIES** | Benches, viewing and fishing dock |
| **DISABLED ACCESS** | None |

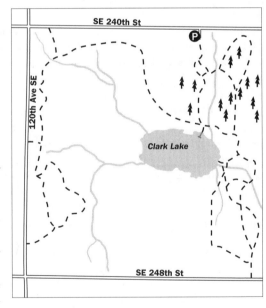

Leave the edge of suburbia and walk through restored meadows where plump heads of lavender clover and bright yellow buttercups brighten the summer greenery. The land is in transition, slowly being reclaimed from its long-ago use as farmland. A quiet dell of Douglas fir and hemlock resounds with birdsong, and bird boxes offer shelter to nesting flickers. Nestled in the center of this passive-use park, 7-acre Clark Lake is home to native bass and rainbow trout. The graveled paths lead you through meadows and shady stands of forest, while nearer the lake's edge you walk on securely built boardwalks over sensitive wetlands and out to the lake's edge on a viewing/fishing platform.

The trail rises from the lake to the north and east, and even with summer's luxuriant growth, the lake is visible. In summer, the once-domestic cherry trees drape with ripe red fruit, which is plundered by resident raccoons. In fall, the leaves stand brilliant with color against a backdrop of blue sky and the white cone of Mount Rainier to the south.

In years past, the stream was home to coho and chinook salmon; with the help of volunteers, the stream is being cleared of invasive plants and re-planted to provide habitat for the fish and other native wildlife. The original 29 acres were first annexed by the city in the early 1990's, and since then Clark Lake Park has been growing bit by bit as more land is purchased. Eagle Scout Troops have built information kiosks at the entrances, and scores of volunteers have created boardwalks, fencing, and loop trails. Although the tannin-brown waters of the lake are tempting on hot summer days, swimming is not allowed due to underwater natural hazards.

**GETTING THERE:** From I-405 in Renton, north- or southbound, take exit 2 (S 167 south). Go south on SR 167 for 4.9 miles. Exit at 84th Ave S/N Central Ave toward Kent city center. Turn left on 84th Ave S. Central Ave. N, which becomes Central Ave N. Turn left onto E. James St which becomes SE 240th St. Continue 3.3 miles and look for the parking lot on the right after crossing 120th Ave SE.

Other trailheads with very limited parking can be found on 120th Ave SE and SE 248th St.

**ADDRESS:** Between SE 240th Street and SE 248th Street, at 127th Avenue SE, Kent

**CONTACT:** Kent Parks (253) 856-5110; www.ci.kent.wa.us

### Pack It In, Pack It Out

Many parks and most natural-surface trails have no trash collection. Carry a plastic bag in your pocket or a day pack for trash. If you've got a dog on leash, you should be carrying plastic bags for scooping.

# 75

# SOOS CREEK TRAIL

**Kent, 4 miles east of downtown**

*Meander along creekside and forested wetlands that are alive with birds year-round.*

| | |
|---|---|
| **TRAIL** | 4.5 miles one way; paved |
| **STEEPNESS** | Level to gentle |
| **OTHER USERS** | Bicycles, horses (horses sometimes on separate trail) |
| **DOGS** | Leash and scoop |
| **CONNECTING TRAILS** | None |
| **PARK AMENITIES** | Restrooms, brochure, interpretive walks, picnic tables |
| **DISABLED ACCESS** | Trail (though parts do not meet ADA standards), restrooms |

Just inches above the marshes, the path cuts a straight dark line through one of the finest wetlands in King County. Chickadees call *chicka dee dee dee* from the branches of alder and oak. A red-tailed hawk soars overhead. Soos Creek Trail is a walker's hidden paradise just minutes from downtown Kent.

Marshes like this one have an all-season appeal. In summer the trail is busy with skaters, cyclists, and walkers, and the marsh plants are tall and thick with green stalks and golden-brown cattails. The landscape feels enclosed and intimate. In winter the wet meadow areas predominate, with hardhack, alder, willow, and many bird species. In winter, too, you can see through the brush to the hillsides of fir and hemlock that rise from the creek.

The park's shape is defined by meandering Soos Creek. The northern end is near Gary Grant Park northeast of Kent; the southern end is near Lake Meridian Park on the Kent-Kangley Road. Along the length of the trail, you pass through several distinct types of wetlands. Ponds are home to great blue herons, ducks, geese, cattails, rushes, skunk cabbage, and wild roses. Scrub wetlands remain flooded year-round. In the forested wetland you'll walk beside vine maple, cedar, salmonberry, and elderberry; then you climb to the upland forest, with its second-growth cedars, maples, and ferns.

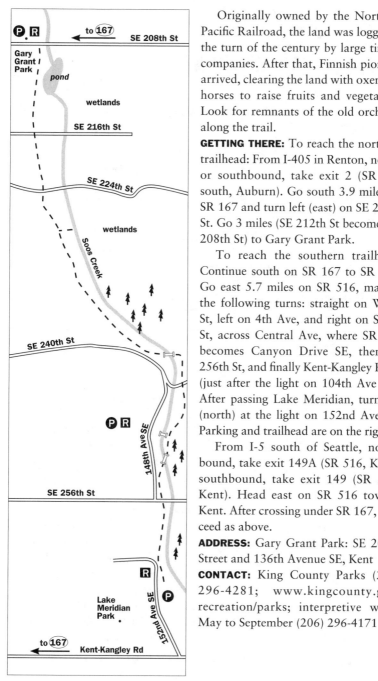

Originally owned by the Northern Pacific Railroad, the land was logged at the turn of the century by large timber companies. After that, Finnish pioneers arrived, clearing the land with oxen and horses to raise fruits and vegetables. Look for remnants of the old orchards along the trail.

**GETTING THERE:** To reach the northern trailhead: From I-405 in Renton, north- or southbound, take exit 2 (SR 167 south, Auburn). Go south 3.9 miles on SR 167 and turn left (east) on SE 212th St. Go 3 miles (SE 212th St becomes SE 208th St) to Gary Grant Park.

To reach the southern trailhead: Continue south on SR 167 to SR 516. Go east 5.7 miles on SR 516, making the following turns: straight on Willis St, left on 4th Ave, and right on Smith St, across Central Ave, where SR 516 becomes Canyon Drive SE, then SE 256th St, and finally Kent-Kangley Road (just after the light on 104th Ave SE). After passing Lake Meridian, turn left (north) at the light on 152nd Ave SE. Parking and trailhead are on the right.

From I-5 south of Seattle, north-bound, take exit 149A (SR 516, Kent); southbound, take exit 149 (SR 516, Kent). Head east on SR 516 toward Kent. After crossing under SR 167, pro-ceed as above.

**ADDRESS:** Gary Grant Park: SE 208th Street and 136th Avenue SE, Kent

**CONTACT:** King County Parks (206) 296-4281; www.kingcounty.gov/recreation/parks; interpretive walks May to September (206) 296-4171

Renton & Kent

# 76

# CEDAR RIVER TRAIL
## (SOUTHEAST SECTION)

**Maple Valley, 8 miles east of Kent**

*Watch birds and spawning salmon along this forested rails-to-trails path.*

| | |
|---|---|
| **TRAIL** | More than 6 miles one way; gravel |
| **STEEPNESS** | Level |
| **OTHER USERS** | Bicycles, horses |
| **DOGS** | Leash and scoop |
| **CONNECTING TRAILS** | Lake Wilderness Trail, Lake Wilderness Arboretum (Walk #77); Cedar River Trail (northwest section) (Walk #67) |
| **PARK AMENITIES** | None |
| **DISABLED ACCESS** | None |

Lined with cottonwoods, alders, and mixed conifers, this converted rails-to-trails path is wide and smooth, offering year-round dry-footed walking. A wild cry might break the stillness as a bald eagle rises from the river, a salmon clutched in its talons. In summer, golden-crowned kinglets call from the trees, swallows dive for insects, and dippers bob along the riverbanks like tireless windup toys.

Running a course straighter than the Cedar River, the trail takes you alternately from forest to riverside to bridge. About 1 mile from Landsburg Park (the easternmost trailhead), a reconstructed 1908 railroad bridge spans the river. High above the water, you have an eagle's-eye view both up- and downstream to cliffs, eddies, and rapids. From here, you can loop back to Landsburg by exploring the sandy path that traces the river's edge.

Alternatively, continue west as long as your feet and time hold out: several hours takes you over Rock Creek, past a stone quarry, and to the underpass of SR 18 and SR 169. At this point, the trail loses its appeal as it borders the Maple Valley Highway for several miles. See Walk #67, Cedar River Trail (northwest section) for another lovely stretch of this trail.

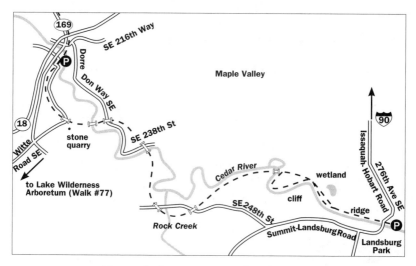

**GETTING THERE:** To reach the western trailhead: From I-405 in Renton, north- or southbound, take exit 4 (SR 169, Maple Valley, Enumclaw). Go south on SR 169 (Maple Valley Hwy) 10 miles to Maple Valley. Go under SR 18 and turn left onto SE 216th Way. Park here (walk behind the Testy Chef Cafe to the river).

From I-5 north of Tacoma, north- or southbound, take exit 142A (SR 18 east to Auburn, North Bend) and go east on SR 18 to the SR 169 (Renton, Maple Valley) exit. At the end of the ramp, take a right on SE 231st St, then turn left (north) on SR 169 toward Renton and Maple Valley. Go about 0.8 mile, cross the Cedar River, and park where possible near the corner of SR 169 and SE 216th Way. (Access is behind the Testy Chef Cafe.)

To reach the eastern trailhead: Continue east on SE 216th Way, which becomes SE 216th St. Go 3 miles and turn right onto 276th Ave SE (Issaquah-Hobart Road). Go 2.4 miles to Landsburg Park (just before the Cedar River crossing). Trail begins on the west side of the road.

From I-90 east of Bellevue, eastbound, take exit 17 (Front St, Issaquah). Turn right (south) on Front St, which becomes the Issaquah-Hobart Road. Go 3 miles past Hobart to Landsburg Park on the Cedar River. The trail begins on the right (west) side.

From I-5 north of Tacoma, north- or southbound, take exit 142A (SR 18 east to Auburn, North Bend) and go east on SR 18 to SR 516 (Kent-Kangley Road). Go east on SR 516 for 1.2 miles. After passing SR 169, turn left (north) on Landsburg Road SE. Go 1.5 miles to Landsburg Park.

**ADDRESS:** Landsburg Park: SE 253rd Street and Landsburg Road SE, Ravensdale

**CONTACT:** King County Parks (206) 296-4281; www.kingcounty.gov /recreation/parks

# 77

# LAKE WILDERNESS ARBORETUM

**Maple Valley, 8 miles east of Kent**

*Admire gardens and natural forests alive with birds near Lake Wilderness.*

| | |
|---|---|
| **TRAIL** | 2.5 miles total; gravel, natural surface |
| **STEEPNESS** | Level (garden) to moderate (forest) |
| **OTHER USERS** | Pedestrians only on Self-guided Loop; horses on Lake Wilderness Trail |
| **DOGS** | Leash and scoop; not allowed on nature loop |
| **CONNECTING TRAILS** | Green-to-Cedar Rivers Trail |
| **PARK AMENITIES** | Classes, guided walks by arrangement, nature trail brochure and map, plant sales; Lake Wilderness Park offers restrooms, beach, meeting rooms, playgrounds, tennis |
| **DISABLED ACCESS** | Garden trails |

Located on the edge of Lake Wilderness Park, the Lake Wilderness Arboretum leases land from the county for a show garden with walking trails and interpretive information. In one walk, you can enjoy both an ornamental garden of native plants and a natural second-growth forest typical of Cascade foothills.

The Lake Wilderness Arboretum Foundation, a nonprofit volunteer group, has created these gardens to provide examples of native plants and to teach why it's important, when choosing non-native ornamental plants, to select those that will thrive here without extra water or fertilizer. On the garden trails, you can see a wide variety of rhododendrons, both species and hybrids, and showy trees such as the purple-leafed smoke tree and unusual maples. Spring is, of course, spectacular with color, but each season offers some new and colorful changes in the garden. Volunteers are needed—there are always more plantings and projects in the works.

North across the old railroad grade (part of the Green-to-Cedar Rivers Trail), you enter a mature second-growth forest. On the Self-guided Loop, you can read about and observe this transitional forest, in which the more shade-tolerant western hemlocks and western red cedars are slowly replacing the Douglas firs. From high in the canopy, secretive warblers sing and tiny

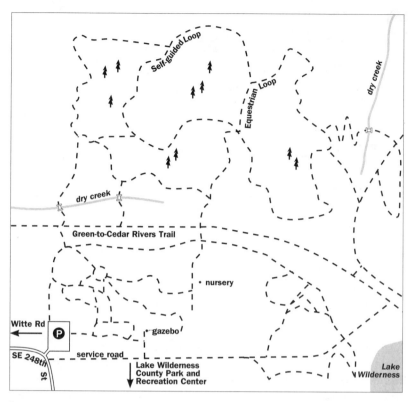

brown creepers spiral their way up the trunks in search of bark-dwelling insects. Orange lichen paint intriguing patterns on the trunks of the bigleaf maples.

**GETTING THERE:** From I-405 in Renton, north- or southbound, take exit 4 (SR 169, Maple Valley). Turn east and go 10 miles on SR 169 to Maple Valley. After crossing SR 18, turn right on Witte Road. Go 0.8 mile and turn left on SE 248th St. Reach the arboretum in 0.5 mile, just before the entrance to Lake Wilderness County Park.

From I-5 north of Tacoma, north- or southbound, take exit 142A (SR 18 east to Auburn, North Bend). Follow SR 18 east to the SR 169 exit. At the end of the ramp, turn right on SE 231st St, then right (south) on SR 169. Go 0.3 mile and turn right again (south) on Witte Road and proceed as above.

**ADDRESS:** 22520 SE 248th Street, Maple Valley

**CONTACT:** City of Maple Valley (425) 413-2572; www.ci.maple-valley.us or www.lakewildernessarboretum.org

# 78

# ISAAC EVANS PARK

**Auburn, 5.5 miles south of Kent**

*Stroll beside the banks of the clear and inviting Green River.*

| | |
|---|---|
| **TRAIL** | 1 mile round trip; paved |
| **STEEPNESS** | Level |
| **OTHER USERS** | Bicycles |
| **DOGS** | Leash and scoop |
| **CONNECTING TRAILS** | None |
| **PARK AMENITIES** | Restrooms, picnic shelters, playground |
| **DISABLED ACCESS** | Trail, restrooms |

Just 6 miles inland as the Northwest raven flies, the Green River makes its final push north toward its confluence with the Duwamish River and Elliott Bay. After flowing among meadows and forests, it enters the urban areas still clear and energetic, shallow and inviting. Although the City of Auburn and King County have set aside a longer swath of riverside parkland, the best walking and viewing are currently at tiny Isaac Evans Park.

Paved trails (all fully accessible) crisscross and form loops across the neat lawns. Start at either the north or the south end and stroll the park. Black cottonwoods line the riverbank, with snowberries creating a decorative skirt around each trunk. Young hemlock and cedar add year-round greenery. In places the brushy bank gives way to a sandy slope. Here the flooding river deposited sand and then receded, its normal current not strong enough or high enough to reclaim the sand. Watch for migrating waterfowl paddling the river.

At the southern end, a picturesque suspension bridge spans the river, leading to Dykstra Park and its playground.

> **What Is That?**
>
> Find out by joining a naturalist-led walk. Most are free. Call your city or county parks department for information. Parks also offer classes in outdoor-related topics such as gardening, birding, geology, animal care, naturalist studies, and science. Fees may apply.

**GETTING THERE:** From I-405 near Renton, north- or southbound, take exit 2 (SR 167 south, Auburn). Go 6.7 miles south on SR 167 to the SR 516 (Willis St) exit. Turn east (left) on W Willis St and go straight through Kent. At the T junction against a wooded hillside, take a right onto S Central Ave. Take the first left (S 259th St), which veers right to become Green River Road. Go about 3.5 miles south on Green River Road to the park, on the right across from the Auburn Golf Course.

From I-5 in Federal Way, north- or southbound, take exit 142A (SR 18 east, Auburn). Go 4 miles east on SR 18 and exit at SR 164, looping around under the freeway and back north on Auburn Way. Go right on Main St E, left on "N" St NE, and then right onto Henry Road and then SE 320th St. After crossing the river, take a left on Riverside Ave, which becomes Green River Road. Go north 1 mile. The park is on the left after you pass 100th Ave SE.

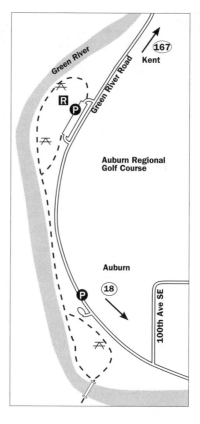

**ADDRESS:** 29627 Green River Road NE, Auburn

**CONTACT:** Auburn Parks (206) 931-3043; www.auburnwa.gov

# 79

# WHITE RIVER TRAIL

**Auburn, 11 miles south of Kent**

*Follow the blue-white waters of the White/Stuck River on a paved
trail under the shade of cottonwoods and conifers.*

| | |
|---|---|
| **TRAIL** | 2.2 miles one way; paved |
| **STEEPNESS** | Level to gentle |
| **OTHER USERS** | Bicycles; horses on soft surface parallel trail |
| **DOGS** | Leash and scoop |
| **CONNECTING TRAILS** | Game Farm Wilderness Park (Walk #80) |
| **PARK AMENITIES** | Restrooms, art, picnic area, playground |
| **DISABLED ACCESS** | Trail, restrooms |

There is something both invigorating and peaceful about walking by the
side of a swiftly flowing river. The slow pace of foot travel contrasts with
the swift motion of the river, the energetic sound of moving water, and the
sight of a lone rock fighting the force of the river flowing over it. Above and
surrounding it all is the freshwater-scented breeze. The White River Trail has
the added attraction of a smooth, paved walkway so that you can watch the
river as you walk, without being over-mindful of your feet. Perhaps you'll

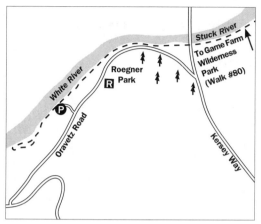

spot a great blue heron wading in an eddy, or a bright blue kingfisher perched on a maple branch searching for its next meal. If you begin in Roegner Park, you can follow a loop trail to the west, return to the park and its amenities, and then walk upstream as far as you like before retracing your steps.

Is it called the White River or the Stuck River? The answer is: both. Until the end of the 19th century, the White River, together with the Green and Black Rivers, formed the Duwamish River, which emptied into Elliott Bay in Seattle. The Stuck River flowed toward Tacoma. Farmers in the Kent Valley, forever worried about flooding, used to dynamite the rivers, and in one mishap, they diverted much of the flow of the White River to the Stuck Valley. A huge flood in 1906 changed the landscape further, and the White River was diverted permanently. Today the White and Stuck are the same river and they flow into the Puyallup River en route to Tacoma's Commencement Bay. The milky color of the river is from the finely ground rock, the glacial till, that is carried by the water as it flows from the glaciers on Mount Rainier.

**GETTING THERE:** From I-5 near Renton, north- or southbound, take exit 2 (SR 167, Kent Auburn). Go south on SR 167. After 14 miles, take the exit toward Algona Pacific. Go 0.3 mile and turn left onto Ellingson Road. Go 1.5 miles and turn right onto A St SE. Go 0.7 mile and turn left onto Lakeland Hills Way. Turn left onto Oravetz Road SE. Go 0.4 mile. Roegner Park is on the left after the high school.

To begin at Game Farm Wilderness Park, follow directions for Walk #80.

**ADDRESS:** Roegner Park: 601 Oravetz Road, Auburn

**CONTACT:** Auburn Parks (206) 931-3043; www.auburnwa.gov

### Don't Get Carried Away

Rivers can change character rapidly from shallow and placid to raging, murky torrents during and after local storms or Cascades storms that increase the snowmelt. Don't walk or play along riverbanks during heavy rain or when flood warnings are in effect. Both controlled rivers (such as the Cedar, Green, and White) and free-flowing rivers (such as the Snoqualmie, Carbon, and Snohomish) are potentially hazardous.

*Renton & Kent*

# 80

# GAME FARM AND GAME FARM WILDERNESS PARKS

**Auburn, 9.5 miles southeast of Kent**

*Glacier-fed White River invites exploration from both landscaped and wilderness parks.*

| | |
|---|---|
| **TRAIL** | 4 miles total; natural surface, paved |
| **STEEPNESS** | Level |
| **OTHER USERS** | Bicycles |
| **DOGS** | Leash and scoop |
| **CONNECTING TRAILS** | White River Trail (Walk #79) |
| **PARK AMENITIES** | Restrooms, art, campgrounds, disc golf course, picnic shelters, playgrounds, playing fields, sports courts |
| **DISABLED ACCESS** | Paved trail in Game Farm Park, restrooms, amphitheater, picnic shelters; Wilderness Park offers short paved trail and campground |

These nonidentical twin parks line both sides of the milky, glacially fed White River (which becomes the Stuck River as it passes the parks). Here you can choose civilization, amenities, and landscaping at Game Farm Park on the north, or a wilder, less gentrified park on the south.

Game Farm Park (named for its past history as a site on which shooting stock was raised) throbs with activity. Colonnades of landscaping trees border playing fields that are interconnected with more than 2 miles of paved walkways. Come for people-watching on weekends, and for solitude on damp winter days. Park near the amphitheater at the southern end and walk past the picnic shelters toward the river. The almost-century-old diversion dam divides park landscaping from river wilderness. Walk along it, or step over it to find an unmaintained but well-used path on the riverbank. Follow this path of sand and rounded river rocks east along the river. Side trails lead to possible wading and picnic areas on the shores. (See sidebar on rivers, page 165.) Beaver-toppled trees, with their telltale gnawing marks, lie jumbled in the river, awaiting removal by the rodents or the next flood.

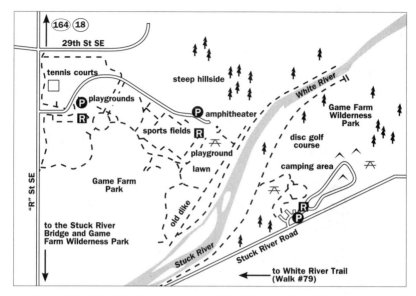

Across the river in Game Farm Wilderness Park, an RV campground, restrooms, and picnic shelters are the only amenities. An actively used disc golf course parallels the sand-and-rock path that leads along the river. Watch for dippers—small brown birds that bob and hunt for food along the rocky rapids. Breathe deeply of this fresh river-scented air. Across the water, 150-foot-high bluffs are a geological window to the past, while today's trees cling tenaciously to the sandy walls. West from the day-use area, a short paved trail invites walkers, baby strollers, and wheelchairs.

**GETTING THERE:** From I-405 near Renton, north- or southbound, take exit 2 (SR 167 south, Auburn). Go about 10 miles south on SR 167 to SR 18. Go east (left) on SR 18 to the SR 164 (Auburn Way) exit. Head south, staying right on the lower part of the road (Howard Road). Turn right onto "R" St SE and go south 13 blocks to Game Farm Park on your left. The Wilderness Park is farther south on "R" St SE, just across the river, also on the left.

From I-5 in Federal Way, north- or southbound, take exit 142A (SR 18 east, Auburn). Go 4 miles east on SR 18, take the SR 164 (Auburn Way) exit, and proceed as above.

**ADDRESS:** *Game Farm Park:* 3030 R Street SE, Auburn.
*Game Farm Wilderness Park:* 2410 Stuck River Road, Auburn
**CONTACT:** Auburn Parks (206) 931-3043; www.auburnwa.gov

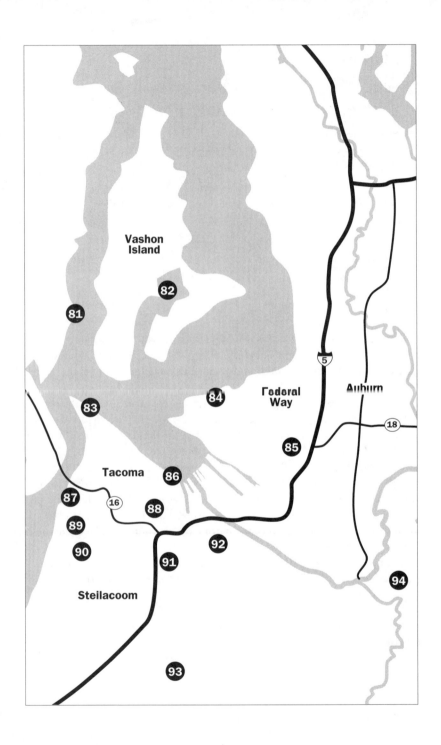

# IN AND AROUND **TACOMA**

# 81

# SUNRISE BEACH PARK

**Gig Harbor, 12 miles northwest of Tacoma**

*Take trails to forest, Colvos Passage beach, and Mount Rainier views.*

| | |
|---|---|
| **TRAIL** | 1.5 miles total; beach, natural surface |
| **STEEPNESS** | Gentle to steep |
| **OTHER USERS** | Pedestrians only |
| **DOGS** | Leash and scoop |
| **CONNECTING TRAILS** | None |
| **PARK AMENITIES** | Restrooms, picnic tables |
| **DISABLED ACCESS** | None |

Stroll a forest path under moss-covered bigleaf maples and nearly 90-year-old Douglas firs, or climb a steep trail to small clearings that single out Mount Rainier and water views. This 82-acre beach park just outside Gig Harbor is a tiny gem tucked away in a back-roads part of Pierce County. A gift from two families, the park forms a patchwork along Colvos Passage, and its southern portion—30 acres of old forest, beach, and wetlands—is as yet undeveloped. For the gentle forest loop, look for trailheads (with limited parking) on both Moller Road and Sunrise Beach Drive.

**Seashells in the Forest?**
Chances are, these shells were brought not by children but by birds. Northwest crows and gulls have learned that the easiest way to open their shellfish meals is to let gravity and impact do the work. They pick up a shell from the beach, fly high, and drop it—repeatedly—until lunch is laid out for them. Oysters on the half shell, anyone?

For the beach and viewpoint trail, continue down Sunrise Beach Drive to the parking field. To the south, you can venture down the grassy slope to the tree-lined beach for some low-tide exploring and views of Mount Rainier and Vashon Island. At high tide the beach disappears, and waves make a song of water on wood as they lap and slap against the wooden seawall.

To hike the steep viewpoint trail, return to the parking field and look on its north side against the hill for the trailhead sign. After you run the

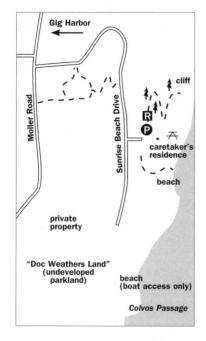

Gig Harbor

Moller Road

Sunrise Beach Drive

cliff

R
P

caretaker's residence

beach

private property

"Doc Weathers Land" (undeveloped parkland)

beach (boat access only)

Colvos Passage

prickly, stinging gauntlet of blackberry and nettle, the trail widens and a lush green forest encircles you. A massive bigleaf maple with multiple trunks borders the steeply climbing trail. Not for the faint of heart or for young children, the now-narrow path ascends along the side of a steep ravine to the first of several viewpoints. Summer foliage masks Rainier but allows tempting glimpses of the water and Vashon far below.

At the second viewpoint, the scene widens and the water shimmers beneath the cliff. Circling the hill, the trail traverses high above a few homes, past old stumps with crevices that house shrews and mice. A wooden sign and an abrupt bluff declare the trail's end. Here, at last, you have a clear, inspiring view of Mount Rainier.

It's best to avoid this trail in wet weather because of its steep, hill-hugging ascent. But try it in fair weather and be rewarded with late-afternoon sunglow on the mountain.

**GETTING THERE:** From I-5 in Tacoma, north- or southbound, take exit 132 (SR 16 west, Gig Harbor). Follow SR 16 west over the Tacoma Narrows Bridge. After the bridge, go 3.7 miles north to Gig Harbor and take the Pioneer Way exit. Go to the T junction at Harborview Drive and turn left, staying on Harborview as it veers right, hugging the water of Gig Harbor. At the T junction with Vernhardson St, turn right. Go to Crescent Valley Drive NW and turn left. Go 0.6 mile and turn right on Drummond Drive (Crescent Valley cutoff). Go 0.8 mile to the T junction at Moller Road. Jog right, then left onto Sunrise Beach Drive at the Sunrise Beach Park sign. Follow the narrow and winding road down to parking on the left.

**ADDRESS:** 10015 Sunrise Beach Drive NW, Gig Harbor

**CONTACT:** Pierce County Parks (253) 798-4176; www.co.pierce.wa.us

Tacoma

# 82

# BURTON ACRES— JENSON POINT PARK

Vashon Island, 14 miles north of Tacoma (including ferry)

*Leave the beach on Quartermaster Harbor for cathedral forest trails.*

| | |
|---|---|
| **TRAIL** | 1.1-mile loop, including center trails; natural surface |
| **STEEPNESS** | Gentle |
| **OTHER USERS** | Bicycles |
| **DOGS** | Leash and scoop |
| **CONNECTING TRAILS** | None |
| **PARK AMENITIES** | Restrooms, boat launch, boat rentals, picnic tables |
| **DISABLED ACCESS** | Restrooms |

Enter a forest cathedral, almost a century old. The deeply furrowed bark of the old Douglas firs leads your eyes upward. Between the pillarlike trunks, neat clusters of sword fern and Oregon grape grow as if arranged like offerings. Walk silently on paths filled with fir needles. The bigleaf maples grow multiple trunks like candelabras.

Saved from the enthusiasm of 19th-century farmers for burning stumps and clearing acreage, these 68 acres belonged to Miles Hatch, a Tacoma businessman who started a college at Burton, where he pioneered in the late 1800s. Although the park has a small beach, picnic area, and boat launch, its allure lies in the forest. Enter it from either of two paths that lead from Burton Drive across from the boat launch. By turning right every time the trail splits, you can experiment with making a loop. If you find that your choice has led you to a house, retrace your steps to the junction and take the other path.

The northern section (the Enchanted Forest) has an open and spacious feel. The squat stumps with their rectangular springboard holes look like sylvan dwarves in a Disney cartoon. Fallen giant trees show the shallow root system of the Douglas firs and how easily they are uprooted in winter windstorms.

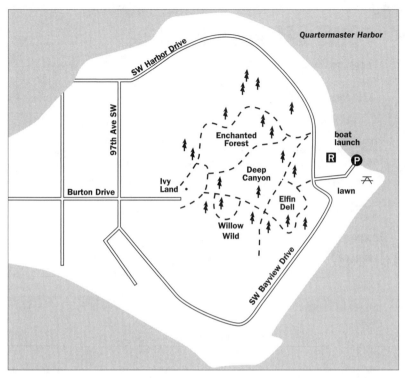

As you take the loop trail, you'll notice subtle changes. In the western section (Ivy Land), English ivy has invaded from the bordering neighborhoods, threatening to engulf the shrubbery and stumps. The brush, too, is higher, composed of blackberry and nettle, and the trees trunks are smaller. A gentle decline in the trail takes you back into the past, back into the cathedral of older trees.

**GETTING THERE:** From Tacoma (Point Defiance), take the ferry to Tahlequah (Vashon Island). Go north on Vashon Island Hwy about 5.5 miles. Turn right on Burton Drive and follow it to the north (at 97th Ave SW) and around the peninsula (on SW Harbor Drive). Look on the left for a boat launch and park sign. The trail begins across the street to the right.

From West Seattle (Fauntleroy Way SW), take the ferry to Vashon Island. Go south on Vashon Island Hwy about 8.8 miles. Turn left on Burton Drive and proceed as above.

**ADDRESS:** SW Bayview Drive and SW Harbor Drive, Vashon Island

**CONTACT:** Vashon Park District (206) 463-9602; www.vashonparkdistrict.org

# 83

# POINT DEFIANCE PARK

**5 miles northwest of downtown Tacoma**

*Stroll along forest trails and saltwater beach; visit gardens and Fort Nisqually Historic Site.*

| | |
|---|---|
| **TRAIL** | 8 miles total; gravel, natural surface, paved |
| **STEEPNESS** | Level to steep |
| **OTHER USERS** | Pedestrians only in forest; bicycles on paved trails |
| **DOGS** | Leash and scoop |
| **CONNECTING TRAILS** | None |
| **PARK AMENITIES** | Restrooms, beach, gardens, picnic shelters; admission fee: aquarium, children's entertainment, logging museum, zoo |
| **DISABLED ACCESS** | The Promenade (1 mile, Owen Beach to Boat-house Marina), park facilities (sawdust-covered trails in Never Never Land) |

It would be hard to choose one trail above all others in this 700-acre park on the northwest tip of Tacoma. Whatever your pleasure in walking trails, you'll find it here. Near the main entrance at N Park Avenue and Pearl Street, paved trails circulate throughout the formal park zone with its pond and gardens. Explore the world-class Rose Garden, the Japanese Garden, and, for a steeper walk, the Native Garden. Stroll the paved Promenade from the boathouse to Owen Beach on Commencement Bay. On Five-Mile Drive, the Rhododendron Garden, ablaze with color in the early spring, leads to more wooded paths. High in the interior of the park, the Spine Trail, bisecting the park through its wild old forest, provides quiet on natural trails and an intimacy with nature not found near the beach and picnic areas.

**Who was Douglas?**

David Douglas was a Scottish naturalist who explored the Pacific Northwest (then called the Columbia District) with the permission of the Hudson's Bay Company in the 1820's. His name is linked in scientific nomenclature to eighty plants and animals, including the Douglas fir and the Douglas squirrel.

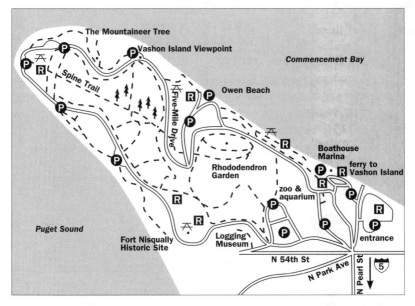

For views of the water and the Olympics, try the walk north from the Vashon Island Viewpoint on Five-Mile Drive. This wooded trail passes wondrous old Douglas firs, cedars, and hemlocks. The earthen path muffles sounds, and as the trail curves farther from the road, the silence settles around you. Because of the age of this forest (more than 100 years), the undergrowth is sparse and a carpet of needles lies on the forest floor. Go past the footpath to the beach, continuing until you come to the immense Mountaineer Tree. This Douglas fir, the largest living tree in the park, measures 218 feet tall and is more than 400 years old. If it survives the forces of nature (and human vandalism), it could still be standing 500 years from now.

**GETTING THERE:** From I-5 in Tacoma, north- or southbound, take exit 132 (SR 16 west, Gig Harbor, Bremerton). Go 3.6 miles west on SR 16 to the 6th Ave/Pearl St exit. Turn left (west) on 6th Ave, then right (north) on Pearl St/ SR 163. Go north 3 miles on N Pearl St, which ends at the Point Defiance Park entrance. On Saturday mornings, Five-Mile Drive is closed to motorized vehicles, but other access points are open.

**ADDRESS:** 5400 N Pearl Street, Tacoma

**CONTACT:** Metropolitan Park District of Tacoma (253) 305-1000; www.metroparkstacoma.org

Tacoma

# 84

# DASH POINT STATE PARK

**Federal Way, 13 miles north of Tacoma**

*A Puget Sound beach and creekside forest feature bird-watching and interpretive activities.*

| | |
|---|---|
| **TRAIL** | 11 miles total; natural surface |
| **STEEPNESS** | Level to steep |
| **OTHER USERS** | Pedestrians only |
| **DOGS** | Leash and scoop |
| **CONNECTING TRAILS** | None |
| **PARK AMENITIES** | Restrooms, camping, picnic shelters |
| **DISABLED ACCESS** | Restrooms, campsites |

The snow-covered peaks of the Olympics jut into the ice-blue sky to the west. Bald eagles glide or beat their wings against the winter wind, holding in place over the whitecaps of the water. Sea-gulls screech and harass the eagles for a share of the meal. Bold and dramatic, this is Puget Sound in winter, seen from the wind-whipped beach at Dash Point.

But whatever the season, the low-tide beach is always inviting with its long strolls (3,300 feet each way) along firm and rippled sand. Views are fine across the East Passage to Maury Island, Vashon Island, and the Olympics. On hot summer weekends, the beach area is crowded with families and children. Driftwood, adorned in black and silver mussel shells and rosettes of barnacles, accents the gently sloping beach. To the north, where the park hillsides pitch steeply to the beach, fir and madrona trees lie across the sand, their roots torn loose from the hill. But at low tide, you can skirt these and walk until your calves ache.

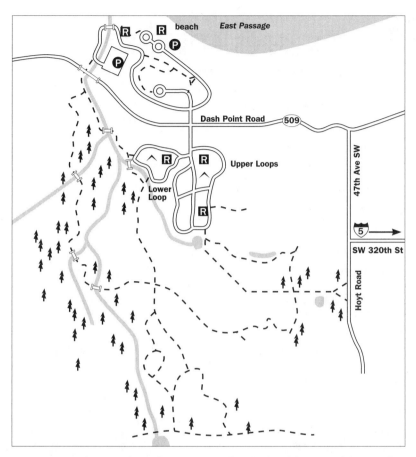

To escape the crowds or the rising tide, head inland for quiet forest walks. From the southwestern corner of the beach parking lot, a dirt-and-sand trail pursues the creek under high maples, firs, and red alders. These miles of trail are for worry-free wandering—some lead nowhere, some to east campground loops. Sturdy wooden bridges span the stream, and steps with railings ease the steep climb from beach to bluff.

**GETTING THERE:** From I-5 north of Tacoma, north- or southbound, take exit 143 (Federal Way, S 320th St). Turn west on S 320th St. Go about 4.7 miles and turn right (north) on 47th Ave SW. At the next T junction, turn left onto Dash Point Road (SR 509), which runs through the park. The park entrance is on the right in about 0.5 mile.

**ADDRESS:** 5700 SW Dash Point Road, Federal Way

**CONTACT:** Washington State Parks (253) 661-4955; www.parks.wa.gov

# 85

# WEST HYLEBOS WETLANDS PARK

**Federal Way, 11.5 miles northeast of Tacoma**

*Walk on boardwalks over 12,000-year-old peat through this urban oasis of wetland and wildlife.*

| | |
|---|---|
| **TRAIL** | 1-mile loop; boardwalk |
| **STEEPNESS** | Level |
| **OTHER USERS** | Pedestrians only |
| **DOGS** | Not allowed |
| **CONNECTING TRAILS** | None |
| **PARK AMENITIES** | Restrooms, interpretive trail |
| **DISABLED ACCESS** | Trail, restrooms |

Nestled in the heart of Federal Way, this small enclave of native wetland is a schoolroom in the wild. Rich, earthy scents accompany you along the dry boardwalk trail. Interpretive markers call attention to wetland plants and common inhabitants of the peat bog and streambank. The walkways "float" on a cushioning of 36 feet of peat that dates back 12,000 to 15,000 years. Moss drapes heavily from the limbs of the bigleaf maples.

This park has caught the attention of environmental groups, research- ers, and nature enthusiasts alike. But

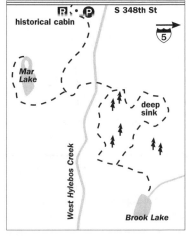

the main thrust of interest in the park came from the Marckx family, who donated 25 acres to the State in the late 1980s with the dream of creating a wetlands preserve. In 2004, Hylebos Wetlands was transferred to the city of Federal Way, and the current 120 acres support dozens of species of moss, lichen, and fungi. Coho salmon have returned to the stream, flashing ruby- red scales against the green of the forest.

Birds, although not easy to see because of the dense vegetation and the low light, raise their voices in a chorus of song in the early morning and serenade the sunset. Hawks and other birds of prey frequent the park and its surroundings. Great blue herons feed at Mar Lake as though it were a breakfast buffet.

Don't plan to visit Hylebos immediately after a heavy winter storm; the stream floods about three times each winter, prohibiting access to Brook Lake and leaving the boardwalks slippery.

**GETTING THERE:** From I-5 north of Tacoma, northbound, take exit 142B (SR 99, Federal Way); southbound, take exit 142B (SR 161 south, Puyallup, Federal Way). Turn west on S 348th St toward Federal Way. Go 0.5 mile and cross Pacific Hwy (SR 99). In another 0.5 mile, turn left onto 4th Ave S (just past St. Francis Hospital). The park is signposted here. Go 2 blocks to the parking lot on the left.

**ADDRESS:** 411 S 348th Street, Federal Way

**CONTACT:** City of Federal Way (253) 835-6900; www.cityoffederalway.com

Tacoma

# 86

# WRIGHT PARK

**Downtown Tacoma**

*Urban paths lead past a pond, a conservatory, an arboretum, and art.*

| | |
|---|---|
| **TRAIL** | 1.5 miles total; gravel |
| **STEEPNESS** | Level to gentle |
| **OTHER USERS** | Bicycles |
| **DOGS** | Leash and scoop; not allowed in conservatory |
| **CONNECTING TRAILS** | None |
| **PARK AMENITIES** | Restrooms, classes, community center, horseshoe pits, lawn bowling, picnic tables, playground, putting green, wading pool |
| **DISABLED ACCESS** | Restrooms, community center, conservatory, paths |

Moist, warm air awakens the sense of smell, and brilliant floral colors stimulate eyes weary of Washington's ever-present green. Birds of paradise, exotic orchids, tropical bromeliads, and poinsettias paint a wild

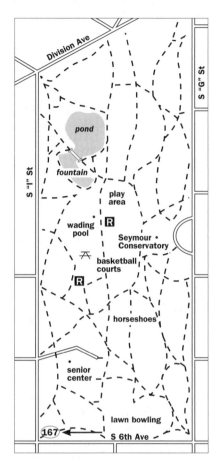

palette of color inside the Seymour Conservatory (open daily 10:00am–4:30pm; free admission). Outside, exotic trees from Asia and Europe add new and unfamiliar forms to the lawns etched by zigzagging paths.

A patch of elegant greenery in historic Tacoma, this 100-year-old park is unique in its spacious landscaping. Follow the paths up and down gentle hillocks. Pause to watch the antics of the mallards on the pond or feel the emotion created by sculptor Larry Anderson's *The Leaf,* south of the community center. But people, more than plants, animals, and art, are the focus of this lively park. As you walk, watch the gyrations of intense young basketball players, the graceful moves of the lawn bowlers, the directed concentration of the horseshoe players. Then carry on your walk—there are lots of tree species to learn.

**GETTING THERE:** From I-5 in Tacoma, north- or southbound, take exit 132 (SR 16 west, Gig Harbor, Bremerton). From SR 16, take the first exit, Sprague Ave, and go north 1.5 miles to S 6th Ave. Turn right (east) on S 6th Ave to S "I" St and the park. There is curbside parking around the park.

**ADDRESS:** S 6th Avenue and S "I" Street, Tacoma

**CONTACT:** Metropolitan Park District of Tacoma (253) 305-1000; www.metroparkstacoma.org

**This Isn't Paris!**
Try saying "Hi." You may not talk to strangers on the street, but camaraderie develops among walkers. Some neighborhood trails have been responsible for creating whole new social groups.

# 87

# TITLOW PARK

**5 miles west of downtown Tacoma**

*Explore wetlands and enjoy Olympic views, forest, and fitness trails from the beach at The Narrows.*

| | |
|---|---|
| **TRAIL** | 2 miles total; gravel, natural surface, paved |
| **STEEPNESS** | Level to gentle |
| **OTHER USERS** | Pedestrians only on forest trails |
| **DOGS** | Leash and scoop |
| **CONNECTING TRAILS** | None |
| **PARK AMENITIES** | Restrooms, community center, fitness course, picnic shelters, playing fields, swimming pools, tennis courts |
| **DISABLED ACCESS** | Restrooms, buildings, pool |

The beauty of Titlow hides behind the busy façade of a swimming pool, playing fields, buildings, and two lagoons, one fresh, one tidal. To leave the high concentration of people, dogs, and ducks, walk past the activities areas,

> **Kid Tip: Choose Walks with Variety**
>
> Avoid long, straight trails when walking with children unless they want to try out their tricycle while you walk. Playgrounds make good bribes for the end of a trail well walked. Streams are fun, but not if they're protected for salmon and can't be played in. You almost can't go wrong with beaches, but you may want the beach to be the destination, not the walk itself. It's hard to get kids to move when there is so much stuff to be picked up and played with.

heading north on the gravel trail that parallels the Burlington Northern tracks. Suddenly the crowds dissipate and you walk in the shade of alders and graceful madronas. A fitness course winds its way over stream and wetlands through the forest.

At the maintenance road, turn left toward the beach. Here, in a secluded strip of forest above the sand, you'll find picnic tables and viewpoints over the water. To explore the beach, follow the old boat-launch ramp down. At low tide you have a half mile of sand and crabs, clams and seaweed to explore before reaching the southern end of Titlow.

Separated from the rest of the park by the railroad tracks, the southwestern corner features views, picnicking, and beachcombing. High on the old ferry dock pilings, wooden birdhouses await nesting martins. Interpretive signs tell about the tidal zones and the creatures living there. This is a favorite point for scuba divers and kayakers, so there's always lots of activity to watch. At high tide, you can walk the quarter-mile access road between the tracks and the beach for fine views of the water and the Tacoma Narrows Bridge.

**GETTING THERE:** From I-5 in Tacoma, take exit 132 (SR 16 west, Gig Harbor, Bremerton). Go about 4.5 miles west on SR 16 and take the Jackson Ave exit. Turn left (south) on Jackson Ave. Go one block and turn right on 6th Ave, which ends at the park.

**ADDRESS:** 8425 6th Avenue, Tacoma

**CONTACT:** Metropolitan Park District of Tacoma (253) 305-1000; www.metroparkstacoma.org

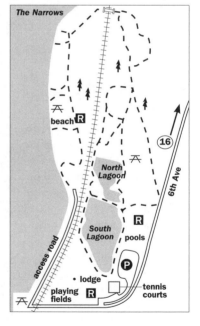

# 88

# TACOMA NATURE CENTER

**3 miles west of downtown Tacoma**

*Snake Lake's wetlands and forest are alive with birds and wildlife.*

| | |
|---|---|
| **TRAIL** | 1-mile Wetland Trail, 1.5-mile Hilltop Forest Loop; natural surface |
| **STEEPNESS** | Level to moderate |
| **OTHER USERS** | Pedestrians only |
| **DOGS** | Not allowed |
| **CONNECTING TRAILS** | None |
| **PARK AMENITIES** | Restrooms, classes, interpretive center, interpretive trail |
| **DISABLED ACCESS** | Westside Trail (0.5 miles one way), restrooms, interpretive center |

The forest here seems intimate, as though nature were wrapping you in earth and lake smells, vine and shrub textures, and the songs of birds. Ten feet from the trail and indifferent to human presence, the wood ducks continue pecking, grooming, and twittering on the muddy bank of Snake Lake. Each line of their vivid, poster-colored heads stands out in sharp contrast to the brown earth.

Winter is a rewarding time to visit this small, snake-shaped lake in the midst of commercial Tacoma. Where only a corner of water remains unfrozen, the ducks, geese, and grebes congregate in massive displays of color

and motion. The snowberry and blackberry thickets stand crisp and naked
without their greenery, letting you watch
the wrens flit from twig to twig.

Warmer weather, though, invites you
to explore all 54 acres. Walk the Wetland Loop, with a stop or two on the
bridges or in the wildlife blinds along the
trail, to see what creatures come to feed
among the reeds. Year-round waterfowl
include mallards, Canada geese, herons,
and wood ducks. A climb up the Hill-
top Forest Loop above the lake promises
more exercise and the refreshing cool of
shade. Early-morning visitors may see
prints of the resident red foxes or raccoons.

The Nature Center has displays,
hands-on activities for adults and kids,
interpretive information, and a gift shop.
The preserve is open daily 8 am to dusk;
the interpretive center is open Monday
through Friday 8 am–5 pm. Saturday 10
am to 4 pm (free admission).

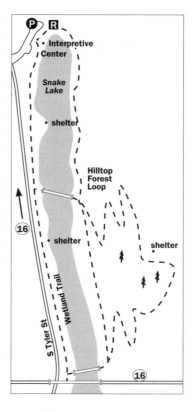

**GETTING THERE:** From I-5 in Tacoma,
north- or southbound, take exit 132 (SR 16 west, Gig Harbor, Bremerton).
Go 2.5 miles west on SR 16 and take the 19th St east exit. Turn right on S
19th St, then right again on S Tyler St. Parking is on the left.

**ADDRESS:** 1919 S Tyler Street, Tacoma

**CONTACT:** Metropolitan Park District of Tacoma (253) 591-6439;
www.metroparkstacoma.org

# 89

# CHAMBERS CREEK CANYON TRAIL

University Place, 12 miles southwest of Tacoma

*A clear creek flows through forest into Chambers Bay on Puget Sound.*

| | |
|---|---|
| **TRAIL** | 1.5 miles one way; natural surface |
| **STEEPNESS** | Steep |
| **OTHER USERS** | Pedestrians only |
| **DOGS** | Leash and scoop |
| **CONNECTING TRAILS** | None |
| **PARK AMENITIES** | None |
| **DISABLED ACCESS** | None |

Hike high on a wildland hillside of moss-covered bigleaf maples and Douglas firs you can hardly fit your arms around. Look out into the canopy of trees and down to the shimmering glimpse of Chambers Creek. Listen to the silence of the forest, broken by the song of a thrush or the rustling of a squirrel in the brush.

An unpretentious beginning leads to this well-traveled trail in a mature forest, just minutes from the I-5 corridor south of Tacoma. In summer, take a moment to walk to the bridge over Chambers Bay before starting up the trail; the forest is so dense with summer greenery that this may be your only chance to see the estuary, which resounds with the calls of the killdeer and shrills of the gulls. In winter, the bigleaf maples drop their screening leaves and allow views from the trail to the stream and estuary below.

This trail is rough and steep. It's not advisable in wet weather, but when it's dry you can follow it to the top, where houses announce the end of

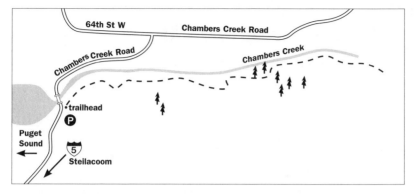

parkland. Along this steep climb up the shoulder of the creek ravine, listen for the forest birds and the chattering squirrels. Pause at the spacious glen where the hillside is carved into an amphitheater of fern and salal.

Several side trails drop down toward the stream. The first leads to a clearing by the bay, the second to a high viewpoint over clear, rushing Chambers Creek. Old stumps make homes for owls and provide food for flickers and sapsuckers.

**GETTING THERE:** From I-5 in Tacoma, southbound, take exit 129 (S 72nd St). Go west (right) on S 74th St (which becomes Custer Road W in 2.3 miles). Go another 1.2 miles and turn right onto Steilacoom Blvd. Follow it west into the town of Steilacoom. Turn right on Main St, then right again onto Lafayette St, which becomes Chambers Creek Road. Follow Chambers Creek Road north to just before it crosses Chambers Bay. Look on the right for a pullout (limited parking) and a signposted footpath into the forest.

From I-5 south of Tacoma, northbound, take exit 119 (Dupont, Steilacoom) and head north on the Dupont-Steilacoom Hwy through Fort Lewis (the road becomes Union Ave after leaving Fort Lewis). In Steilacoom Union Ave becomes Lafayette St, then Chambers Creek Road; then proceed as above.

**ADDRESS:** 7100 block of Chambers Creek Road W, University Place

**CONTACT:** Pierce County Parks (253) 798-4176; www.co.pierce.wa.us

Tacoma

# 90

# FORT STEILACOOM PARK

**Steilacoom, 11 miles southwest of Tacoma**

*Meadows by Waughop Lake offer bird-watching, historical sites, and Rainier and Olympic views.*

| | |
|---|---|
| **TRAIL** | More than 10 miles; natural surface, paved |
| **STEEPNESS** | Level to moderate |
| **OTHER USERS** | Bicycles, horses |
| **DOGS** | Leash and scoop |
| **CONNECTING TRAILS** | None |
| **PARK AMENITIES** | Restrooms, off-leash areas, picnic areas, playground, playing fields |
| **DISABLED ACCESS** | Waughop Lake trail, picnic area, playground |

From fort to mental hospital to county park, these grounds represent a chronicle of Washington history. Parade grounds from the 1850s have given way to meadow grasses, and old buildings have succumbed to the weight of time. There was never a stockade at Fort Steilacoom, which protected the settlers at the bustling Steilacoom port from 1849 to 1868. When soldiers left, it became a mental hospital (the grounds to the north still are). Today, as you walk these spacious

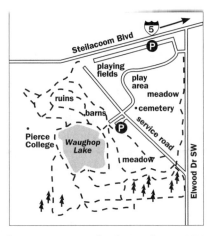

meadows, you can see the old hospital cemetery grounds, dating from 1876 to 1953, and the restored 1930s farm buildings and barns.

From the southwestern corner of the parking area near the barns, head west toward Waughop Lake. A wheelchair-accessible, 1-mile trail circumnavigates the lake under the shade of elms and redwoods. Willows gracefully dip their branches to the water, and mallards paddle about.

Climb the knoll on well-worn footpaths, past several old orchards and lines of poplars. At the top, you'll find the imposing ruins of the 1940s patients' ward, now used as a site to train emergency personnel in earthquake or bombing preparedness. Views here expand west to the Olympics and to Fox, McNeil, and Anderson Islands in the Tacoma Narrows. To the east Mount Rainier looms, and below you see Waughop Lake and the Pierce College campus.

Other trails weave like a spiderweb through the meadows up to the southern forest boundary. Though you have 360 acres to explore, you're not likely to get lost: There's plenty of long-distance visibility across the meadows and from the hillocks.

**GETTING THERE:** From I-5 in Tacoma, southbound, take exit 129 (S 72nd St). Go west (right) on S 74th St, which becomes Custer Drive in 2.3 miles (after crossing Lakewood Drive SW). Go another 1.2 miles and turn right on Steilacoom Blvd. Go about 1.5 miles west and turn left onto Elwood Drive SW (across from 87th Ave SW). Turn right immediately on Dresden Lane into the park.

From I-5 south of Tacoma, northbound, take exit 125 (Lakewood). Turn left onto Bridgeport Way W. Go north on Bridgeport Way W, crossing 100th St SW and Gravelly Lake Drive SW. Turn left on Steilacoom Blvd and go west; then proceed as above.

**ADDRESS:** 8714 87th Avenue SW, Lakewood

**CONTACT:** City of Lakewood (253)983-7887; www.cityoflakewood.us

Tacoma

# 91

# WAPATO PARK

**6.5 miles south of downtown Tacoma**

*Walk Wapato Lake's bird sanctuaries in wetlands and mature forest.*

| | |
|---|---|
| **TRAIL** | 1.4 miles total; natural surface, paved |
| **STEEPNESS** | Level to gentle |
| **OTHER USERS** | Bicycles |
| **DOGS** | Leash and scoop |
| **CONNECTING TRAILS** | None |
| **PARK AMENITIES** | Restrooms, fishing pier, picnic shelters, playground, playing fields<br>Summer only: beach, concessions, paddleboats |
| **DISABLED ACCESS** | Paved trail along lake, restrooms, picnic area |

Formal gardens and a white-trellised pergola welcome you to 30-acre Wapato Lake, set in an 80-acre park in suburban Tacoma. Away from the picnic areas and playing fields, you can find sanctuaries of marshland and mature forest.

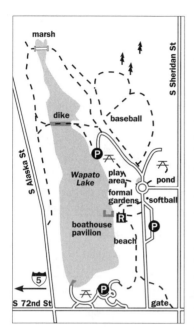

At the garden entrance, turn right to the northern parking lot. Walk the paved road north over an old 1933 WPA-project bridge. To the right, in the forest, follow footpaths to the two-thirds-of-a-mile fitness course, or continue on the road, cutting left toward the marshland. A high footbridge lifts you over the cattails where red-winged blackbirds nest. Marsh wrens call *tsuck, tsuck* and flit from bush to bush. On the western side of the lake, join the paved trail that borders the water until it ends at private homes.

Return over the dike structure, where kids can fish year-round and from which you can watch the bottoms-up antics of the coots and mallards feeding among the water lilies. From the parking area, walk south under hundred-year-old fir and hemlock, past the swimming area and summer concessions. Footpaths connect the open lawns, playing fields, southern picnic area, and parking lot. Look for the old wrought-iron lightpost slowly being absorbed by the dense bark of a Douglas fir. The park derives its name from *wapato,* a previously abundant aquatic root the Native Americans harvested from the lake.

**GETTING THERE:** From I-5 in Tacoma, north- or southbound, take exit 129 (S 72nd St). Go east on S 72nd St 2 blocks and turn left (north) on S Sheridan St. Entrance is on the left at S Sheridan St and S 68th St.

**ADDRESS:** S 68th Street and S Sheridan Avenue, Tacoma

**CONTACT:** Metropolitan Park District of Tacoma (253) 305-1000; www.tacomaparks.com

### Finding Your Way

Not all trails remain as they were originally built. Trees fall down. Trails get flooded out. Signs fall down or are faded. New neighborhoods crop up like dandelions, so driving directions can also change. Keep a sense of direction, and always walk with someone else.

# 92

# SWAN CREEK PARK

**6 miles east of downtown Tacoma**

*Soft forest trails hug the side of a lush ravine above a clear stream, which teems with salmon in the fall.*

| | |
|---|---|
| **TRAIL** | 2 miles one way; natural surface |
| **STEEPNESS** | Gentle to steep |
| **OTHER USERS** | Bicycles allowed, but not advised on narrow trails |
| **DOGS** | Leash and scoop |
| **CONNECTING TRAILS** | None |
| **PARK AMENITIES** | Benches, picnic area |
| **DISABLED ACCESS** | None |

Traverse a fern-covered and forested hillside above a salmon-spawning creek that has carved a pebbled gully for itself. Listen to the call of birds over the soft murmuring of the water. Tacoma's Swan Creek Park is most often visited by people wanting to cool off on a hot summer's day, let the kids play in the detention pond fed by Swan Creek, or watch the coho and

### Love That Dog!

I'm sure we'd like your dog if we knew him or her. But dogs belong on a leash (where posted) to protect wildlife, minimize their impact on the habitat, and avoid disturbing other walkers and pets. Many parks now patrol and ticket leash offenders.

chinook salmon make their arduous way up the stream in the fall. But past the pond and the footbridge, a trail leads deep into a fine old forest of towering Douglas firs and moss-bedecked bigleaf maples leaning elegantly over the stream.

Saved from becoming a landfill back in the 1960's, Swan Creek is now a showcase of mature Northwest forest and an active salmon stream. Even in summer, when there are no salmon in the stream, the water runs clear and bright over a pebbled streambed, and the old logs and rocks guarantee good hiding places for the newly hatched fry in winter. The trail begins near the pond and climbs slowly, staying near the level of the stream. Numerous "social trails" lead to the water's edge where you can rest on a downed log or picnic on a shady bank.

The wet season brings standing water to parts of the trail, so while the boardwalks are welcome, they can be slippery. This is a good place to practice "Walk or Look," because if you try and take in the beauty of the forest while walking, it is easy to fall on the narrow trail crisscrossed with tree roots. Two spur trails, buttressed with sturdy railroad ties, zigzag uphill and join at an old meadow on the ridge. The site of housing for shipping workers during World War II, today this meadow is home only to broom and blackberries. It would be easy to get disoriented

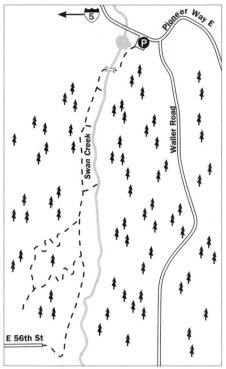

in here, so if you wish to walk the full two miles of trail, it is best to leave the meadow and follow the well-worn earth trail below the ridge until you reach the large tractor tires that mark the trail entrance at 56th Street. Although a bright open forest of conifers beckons from the end of 56th, there are many "social trails" (some of which lead back to the meadow), but without trail markings it is easy to get confused. The surest way to return to the pond and parking area is to retrace your steps down the ravine.

**GETTING THERE:** From I-5 north of Tacoma, southbound, take exit 135 (Bay St, River Road, SR 167 north, Puyallup). Take the first left onto Bay Street (before the light), crossing under I-5. Continue straight through the light where Bay becomes River Road. Stay right past the cemetery and merge onto Pioneer Way E. The parking lot is just past the Clay Art Center on the right.

From I-5 in Tacoma, northbound, take exit 135 (River Road, SR 167 north, Puyallup). Stay straight on River Road and continue as above.

**ADDRESS:** Pioneer Way E and Waller Drive

**CONTACT:** Metropolitan Park District of Tacoma (253) 305-1000; www.tacomaparks.com

# 93

# SPANAWAY PARK AND BRESEMANN FOREST

### Spanaway, 15 miles south of Tacoma

*Walk wetland trails by the creek, or wander miles of sylvan trails in Bresemann Forest.*

| | |
|---|---|
| **TRAIL** | About 6 miles total; gravel, natural surface, paved |
| **STEEPNESS** | Level to gentle |
| **OTHER USERS** | Bicycles on designated trails |
| **DOGS** | Leash and scoop |
| **CONNECTING TRAILS** | None |
| **PARK AMENITIES** | Restrooms, interpretive signs, picnic shelters, playground, playing fields, Sprinker Recreation Center, swimming beach |
| **DISABLED ACCESS** | Restrooms, beach, boat launch, fishing, picnic shelters, playground, playing fields |

Follow a wide, graveled trail along the edge of this expansive lake, or explore shaded trails through a wetland or forest—all just minutes from downtown Tacoma.

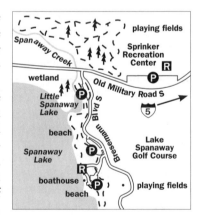

Like a mink changing color for the winter, this park, too, changes with the seasons. In summer the manicured lawns resound with the sound of families and children playing, motorboats, and Jet-Skis on the lake. The snack bar attracts crowds, and the aromas of ketchup and grilling supper fill the air. You can walk here then, but sometimes it's an effort: it's easy to rely on the car to move from one end of the long park to the other.

Off-season, though, the park regains a more natural feel. Fishermen cast their lines in hope of bass or trout. Migrant waterfowl glide on the still

waters, and you can stroll the waterfront trail, then return by the upper play-ing fields, beneath majestic Douglas firs.

To the north, where the lake empties to a stream, two footbridges lead into a more sylvan setting of alders and willows, salal and ferns. The dirt trail is narrow, with exposed roots and rocks, climbing a gentle hill and then dropping to a wetland. The park boundary fence, the stream, and Old Military Road ensure that you can't get lost. Follow a stone-lined, narrow footpath along the edge of the wetland, and then return over the footbridges.

North across Old Military Road S, explore the many miles of interpretive trail and informal forest paths in Bresemann Forest. The trails begin near SPIRE climbing wall, looping into the forest and along Morey Creek.

**GETTING THERE:** From I-5 south of Tacoma, north- or southbound, take exit 127 (SR 512 east, Puyallup). Go east for 2 miles on SR 512 and turn right (south) on SR 7 (Pacific Ave S). Go 4.8 miles and turn right on Old Military Road S (152nd St E). Go 0.5 mile to the park's main gate on the left. Sprinker Recreation Center and forest trails are on the right (north) side; the lake is on the left. Parking fee of $3 may apply.

**ADDRESS:** 14905 Gus Bresemann Road S, Tacoma

**CONTACT:** Pierce County Parks (253) 798-4176; www.piercecountywa.org

# 94

# FOOTHILLS TRAIL

McMillan, 14 miles southeast of Tacoma, to Buckley, 22.5 miles
southeast of Tacoma

*Visit Carbon River farmland and small historic towns with
Mount Rainier views.*

| | |
|---|---|
| **TRAIL** | 26 miles total; gravel, natural surface, paved |
| **STEEPNESS** | Level |
| **OTHER USERS** | Bicycles; horses on soft shoulder |
| **DOGS** | Leash and scoop |
| **CONNECTING TRAILS** | None |
| **PARK AMENITIES** | Restrooms, picnic areas where trail enters a town |
| **DISABLED ACCESS** | Paved trail |

Imagine riding with the engineer in the locomotive of a Burlington Northern train along the floodplain of the glacial-silted Carbon River. Ahead looms Tahoma, mighty volcano of ice and snow. The river beside you is white and rushing, cutting its path through a millennium of rocky till. Tannin-brown streams swirl and join the opaque river.

Now, although the railroad runs no more, the route is open to those seeking a slower mode of transport. Thanks to the Foothills Rails-to-Trails Coalition and Pierce County, 17 miles of long-abandoned railbed are available for recreation from McMillan to Buckley, with a spur from lower Cascade Junction to Wilkeson and Carbonado. The coalition and county are working to fulfill their vision of a 12-foot-wide nonmotorized asphalt trail and linear park system throughout Pierce County.

Riverside scenery and mountain views are just two of the pleasures of walking the Foothills Trail. Picnic areas dot the trail, as well as cow pastures, footbridges over the river—and there's even a bison and pygmy goat farm. From McMillan, the paved trail heads south through Orting, then swings east to cross the Carbon River; here the pavement ends. Gravel and natural surfaces continue northeast along South Prairie Creek, crossing the creek several times through the towns of South Prairie and Cascade Junction, where

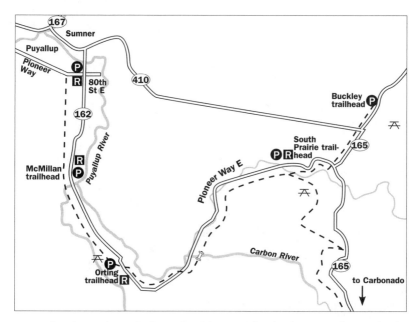

a spur heads south to Carbonado. After another bridge over the creek, the pavement resumes for the last 2 miles into Buckley.

To enjoy the full length of the trail, bicycles may be in order, but numerous access points (the trail runs parallel to SR 162 in many places) allow you to explore on foot a few miles at a time. Near the towns, there are many street crossings: be sure to keep children and pets closely supervised.

**GETTING THERE:** McMillan trailhead: From I-5 south of Tacoma, north- or southbound, take exit 127 (SR 512 east) and continue east; take the SR 410 exit. Go east on SR 410 about 2 miles, then take the Orting/Sumner exit (SR 162). Turn right (south) toward Orting. Go about 4.5 miles. The McMillan trailhead is on the right directly after the cement bridge at the confluence of the Puyallup and Carbon Rivers.

Alternatively, from I-5 east of Tacoma, north- or southbound, take exit 135 (SR 167 south) and continue south to the SR 410 exit and proceed as above.

Orting trailhead: Continue 2.2 miles farther south on SR 162; the trailhead is on the right, located in the Orting City Park.

South Prairie trailhead: Continue east on SR 162 8 miles. The junction with SR 165 is just a little farther east.

Buckley trailhead: Stay on SR 410 east into Buckley; the trailhead is located at the armory. The trail heads south along SR 165.

**ADDRESS:** SR 162, McMillan

**CONTACT:** Pierce County Parks (253) 798-4176; www.piercecountywa.org/ccp

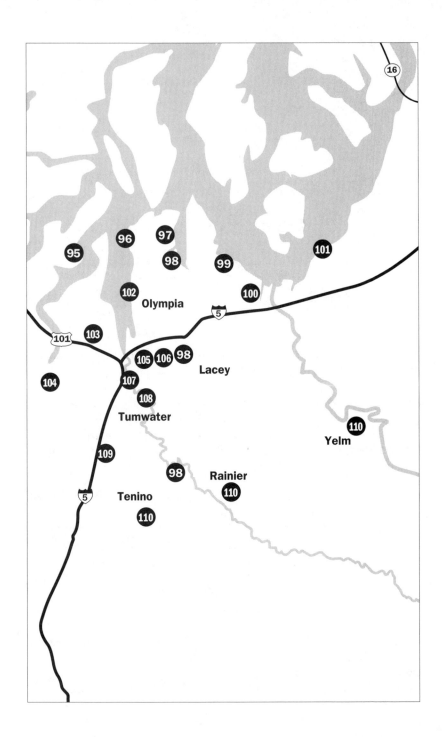

# IN AND AROUND **OLYMPIA**

# 95

# FRYE COVE PARK

## 12 miles northwest of Olympia

*Forested trails lead to South Sound views at an Eld Inlet beach.*

| | |
|---|---|
| **TRAIL** | 3 miles total; gravel, natural surfaces |
| **STEEPNESS** | Level to gentle |
| **OTHER USERS** | Pedestrians only |
| **DOGS** | Leash and scoop |
| **CONNECTING TRAILS** | None |
| **PARK AMENITIES** | Restrooms, picnic area, shelters |
| **DISABLED ACCESS** | Gravel trail from parking lot to picnic area, restrooms |

Tucked away on one of many finger-inlets of southern Puget Sound, this forest and beach park entices with the twin luxuries of silence and seclusion.

When you enter the forest in summer, the bigleaf maples and alders shield you from the brilliance of the sun on the Sound. Licorice ferns adorn the moss on the maples like miniature Dr. Seuss characters on parade around the tree trunks. Catkins from the red alders dangle above the trail and speckle the path.

Last logged a hundred years ago, the forest has a mature presence, and the air carries the heady scent of cedar and salt. Hemlocks, some more than 200 feet tall, drape their graceful branches above the trail. Benches and observation decks are placed for glimpses of the Sound and beach below, and a raised walkway carries you over a dense ravine of sword ferns.

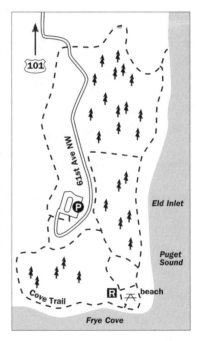

After you complete a forest loop and return to the parking lot, then descend Cove Trail, at first gentle, then steep, to arrive at the southern end of the beach. Air holes of a million clams dapple the sand-and-mud beach at low tide, and palm-sized clams and oysters provide feasts for crows and gulls.

**GETTING THERE:** From I-5 in Olympia, north- or southbound, take exit 104 (US 101 north, Aberdeen). Stay on US 101 toward Shelton, and take the Steamboat Island Road exit. Go north on Steamboat Island Road NW about 5.8 miles and turn right on Young Road NW. Go about 2 miles and turn left on 61st Ave NW into the park.

**ADDRESS:** 5945 61st Avenue NW, Olympia

**CONTACT:** Thurston County Parks (360) 786-5595; www.co.thurston.wa.us /parks

Olympia

# 96

# BURFOOT PARK

**6 miles north of Olympia**

*Forest trails lead to a Budd Inlet beach with State Capitol views.*

| | |
|---|---|
| **TRAIL** | 3.8 miles; natural surface |
| **STEEPNESS** | Moderate to steep |
| **OTHER USERS** | Pedestrians only |
| **DOGS** | Leash and scoop |
| **CONNECTING TRAILS** | None |
| **PARK AMENITIES** | Restrooms, interpretive trail, picnic shelters, playground |
| **DISABLED ACCESS** | Horizon Trail and Braille Trail (0.25 miles), restrooms, Meadow Shelter, picnic area |

Most of the wonder of Burfoot Park is hidden from the casual first-time visitor. The central lawn/picnic area is so large and appealing that you might believe it's all there is to the park. But drive or walk the parking loop, and you'll discover the three trail entrances into the cool enchantment of the forest, which descends to the beach on Budd Inlet.

For an easy stroll, start on the Horizon Trail nature loop, which documents the changes in the forest since it was logged in the 1890s. Moisture encourages moss and old man's beard to grow prolifically, and they cover the trees with a thick green shawl.

To the north, from the Rhododendron Trail, the right-fork Beach Trail descends the ridge of a ravine carpeted with sword fern. Here, the wrens call and hop on downed logs, their short perky tails bobbing. A clear *rat-a-tat-tat* may sound from above. High on a snag, pileated woodpeckers with iridescent red crests may be circling the tree, probing the bark for grubs. Farther

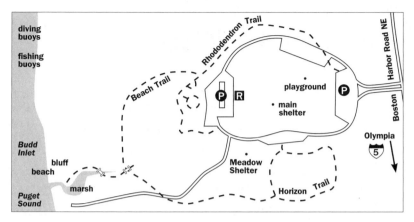

along the fern-bedecked ravine, more snags bear the characteristic rectangular holes made by these birds, the largest western woodpeckers.

Though there are several trails, there is no need for signs: all trails lead to the beach. At low tide, crows stride the shore, and great blue herons may be feeding on small fish in the shallows. To the south, the dome of the State Capitol rises between forested hills.

**GETTING THERE:** From I-5 in Olympia, northbound, take exit 105 (City Center, Port of Olympia). Stay hard right, following Port of Olympia signs. At the end of the ramp, take a right and go under the freeway. Go straight onto Plum St (which becomes E Bay Drive, and then Boston Harbor Road NE). Go 6 miles and look for the park on the left.

From I-5 in Olympia, southbound, take exit 105B. Follow signs for the Port of Olympia, staying right toward Plum St. Follow Plum St north and proceed as above.

**ADDRESS:** 6927 Boston Harbor Road NE, Olympia

**CONTACT:** Thurston County Parks (360) 786-5595; www.co.thurston.wa.us /parks

# 97

# WOODARD BAY PRESERVE

**5 miles northeast of Olympia**

*Forest trails lead to beaches, birds, and seals on Henderson Inlet.*

| | |
|---|---|
| **TRAILS** | 2.5 miles total; boardwalk, natural surface, paved |
| **STEEPNESS** | Level |
| **OTHER USERS** | Pedestrians only |
| **DOGS** | Not allowed |
| **CONNECTING TRAILS** | Chehalis Western Trail (Walk #98) |
| **PARK AMENITIES** | Restrooms, interpretive signs, nature classes, picnic shelter |
| **DISABLED ACCESS** | Whitham Road to Henderson Inlet, parking lot to picnic area on Sound via Whitman Road |

Beginning at the paved access road (gated for all vehicles except DNR maintenance), stroll the half mile through moss-draped second-growth forest to Henderson Inlet. You may hear the sharp hammering of woodpeckers or the hoarse, barking sound of the green-backed heron. If the breeze is right, you'll smell the salt water before you see it. The state of the tide determines

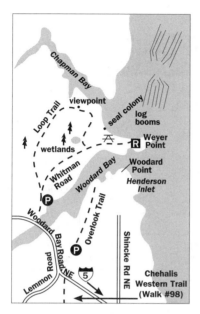

whether you see shimmering, wet mud or hear the lapping of wavelets on the shore. The clearing at the tip of land called Weyer Point was once a bustling log dump where timber was transferred from railroad cars to the water, to be floated to mills in Everett.

The logging sounds are gone now, giving way to the persistent chatter of belted kingfishers as they hover, searching for lunch below. Soon you may hear the yarps and groans of harbor seals, 300 to 400 of them. In this maternity colony, females and their pups rest on the log booms or sun themselves on the shores. They are easily stressed, so enjoy them from afar. With binoculars, you can watch the cormorants and gulls standing like nursemaids on old pilings above sleeping seals.

For variety, take the Loop Trail through the forest back to the entrance. This natural path ranges up and down gentle hillocks and through forest wetlands over wooden boardwalks. Overhead stand massive maples with spreading branches that could hold swings for giants. Sturdy cedars and hemlocks embrace their nurse logs, or form their own colonies of two or three trunks growing together. When the trail parallels the shore of Chapman Bay high on a ridge, you can look down on the flocks of shorebirds or solitary great blue herons feeding.

**GETTING THERE:** From I-5 north of Olympia, north- or southbound, take exit 108 (Martin Way, Sleater-Kinney Road NE). Go north (left) on Sleater-Kinney Road NE about 5 miles, until it takes a sharp turn to the left, becoming 56th Ave NE. Go immediately right on Schinke Road NE, which becomes Woodard Bay Road NE and crosses upper Woodard Bay on a bridge. Park immediately on the right in front of the bright yellow gates to the authorities-only entrance road, Whitham Road.

**ADDRESS:** Woodard Bay Road NE and Lemmon Road NE, Olympia

**CONTACT:** Washington State Department of Natural Resources (360) 577-2025; www.dnr.wa.gov

# 98

# CHEHALIS WESTERN TRAIL

**5 miles northeast of Olympia via Lacey, to 14 miles southeast of Olympia**

*A rails-to-trails amid farmland, wetlands, ponds, and forests leads from Woodard Bay to the Deschutes River.*

| | |
|---|---|
| **TRAIL** | 20 miles; paved |
| **STEEPNESS** | Level |
| **OTHER USERS** | Bicycles; horses north of S Bay Road and south of Fir Tree Road |
| **DOGS** | Leash and scoop |
| **CONNECTING TRAILS** | Olympia Woodland Trail (Walk 106), Woodard Bay (Walk #97), Yelm to Tenino Trail (Walk #110) |
| **PARK AMENITIES** | Restrooms, benches, picnic area |
| **DISABLED ACCESS** | Trail, restrooms |

Located in rural Western Washington just minutes from shopping-center madness on Martin Way to the south, the woods and wetlands replace the gunning of engines with the sweet chirping of crickets. Horses come to the fence to greet you, and raptors may be soaring over the meadows in search of mice. Small ponds and wetlands add more tranquil greenery. Near Shincke Road, a large marsh-rimmed pond hosts the usual colorful assortment: kingfishers, red-winged blackbirds, marsh wrens, and great blue herons. Recent construction on the trail now allows users to safely "bridge the gap" from the northern section (north of I-5 and Martin Way) to the southern section

of this 20-mile thoroughfare. Plans are underway to build the final bridge, which will cross Pacific Avenue.

Farmlands, scrub forest, and meadows rim the trail as it journeys southward. Several trailheads exist south of I-5; the northern one at Chambers Lake is the most popular, with amenities on the edge of the lake. Other trailheads are located at 67th Avenue, Fir Tree Road, and 89th Avenue. The final stretch south of 103rd

Avenue follows the Deschutes River upstream before intersecting the Yelm to Tenino Trail.

**GETTING THERE:** To reach the northern trailhead: From I-5 north of Olympia, southbound, take exit 109 (Martin Way, Sleater-Kinney Road N). Go north on Sleater-Kinney Road. Go about 3.7 miles to 56th Ave NE. Go left on 56th Ave NE for about 0.5 mile to the junction with Shincke Road. Go right on Shincke Road to Woodard Bay Road. Turn left on Woodard Bay Road to the junction with Lemon Road. Park on the right.

To reach Chambers Lake: From I-5 north of Olympia, northbound, take exit 108 (Sleater-Kinney Road S). Turn right on Sleater-Kinney. Cross Pacific Ave. At the 4-way stop sign, turn right onto 14th Ave. The entrance is after the trestle on the left.

From I-5 north of Olympia, southbound, take exit #109 (Martin Way College St Sleater-Kinney Road N) and head south on College St SE and proceed as above. Parking, restrooms, and picnic area are available.

To reach the 67th Avenue Trailhead: From I-5 north of Olympia, northbound, take exit 108 (Sleater-Kinney Road S). Turn right at Sleater-Kinney Road. Turn left at 14th Ave SE then right onto College St SE. Cross the Yelm Highway and stay on College St, which becomes Rainier Road SE. Turn right onto 67th Ave and follow it to the end.

From I-5 north of Olympia, southbound, take exit 109 (College Street). Turn left on College St SE and proceed as above. No restroom facility.

**ADDRESS:** Northern Trailhead: Shincke and Lemon Roads, Olympia

Chambers Lake Trailhead: 3725 Elizabeth Avenue SE, Olympia

**CONTACT:** Thurston County (360) 754-4371; www.co.thurston.wa.us /parks

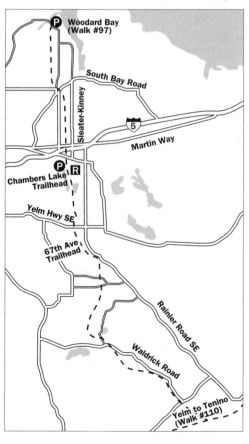

## 99

# TOLMIE STATE PARK

**11 miles northeast of Olympia**

*Explore forests, salt marshes, and beaches along the Nisqually Reach.*

| | |
|---|---|
| **TRAIL** | 4.3 miles; natural surface, paved |
| **STEEPNESS** | Level (beach) to steep |
| **OTHER USERS** | Pedestrians only in forest; bicycles on paved trails |
| **DOGS** | Leash and scoop |
| **CONNECTING TRAILS** | None |
| **PARK AMENITIES** | Restrooms, amphitheater, picnic shelters, underwater park; park closed Mondays and Tuesdays October 1 to March 31 |
| **DISABLED ACCESS** | Restrooms, edge of marsh, picnic area |

Jellyfish, sculpin, and rock crabs share the saltwater marsh with eelgrass and pickleweed. On the tidal flats, young geoducks have been planted in plastic tubes to protect them from crabs and seagulls until they are a year old. Divers head offshore to explore the sunken barges that have created an underwater reef. You can explore the beach or head inland for miles of forest walking.

The upper parking lot offers the best views across Puget Sound to the Olympic Mountains. From there, a steep trail with railroad-tie steps leads to the beach and the lower picnic areas. As at other recreational beaches on the Sound, the best time for quiet and solitude is any day but a hot, sunny one.

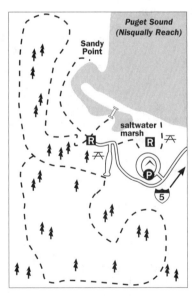

If the tide is in, you can stop on the footbridge over the marsh for a view of

the inhabitants. Offshore the usual waterfowl gather—more during fall and winter migration than in summer.

From the beach, a long loop trail takes you west into the forest of lichen-covered trees. Boardwalk keeps your feet dry while letting you examine the plant life along the way. Benches make good snack stops or resting points. A shortcut about halfway brings you back to the parking lot.

The park honors Dr. William Fraser Tolmie, a pioneer physician with the Hudson's Bay Company who served for 18 years at Fort Nisqually, just east of the present-day park. Married to a daughter of Chief Factor, Tolmie was instrumental in returning peace to the region after the Indian Wars of 1855–56.

**GETTING THERE:** From I-5 north of Olympia, north- or southbound, take exit 111 (SR 510, Yelm, Marvin Road) and head west on Marvin Road NE. Go about 3.5 miles and turn right on 56th Ave NE. Go 0.4 mile to Hill Road NE and turn left, then left again on 61st Ave NE to the park.

**ADDRESS:** 7730 61st Avenue NE, Olympia

**CONTACT:** Washington State Parks (360) 456-6464; www.parks.wa.gov

Olympia

# 100

# NISQUALLY NATIONAL WILDLIFE REFUGE

### 9.5 miles northeast of Olympia

*Farmland meets an estuary, offering many bird-watching opportunities.*

| | |
|---|---|
| **TRAIL** | 1-mile loop; boardwalk |
| **STEEPNESS** | Level |
| **OTHER USERS** | Pedestrians only; no jogging |
| **DOGS** | Not allowed |
| **CONNECTING TRAILS** | None |
| **PARK AMENITIES** | Restrooms, education center (admission fee, except holders of Senior Pass or Interagency Annual Pass), observation decks |
| **DISABLED ACCESS** | Twin Barns boardwalk loop trail, restrooms, interpretive area |

Completing its journey from the heights of Mount Rainier, the Nisqually River releases its pent-up energy into the broad expanse of the estuary. The air is rich with the scent of salt from Puget Sound and fresh water from

the river. The open meadows and wetlands are vast, inviting exploration.

Snow geese and white-fronted geese huddle into the receding tide line. Dozens of great blue herons stand like sentries of the wetland below, some intent on the fish that dart between their stiltlike legs, others staring as though trying to comprehend the human forms with binocular eyes. Green-belted kingfishers

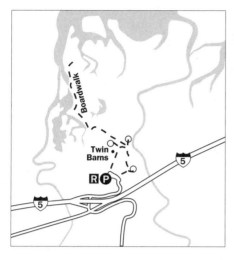

hover above their prey, while over the grasslands immature bald eagles practice soaring and diving. Most visitors to the refuge come for the birds: there are more than 100 species of resident waterfowl, raptors, and songbirds, as well as more than 20,000 migratory birds that gather here during fall and winter.

In years past, the five-mile Brown Farm Dike Trail offered some of the finest walking in the region. Now the trail is closed for the rehabilitation of the sanctuary, with no foreseeable reopening. Although it doesn't feel as wild as the Dike Trail, the totally accessible Twin Barns Loop Trail allows you to get out into the wetlands and still keep your feet dry. The birding is great, too, and with two overlooks and a viewing platform, you have an increased chance of spotting and photographing wildlife. Even around the old farm buildings near the parking lot, the dense vegetation gives refuge to wrens and sparrows.

The new Education Center offers a free summer evening lecture series and throughout the year there are daytime guided walks focusing on the birds, plants, or history of the area. (See the website for details.) While the classes and guided walks are free, the $3 Refuge entrance fee still applies.

**GETTING THERE:** From I-5 north of Olympia, north- or southbound, take exit 114 (Nisqually). Turn west at the end of the ramp and go under the freeway. Turn right (following signs) to the refuge.

**ADDRESS:** 100 Brown Farm Road, Olympia

**CONTACT:** National Wildlife Refuge (360) 753-9467; www.fws.gov/nisqually

# 101 SEQUALITCHEW CREEK

### DuPont, 15 miles northeast of Olympia

*Huge moss-bedecked maples tower above a canyon where the clear stream makes its last journey to the waters of Puget Sound.*

| | |
|---|---|
| **TRAIL** | 1.5 miles one way; gravel, paved |
| **STEEPNESS** | Gentle |
| **OTHER USERS** | Bicycles |
| **DOGS** | Leash and scoop |
| **CONNECTING TRAILS** | None |
| **PARK AMENITIES** | None; restrooms and map at DuPont City hall, when open |
| **DISABLED ACCESS** | None |

In a mighty forest of green canopy, green trunks, and green undergrowth, you can stroll gently downhill next to a murmuring creek on its last mile and a half to Puget Sound. This satisfyingly rich forest is a remnant of what surrounded a trading post of the Hudson's Bay Company in the early 1830's. Nisqually Indians fished the creek for coho salmon, and traded blankets, potatoes, and seeds. Now, the nearby town of DuPont is bustling with shops and schools, but they have preserved this gem of a walk.

Stop in at City Hall for a trail map, then follow signage at the far end of the parking lot to cross the creek and turn north (left), downhill. Although much of the trail is a gentle gradient, there are steeper parts where the pavement has been replaced by deep gravel to combat slippage problems. Parents with strollers may have trouble here.

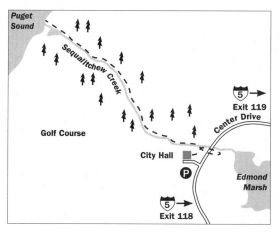

This is a gloriously quiet walk, with just the sound of the creek in the deep cleft of forest. Near the wetlands is an old railroad tunnel, in which kids of all ages will love hooting and yodeling to create a symphony of echoes. Emerging from the tunnel you'll find an expansive stretch of Puget Sound beach complete with pebbles, driftwood, and bits of the old narrow gauge railway. If you want a short, but heart-pumping workout, you can follow the switchbacks up a path on the south side that leaves the main trail just inland of the tunnel and wetlands.

**GETTING THERE:** From I-5 north of Olympia, north- or southbound, take exit 119 (Steilacoom Road, DuPont). Turn left (if northbound) or right (if southbound) onto Steilacoom Road. Continue onto Barksdale Ave. Go 0.3 mile to City Hall on the right. To find the trailhead, park behind City Hall, at the far end.

**ADDRESS:** 303 Barksdale Avenue, DuPont, WA

**CONTACT:** City of DuPont Parks (253) 964-8121; www.ci.dupont.wa.us or www.ci.dupont.wa.us/public-works/parks-recreation/index.html

# 102

# PRIEST POINT PARK

**2.5 miles north of downtown Olympia**

*This meandering woodland trail leads out onto the bluffs above southern Puget Sound.*

| | |
|---|---|
| **TRAIL** | 6 miles round trip; natural surface |
| **STEEPNESS** | Gentle to moderate |
| **OTHER USERS** | Pedestrians only |
| **DOGS** | Leash and scoop |
| **CONNECTING TRAILS** | None |
| **PARK AMENITIES** | Restrooms, picnic shelters, playground, wading pool |
| **DISABLED ACCESS** | Restrooms, picnic areas |

Warm sun filters through the summer canopy of bigleaf maples and Douglas firs. The air feels cool and then warm, and is fragrant with the delicious, almost imperceptible scent of blackberry blossoms. Ellis Cove Trail, the primary walking trail of Priest Point Park, meanders for 3 miles through woodland magic, passing creeks and ravines and then traversing bluffs above southern Puget Sound. Sword ferns, huckleberry, and salal weave a lush green carpet beneath towering western red cedars. This forest so well cocoons you in a sylvan spell that it's hard to believe urban Olympia lies just minutes away.

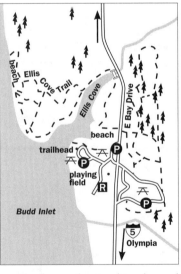

The wide, soft, wood-chip path is easy on the feet and quiet: bicycles and horses are prohibited. The sculptured wooden trail signs are imaginative and playful. At one junction, a carved squirrel shows the way out, and elsewhere a sea otter perches on the trail post. Look for the unexpected sculpture of the small black bear climbing a trunk high above the trail.

Although you must retrace the trail to return to the parking lot, there are several internal loops to explore. There's no fear of getting lost, what with all the wooden animals to give directions. Sturdy wooden bridges lead you down into the cool ravine where Ellis Creek ends in a tidal estuary.

Interpretive signs explain the life of the estuary and the native peoples who traveled to this point on Budd Inlet to trade. A French missionary lived here from 1848 to 1860. After he left, the virgin forest was reduced to stumps within 40 years. In 1905 the City of Olympia bought Priest Point Park, and 75 years later created Ellis Cove Trail. This is one trail to savor, over and over again.

**GETTING THERE:** From I-5 in Olympia, northbound, take exit 105 (City Center, Port of Olympia). Stay hard right, following Port of Olympia signs. At the end of the ramp, take a right and go under the freeway. Go straight onto Plum St (which becomes E Bay Drive, then Boston Harbor Road NE). The park is about 2 miles north of town, with the entrance on the right. Enter the park and pass over Boston Harbor Road NE, following signs to the Ellis Cove Trail.

From I-5 in Olympia, southbound, take exit 105B. Follow signs for the Port of Olympia, staying right toward Plum St. Follow Plum St north and proceed as above.

**ADDRESS:** 2600 E Bay Drive NE, Olympia

**CONTACT:** Olympia Parks (360) 753-8380; www.ci.olympia.wa.us /city-services/parks.aspx

# 103

# YAUGER PARK

**1.5 miles west of downtown Olympia**

*Power walk a jogging trail, or stroll a nature trail through a young forest and a demonstration garden.*

| | |
|---|---|
| **TRAIL** | 1.5 miles total; natural surface |
| **STEEPNESS** | Level |
| **OTHER USERS** | Pedestrians only |
| **DOGS** | Leash and scoop |
| **CONNECTING TRAILS** | None |
| **PARK AMENITIES** | Restrooms, classes, disc golf course, picnic shelter, playing fields, playground; park open until 10 pm |
| **DISABLED ACCESS** | Restrooms |

This community park near Olympia's apartments and shopping malls offers green respite with a three-quarter-mile jogging trail (also great for walking) and a nature trail through a young red alder and maple forest.

For the longest walk, make a full loop on the jogging trail past the sports fields, skate park, and playground. At the northern end, look for a sign that leads north into the young forest. This level, winding nature trail was built by students from Capitol High School in 1986. They cleared the trail, built the platforms and boardwalks, and created the map at the trailhead.

The trail makes two small loops through this forest of saplings. Look in the branches for American robins, rufous-sided towhees, or dark-eyed juncos.

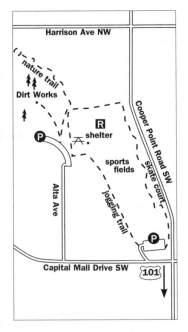

In summer, American goldfinches often alight on the slender branches. The trail crosses a seasonal stream and pauses at viewing platforms, where you can bird-watch or just relax under the open sky. Enjoy the cool of the grove of western red cedar with its lichen-covered stumps.

After reaching the end, return to the northern trailhead, then turn right on the gravel maintenance road. Behind a fence, you'll find Dirt Works, a city demonstration garden (open Saturdays and some weekdays May through September) with lilies, a Shakespearean herb garden, groundcovers, worm bins, and information signs. You can loop back to the southern trailhead on the jogging trail on the west side of the sports fields.

**GETTING THERE:** From I-5 in Olympia, north- or southbound, take exit 104 (US 101, Aberdeen). Head north on US 101 and take the Black Lake Blvd SW exit. Turn right on Black Lake Blvd SW, then left at the next light on Cooper Point Road W. Turn left onto Capital Mall Drive. Yauger Park's southern trailhead parking is immediately on the right; continue a bit farther west on Capital Mall Drive and turn right on Alta Ave to the northern parking lot.

**ADDRESS:** 3100 Capital Mall Drive SW, Olympia; 530 Alta St SW, Olympia
**CONTACT:** Olympia Parks (360) 753-8380, www.ci.olympia.wa.us; Dirt Works (360) 786-5441

Olympia

# 104 MCLANE CREEK NATURE TRAIL

**7 miles southwest of Olympia**

*Beaver pond wetlands lead to a forest alive with birds, salmon, and wildlife.*

| | |
|---|---|
| **TRAIL** | 0.6-mile loop, 0.75-mile loop; natural surface, paved |
| **STEEPNESS** | Level to gentle |
| **OTHER USERS** | Pedestrians only |
| **DOGS** | Not allowed |
| **CONNECTING TRAILS** | None |
| **PARK AMENITIES** | Restrooms, demonstration forest, interpretive signs |
| **DISABLED ACCESS** | Portions of trail, restrooms |

Enter a forest in healing, more than 70 years after loggers took out the giants. Huge stumps show the scars of springboards but now serve as nurse logs for new saplings. Beavers maintain their ponds, and black-tailed deer and coyotes roam the open grassland at dawn and dusk.

Starting the loop to the left of the parking lot brings you first to the beaver ponds. These elusive but energetic rodents may not be easy to see, but you can observe the evidence of their work: freshly gnawed alders and cottonwoods lie tumbled along the water's edge. In winter the pond is full, almost overflowing, and alive with ducks, geese, herons, frogs, otters, muskrats, and

---

### It's a Bird, It's a Plane . . .

Well, most of us can tell the difference. But can you tell one bird from another? If you're a beginning birder, start by learning general shapes, sizes, and obvious color patterns. A bird's habitat is also a clue to its identity, whether you find it in a forest, meadow, wetland, or Puget Sound beach. The longer you study birds, the better you'll get at the specifics, such as telling one gull from another (they're tricky, though, with several years of plumage changes!) or one duck from another, and moving past the L.B.J. (Little Brown Job) category for all the smaller songbirds. Learn more by walking with more experienced birders, such as on Audubon Club outings or ranger-led interpretive walks.

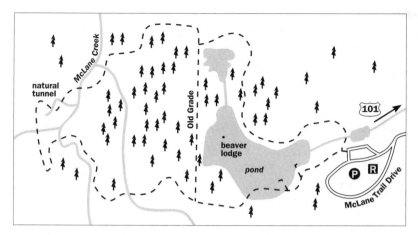

salamanders. Sometimes fall floods wash the dam out and the pond drains, but within six months the beavers can rebuild and refill the pond.

A cutoff trail, the Old Grade, makes a shorter loop or can be explored as a side trip from the main trail. This is a remnant of old logging days, when locomotives chugged through here on their way to the Mud Bay Timber Company on Puget Sound, just 5 miles away.

On the southern edge of the loop, you walk in a forest of western red cedar and Douglas fir. Moss and lichen adorn the massive limbs, and woodpeckers leave their markings where they have bored for insects. Sparkling-clear McLane Creek is home to spawning salmon. Interpretive signs along the trail help you envision the creek and surrounding habitat in all their seasonal changes.

**GETTING THERE:** From I-5 in Olympia, north- or southbound, take exit 104 (US 101 north, Aberdeen). Go 4 miles and take the Mud Bay/2nd Ave exit. Turn left at the stop and go over the freeway. Take the first left onto McKenzie Road (which becomes Delphi Road). Go about 3 miles to the sign for McLane Creek Demonstration Forest and Nature Trail. Parking is on the right.

**ADDRESS:** No street address

**CONTACT:** Washington State Department of Natural Resources (360) 748-2383; www.wa.gov/dnr

# 105

# WATERSHED PARK (OLYMPIA)

**1 mile south of downtown Olympia**

*Watch spawning salmon in Moxlie Creek and birds in forested wetlands nearby.*

| | |
|---|---|
| **TRAIL** | 2.8 miles total; natural surface |
| **STEEPNESS** | Moderate to steep |
| **OTHER USERS** | Pedestrians only (no jogging) |
| **DOGS** | Leash and scoop |
| **CONNECTING TRAILS** | Olympia Woodland Trail (Walk #106) |
| **PARK AMENITIES** | None |
| **DISABLED ACCESS** | None |

This green and mossy basin just minutes from downtown Olympia encircles you with a rich scent of wetland forest and the soothing sounds of birds and water. Bracken, horsetail, maples, and alder line the natural pathway that stretches from the rim to the streambed of Moxlie Creek and back. Trees tumbled by winter's windstorms lie like giant matchsticks, their roots exposed like pinwheels.

From the parking lot, descend into the forest, taking the loop in either direction. Steps lead down to marshes where green

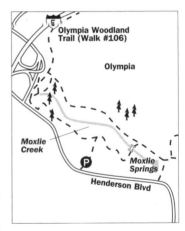

algae create an impressionist painting on the water's surface. Sword ferns, bracken, and maidenhair ferns line the trail. In this deep, shady forest of Douglas fir, bigleaf maple, and alder, be ready for banana slugs and skunk cabbage, natural inhabitants of so wet and lush a place.

This is a popular walk, despite its ruggedness—or perhaps because of it. Young families come with children in tow, teaching them the wonders of the streambed, where salmon spawn and tadpoles scoot about like tiny bumper cars gone crazy. Dogs are welcome, but only on leash, to protect the fragile

habitat and sensitive replanting areas. Boardwalks, too, protect the wetlands and help you keep your feet dry; sturdy wooden bridges offer vantage points above the clear, sandy-bottomed creek.

**GETTING THERE:** From I-5 in Olympia, northbound, take exit 105 (City Center, Port of Olympia). Stay hard right, following Port of Olympia signs. At the end of the ramp, turn left (onto Henderson Blvd, not marked) and go 0.25 mile to the trailhead on the left.

From I-5 in Olympia, southbound, take exit 105B. Follow signs for the Port of Olympia, staying left for Henderson Blvd. Go under the freeway and in 0.25 mile look on the left for the trailhead.

**ADDRESS:** 2500 Henderson Boulevard SE, Olympia

**CONTACT:** Olympia Parks (360) 753-8380; www.ci.olympia.wa.us

Olympia

# 106

# OLYMPIA WOODLAND TRAIL

**1 mile south of downtown Olympia**

*Miles of accessible trail follow an old railway line through a forest of towering maples and firs.*

| | |
|---|---|
| **TRAIL** | 2.5 miles one way; natural surface, paved |
| **STEEPNESS** | Level |
| **OTHER USERS** | Bicycles; horses on parallel natural trail |
| **DOGS** | Leash and scoop |
| **CONNECTING TRAILS** | Olympia's Watershed Park (Walk #105); Chehalis Western Trail (Walk #98); Lacey Woodland Trail (extension to the east) |
| **PARK AMENITIES** | Restrooms, benches, map signs, picnic area |
| **DISABLED ACCESS** | Paved trail, restrooms, picnic area |

Birdsong rings brightly in this emerald thoroughfare of old Olympia forest. Huge maples, dressed in soft green moss-velvet stand sentinel over the smoothly paved trail, and deep in a green cleft a stream rushes through a canopy of ferns. Just over half a mile from the trailhead, near the Frederick Street trailhead (pedestrian only), a spur trail leads to a waterfall along East Indian Creek. Other small natural-surface nature trails have been built by

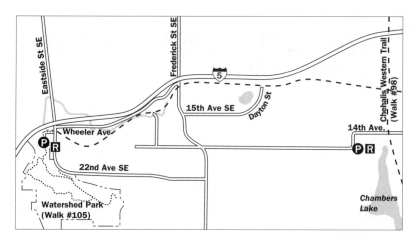

volunteers and lead into the creek canyon or onto the surrounding ridges. Although never far from the interstate highway, the traffic blurs to white noise, and, surprisingly, the sound of birdcalls and the rushing stream can be clearly heard.

Over twenty years ago, this abandoned railway line began tempting Olympian residents with the dream of creating an accessible trail from Olympia to Lacey and beyond. The trail opened in 2007 and now extends almost 5 miles from the state capitol. Hundreds of volunteers of all ages have planted over 15,000 shrubs and saplings to help restore native flora. The idea of "green" is a theme with the trail: the parking lot is porous pavement, the restrooms are lighted with solar tubes, and the entire roof of the restroom/picnic shelter at the Eastside Street trailhead is covered in plants.

The entire trail runs from Watershed Park in Olympia to central Lacey, for a total of 4.75 miles. Although the eastern trailhead is in Lacey's Woodland Park with a pond and meadow trails, the 2.3 miles of interim trail traverses the business district and shops. For bicycling, the whole trail is a dream, but walkers seeking a natural venue should stick to the 2.5 miles between Olympia's Eastside Street and the Chehalis Western Trail, or take short strolls at the Lacey end near Woodland Park.

**GETTING THERE:** From I-5 north of Olympia, southbound, take exit 105 (Port of Olympia). Stay right for 105B (Port of Olympia). Go straight through the light onto Plum Street. Go 0.1 mile and turn right onto Union Ave SE. Go 0.2 mile and turn right onto Eastside St SE. Cross the bridge and look on the left for the parking lot and a low building with plants on its roof.

**ADDRESS:** Olympia vehicle trailhead: 1600 Eastside Street SE, Olympia (corner of Wheeler Avenue). Pedestrian and bicycle only trailheads are at Frederick Street, Boulevard Road and Dayton Avenue.

**CONTACT:** Olympia Parks (360) 753-8380; www.ci.olympia.wa.us

Olympia

# 107

# TUMWATER HISTORICAL PARK AND CAPITOL LAKE

**Tumwater, 2 miles south of Olympia, to downtown Olympia**

*Deschutes River wetlands offer lakeshore trails, Mount Rainier views, salmon, and birds.*

| | |
|---|---|
| **TRAIL** | 2 miles one way, with 0.8-mile loop; mostly paved |
| **STEEPNESS** | Level |
| **OTHER USERS** | Bicycles |
| **DOGS** | Leash and scoop |
| **CONNECTING TRAILS** | None |
| **PARK AMENITIES** | Restrooms, fishing docks, picnic shelter, playgrounds, viewpoints |
| **DISABLED ACCESS** | Trail (except loop trail east of Marathon Park and marsh trail in Historical Park), restrooms |

Nestled in a pocket of marsh and greenery beneath the ramparts of I-5, tiny Historical Park may not be a long-distance destination in itself, but after strolling its gardenlike setting of wild roses and marsh walks, you can head north under the freeway to the shores of Capitol Lake and on to Marathon Park and Percival Landing for a longer walk.

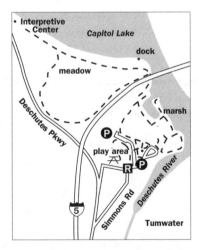

Near the underpass by Historical Park, a dock provides access to the lake and a close-up view of the reeds that adorn its edges. Blackbirds whistle *tse-er, tse-er* and great blue herons study the water for lunch. The trail continues around the southern edge of the lake, through meadows and past the hives of honeybees established by local beekeepers in 1989. Despite its proximity to the freeway, this stretch of trail is surprisingly quiet except for the undulating song of robins and the chirps of wrens.

The lake was first proposed in 1911 as a means of trapping sediment from the Deschutes River, but was not created until 1951. Today this lake is home to migrating and resident flocks of, among others, western grebes, red-winged blackbirds, juncos, pied-billed grebes, scaups, ruddy ducks, and swallows.

On reaching the Deschutes Parkway, the sidewalk trail borders the lake, with fine views of Mount Rainier and the Capitol buildings. For a northern loop, cut through Marathon Park, an oasis of lawn and cattails. Take the wooden bridge east to the gravel road that leads to Percival Landing. Complete the circle around the northern end, where the salt scent of Budd Inlet mixes with the freshwater air from the lake.

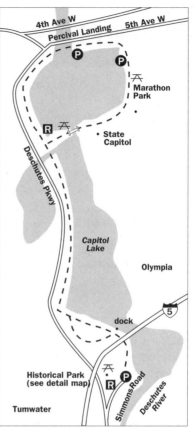

**GETTING THERE:** To reach Historical Park: From I-5 just south of Olympia, northbound, take exit 103 (Deschutes Way). Continue straight from the ramp through 1 stop sign, then turn right on Simmons Road, which leads into the park.

From I-5 just south of Olympia, southbound, take exit 103 (2nd Ave). At the flashing light, turn left on Custer Way, which crosses the freeway. Immediately at the end of the overpass, take a sharp right, curving down to a stop sign on Deschutes Way. Turn right on Deschutes Way, then right again onto Simmons Road into the park.

**ADDRESS: HISTORICAL PARK:** 777 Simmons Road SW, Tumwater

**CONTACT:** Tumwater Parks (360) 754-4160; www.ci.tumwater.wa.us /parks.htm

Olympia

# 108 PIONEER PARK (TUMWATER)

**Tumwater, 4 miles south of Olympia**

*Enjoy views of Mount Rainier from the Deschutes River's shores and meadows.*

| | |
|---|---|
| **TRAIL** | 1.5 miles total; gravel, natural surfaces, paved |
| **STEEPNESS** | Level |
| **OTHER USERS** | Bicycles |
| **DOGS** | Leash and scoop |
| **CONNECTING TRAILS** | None |
| **PARK AMENITIES** | Restrooms, playground, playing fields |
| **DISABLED ACCESS** | Paved trail, restrooms |

This small community park with a rural feel and open meadows lies only minutes south of downtown Olympia. Here you can walk well-defined trails through open grassland or explore the banks of the Deschutes River. A trail system completed in 1996 has enlarged the park, and now it appeals not only to playground users and ball players but also to lovers of easy walks.

Nestled in a curve of the clear but shallow-running river, the meadow hosts rabbits and shrews, food for the hunting hawks overhead. From the parking lot, turn south from the playing fields and cross the natural meadow. The row of cottonwoods and alders defines the riverbank, where you can wander the sandy edge or picnic on the graveled bar. No swimming is allowed, but you can stop and throw a fishing line. Back in the meadow, take a different loop to return to the cars. If it's a clear day, look for the white crown of Mount Rainier to the east.

**GETTING THERE:** From I-5 south of Olympia, northbound, take exit 101 (Airdustrial Way). Turn right (east) on Airdustrial Way and follow it to the end (about 1 mile). Turn left on Henderson Blvd and go about 0.6 mile. The park is on the left just past the Deschutes River.

From I-5 just south of Olympia, southbound, take exit 103 (2nd Ave). At the flashing light, turn left on Custer Way, which crosses the freeway. Continue on Custer Way through 1 light, then turn right at Cleveland Ave. Go 1.2 miles and turn right on Henderson Blvd. Go 0.5 mile, across Yelm Hwy and the railroad tracks. The park is on the right at the bottom of the hill.

**ADDRESS:** 5800 Henderson Boulevard, Tumwater

**CONTACT:** Tumwater Parks (360) 754-4160; www.ci.tumwater.wa.us /parks.htm

Olympia

# MILLERSYLVANIA STATE PARK

**10 miles south of Olympia**

*Wetlands, old-growth forests, and lakeside beaches provide varied habitat for wildlife, and many miles of walking.*

| | |
|---|---|
| **TRAIL** | 8 miles; natural surface |
| **STEEPNESS** | Level |
| **OTHER USERS** | Bicycles |
| **DOGS** | Leash and scoop |
| **CONNECTING TRAILS** | None |
| **PARK AMENITIES** | Restrooms, beaches, camping, fitness trail, nonmotorized boat rentals, picnic areas |
| **DISABLED ACCESS** | Restrooms, campgrounds |

Stroll under immense old Douglas fir and western red cedar trees on miles of soft, needle-lined trails. Cross a wetland on a puncheon boardwalk. Enjoy the quiet of this state park forest in a section far from the bustle of the beaches (the park has 3,300 feet of lakefront). Here you may see pileated woodpeckers or their dainty cousins, the downy woodpeckers. Even if the birds elude you, you'll see evidence of work in the large holes pecked into snags throughout the forest.

> **Anyone Home in the Alder Cone?**
> Alder cones may be tiny, but they harbor tasty food. Chickadees fly from cone to cone listening for a meal. If they tap and hear a hollow sound, it means there's a tasty bug burrowed in the cone. Oh yum!

For those with a mind for exercise, in addition to walking, follow the blue-and-white arrows to the 1-mile fitness trail. Millersylvania's trail uses natural stumps for steps and logs for balance, an interesting (but possibly slippery) version of the normal exercise equipment found on other fitness trails.

Those arriving early or staying in the campgrounds might find scat or tracks of martens, raccoons, or coyotes. Around the borders of Deep Lake you may see evidence of muskrats or otters. Bird life is prolific. On and over the lake, look for ducks, geese, ospreys, and eagles. In summer, hummingbirds frequent bushes by the orchard and lakeshore.

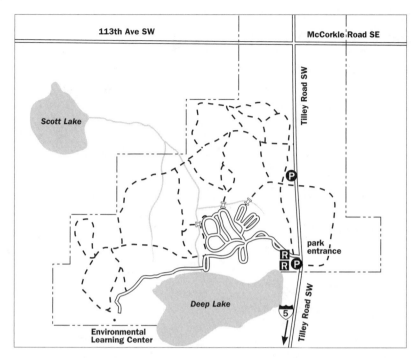

The park's structures were constructed almost entirely by hand in 1935 by the Civilian Conservation Corps. Paved trails around the campgrounds and shelters are ADA accessible. There is a separate parking lot, in an old orchard, for walkers on Tilley Road north of the main entrance.

**GETTING THERE:** From I-5 south of Olympia, southbound, take exit 99 (93rd Ave S, SR 121 S). Turn left on 93rd Ave S/SR 121 S. Drive 1.5 miles and turn right on Tilley Rd S/SR 121 S. The park entrance is on the right in 2.9 miles.

**ADDRESS:** 12245 Tilley Road S, Olympia

**CONTACT:** Washington State Parks (360) 753-1519; www.parks.wa.gov

# 110 | YELM TO TENINO TRAIL

**Yelm, 20 miles southeast of Olympia, to Tenino, 13 miles south of Olympia**

*Visit historic towns, farmland, forest, the Deschutes River, and McIntosh Lake.*

| | |
|---|---|
| **TRAIL** | 14 miles one way; gravel, paved |
| **STEEPNESS** | Level to gentle |
| **OTHER USERS** | Bicycles; horses on parallel trail |
| **DOGS** | Leash and scoop |
| **CONNECTING TRAILS** | Chehalis Western Trail (Walk #98) |
| **PARK AMENITIES** | Restrooms at all trailheads, picnic tables at Yelm trailhead, trailhead information |
| **DISABLED ACCESS** | Paved trail |

Walk through historic Yelm, and then into the countryside with great views of Mt. Rainier. One of the newest rails-to-trails conversions in Western Washington, this bicyclers' paradise (and walkers' long-distance challenge) connects the rural towns of Yelm, Rainier, and Tenino, along the route followed for more than 100 years by the Burlington Northern Railroad. Although the trail parallels SR 507 fairly closely, it is pleasantly quiet. You pass orchards, farms, and backyards.

The first paved section runs 7 miles, from Yelm southwest through the town of Rainier's Wilkowski Park, and a bit beyond, with further paving expected. The currently unpaved section continues east from Rainier, crossing the Deschutes River near the Chehalis Western Trail (Walk #98), then borders Lake McIntosh for three-quarters of a mile, passes under historic trestles, and traverses tranquil sections of Douglas fir

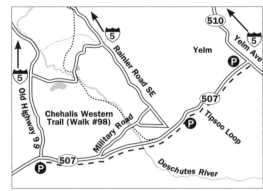

forest and agricultural land. The trail ends at Tenino City Park. Parts of the trail cross driveways and small roads, so keep kids and pets close.

**GETTING THERE:** From I-5 north of Olympia, north- or southbound, take exit 11 (Marvin Way/SR 510). Go 13 miles southeast on SR 510 into Yelm. Before the first stoplight in Yelm, turn right into the City Hall parking lot. The trailhead is on W Yelm Ave, next to the Timberland Library attached to Yelm City Hall.

From Hwy 101 west of Olympia, eastbound, before entering I-5, take the Tumwater exit. Cross over I-5, then go past the brewery and across Capitol Blvd to the light at Cleveland Ave. Turn right onto Yelm Hwy until it intersects with SR 510 near the Nisqually Indian Reservation. Turn right onto SR 510 and go into downtown Yelm. Just before the first stoplight, turn right and proceed as above.

**ADDRESS:** 105 W Yelm Avenue, Yelm

**CONTACT:** Thurston County Parks (360) 786-5595; www.co.thurston.wa.us /parks

# VOLUNTEERING FOR PARKS AND TRAILS

Almost every weekend, year-round, be it sunny, overcast, or drizzling, hundreds of volunteers emerge to work on the trails we all love to walk. Dozens more volunteer their time as docents, guides, or citizen patrols to inform and aid other walkers. Still others lead youth groups on outdoor projects, advocate for our parks, wetlands, and wild spaces, and work to restore the natural habitat of the forests and wetlands surrounding our trails. Without volunteers, our region's trails, parks, wetlands, and shoreline would not be what they are today. If you've never made the time to volunteer, now is a great time to think about it! Your effort *will* count, and it *will* be appreciated!

## GOOD REASONS TO VOLUNTEER

- **IT'S OUTSIDE:** Away from your desk, you'll be surrounded by all that fresh, fragrant Pacific Northwest air.

- **IT'S COMPANIONABLE:** Volunteers work in groups, make new friends, and find others with common interests. Lots of families work together on projects, too.

- **IT BUILDS TEAMWORK:** Working outdoors on a common project teaches kids about cooperation and teamwork. Youth organizations and whole school classes can be found working on trails. For adults, trail building and replanting are great team-builders, which allow businesses to give back to the community.

- **IT'S EDUCATIONAL:** Do know the difference between invasive Himalayan blackberry and our native trailing blackberry? Do you know a white-crowned sparrow from an Oregon junco? Or how to use a Pulaski or a McLeod? Volunteers get a chance to learn about so many things, including flora and fauna and how to handle tools. If you already know how to answer questions like these, then you can share your knowledge and teach.

- **IT'S GOOD FOR THE ECONOMY:** Many volunteer hours are logged and matched by funds from the Federal government or other agencies. Your time IS valuable.

- **IT HELPS THE ENVIRONMENT:** Volunteers remove invasive flora and plant native species to make the Northwest better for our native animals. When barren places are replanted, it increases the green of our world, and everyone benefits. Repaired trails are less likely to erode and build up sediment in our salmon streams. Restoring streams to their natural state, including downed logs and rocks, creates more habitat in which young fish can thrive. Monitoring salmon streams helps scientists gather needed information about the health of our salmon population.

- **IT'S FUN AND HEALTHY:** You get to do something you love that is also good for you: walk, use your body, and be outdoors.

## WHERE TO VOLUNTEER

### Your City:

If you want to put time in on the trails and parks you love or new ones just in the creation stage, start with your local city. From Everett to Tacoma, Shoreline to Issaquah, Renton to Olympia—you name your city and chances are they'll have a program for park and/or trail volunteers. Call your City Hall or surf your city's website—volunteer information is usually under a parks and recreation section.

### Your County:

All four of our regional counties—Snohomish, King, Pierce, and Thurston—have extensive volunteer programs. Do a web search for "parks volunteer" and your county name. In King County you can become an "ambassador" to a favorite park, a place you spend lots of your time anyway. While walking the trails you can assist and educate other visitors, monitor restoration projects, and report on trail conditions. In Snohomish County, Lord Hill Regional Park has bicycle, hiker, and horseback patrols: volunteers monitor the trail conditions, report problems, and assist visitors. Pierce County has a "Courtesy Patrol" for which volunteers aid and assist other hikers.

- **SNOHOMISH:** www1.co.snohomish.wa.us/Departments/Parks /Get_Involved/Volunteer/
- **KING:** www.kingcounty.gov/recreation/parks/volunteer.aspx.
- **PIERCE:** www.piercecountytrails.org/vol.php
- **THURSTON:** www.co.thurston.wa.us/parks/volunteer/index.htm

### Your State

Washington State runs the Washington State Parks Volunteer Stewardship program, which utilizes volunteers in a range of activities to monitor and maintain State Parks. State Parks Volunteer Stewards may work on projects like pulling noxious weeds, securing grants, or studying the impact of rock climbing on plants and animals. Contact Robert A. Fimbel for more information.

- **PHONE:** (360) 902-8592
- **EMAIL:** robert.fimbel@parks.wa.gov
- **ADDRESS:** Washington State Parks, 7150 Cleanwater Lane, Olympia, WA 98504
- **WEBSITE:** www.parks.wa.gov/stewardship

## Not-For-Profit Organizations

### AUDUBON WASHINGTON
Audubon volunteers help with bird counts, and advocate for our wetlands, wildlands, and forests.
> **WEBSITE:** wa.audubon.org

### CASCADE LAND CONSERVANCY
This agency brings leaders, communities, and individuals together in a broad coalition to protect and improve our natural heritage in the Pacific Northwest. Among other things, volunteers help with park restoration at events like Green Seattle Day or at individual sites like the Duwamish Hill.
> **PHONE:** (206) 292-5907
> **ADDRESS:** 615 2nd Avenue, Suite 600, Seattle, WA 98104
> **WEBSITE:** www.cascadeland.org

### EARTHCORPS
EarthCorps is an AmeriCorps affiliate, with intensive programs in conservation techniques and training skills for leading volunteers. They employ people from over sixty countries, of all ages, on habitat restoration and conservation projects throughout the region.
> **PHONE:** (206) 322-9296
> **ADDRESS:** 6310 NE 74th Street, Suite 201E, Seattle, WA 98115
> **WEBSITE:** www.earthcorps.org

### ENVIRONMENTAL COALITION OF SOUTH SEATTLE (ECOSS)
ECOSS works with neighborhoods to raise awareness of environmental issues. They do extensive habitat restoration along the Duwamish River.
> **PHONE:** (206) 767-0432
> **ADDRESS:** 8201 10th Avenue S, #3, Seattle, WA 98108
> **WEBSITE:** www.ecoss.org

### EVERGREEN MOUNTAIN BIKE ALLIANCE
Evergreen volunteers put in thousands of hours of trail maintenance for walking/biking trails, including those on Paradise Valley Conservation Area and Tiger Mountain.
**WEBSITE:** www.evergreenmtb.org

### GREEN SEATTLE PARTNERSHIP
Green Seattle works with the Cascade Land Conservancy and city parks to remove invasive plants in an effort to restore city forests to health.
**WEBSITE:** www.greenseattle.org

### HERON HABITAT HELPERS
Part of the Associated Recreational Council, HHH volunteers restore heron habitat and facilitate heron watching at places such as Seattle Discovery Park.
**PHONE:** (206) 684-7083
**ADDRESS:** 100 Dexter Avenue North, Seattle, WA 98109
**WEBSITE:** www.heronhelpers.org

### ISSAQUAH ALPS TRAILS CLUB
IATC works on the trails on Tiger and Cougar Mountains, plus farther afield.
**CONTACT:** Scott Semans, Volunteer Trail Maintenance Coordinator
**PHONE:** (425) 369-1725
**ADDRESS:** P.O. Box 351, Issaquah, WA, 98027
**WEBSITE:** www.issaquahalps.org

### IVY OUT
English ivy is an invasive plant that creates ivy deserts and provides habitat in the Northwest for rats. "Ivy pulls" are organized by many local cities in conjunction with Ivy Out.
**WEBSITE:** www.ivyout.org/volunteer.htm

### MOUNTAINS TO SOUND GREENWAY
Started in 1991 by concerned citizens, Mountains to Sound Greenway Trust is dedicated to creating and maintaining a viable greenway from the Cascades to Puget Sound. Volunteers help with environmental education, trail maintenance, habitat restoration, youth camps, and more.
**PHONE:** (206) 812-0122
**ADDRESS:** 911 Western Avenue, Suite 523, Seattle, WA 98104
**WEBSITE:** www.mtsgreenway.org/volunteer

## NATURE CONSORTIUM
Nature Consortium is a grassroots organization that teaches environmental lessons through the creative arts and hands-on conservation projects, such as their Urban Forest Restoration Project.
**ADDRESS:** 4408 Delridge Way SW #107, Seattle, WA 98106
**WEBSITE:** www.naturec.org/restoration.htm

## PEOPLE FOR PUGET SOUND
People for Puget Sound is a citizens' group dedicated to protecting and restoring our land and water through education and action.
**WEBSITE:** www.pugetsound.org/act/volunteer/volunteer-opportunities

## PUGET SOUND RESTORATION FUND
Puget Sound Restoration Funs is a nonprofit organization that works with volunteers to restore marine habitat, water quality, and native species in Puget Sound.
**WEBSITE:** www.restorationfund.org

## RESTORATION ECOLOGY NETWORK (UW-REN)
UW-REN is a tri-campus program through the University of Washington, which brings together university students, staff and faculty with community volunteers interested in ecological restoration and conservation. Projects include parks throughout the Puget Sound Region.
**WEBSITE:** www.depts.washington.edu/uwren/volunteer.html

## THE SIERRA CLUB, CASCADE CHAPTER
The Sierra Club is a bit more political than hands-on, but they do organize trail restoration trips for volunteers.
**PHONE:** (206) 378-0114
**EMAIL:** cascade.chapter@sierraclub.org
**ADDRESS:** 180 Nickerson Street, Suite 202, Seattle 98108

## URBAN WILDERNESS PROJECT
The Urban Wilderness Project works with Seattle middle and high schools and other youth groups to promote awareness with hands-on opportunities, including work parties for habitat restoration.
**PHONE:** (206) 464-8364 Office
**ADDRESS:** P.O. Box 18874, Seattle, WA 98118
**WEBSITE:** www.urbanwildernessproject.org/volunteer.htm

**VOLUNTEERS FOR OUTDOOR WASHINGTON**
Volunteers for Outdoor Washington is a training organization that
works with local land managers, including the City of Seattle, to build
trails and restore habitat.
> **PHONE:** (206) 517-3019
> **ADDRESS:** 12345 NE 30th Avenue, Suite I, Seattle, WA 98125
> **WEBSITE:** www.trailvolunteers.org

**WASHINGTON TRAILS ASSOCIATION**
Washington Trails Association is one of the biggest supporters of our
local trails and parks. Thousands of volunteer hours are contributed
every year to many of the region's trails.
> **PHONE:** (206) 625-1367
> **ADDRESS:** 2019 3rd Avenue, Suite 10, Seattle, WA 98121
> **WEBSITE:** www.wta.org

## Citizens' Groups and "Friends of..."

Citizen' Groups and "Friends of..." organizations are usually started by individuals interested in giving time to their own local parks and trail systems.
(Just a heads up: occasionally a "Friends of..." organization is established
primarily for fund-raising—a much needed activity!—but may have no outdoor volunteer opportunities.) Search the websites of your favorite walks to
see if there are local advocacy/volunteer groups.

Here are examples of some of the individual parks that have active volunteer groups:

- **BRIDLE TRAILS PARK FOUNDATION:** www.bridletrails.org
- **FRIENDS OF DISCOVERY PARK:** www.friendsdiscoverypark.org
- **FRIENDS OF LORD HILL REGIONAL PARK:** www.friendsoflordhill.org
- **FRIENDS OF SEWARD PARK:** www.sewardpark.org
- **FRIENDS OF THE CEDAR RIVER WATERSHED:** www.cedarriver.org
- **FRIENDS OF THE HYLEBOS (PARK AND WETLANDS):** www.hylebos.org
- **MAGNUSON (PARK) ENVIRONMENTAL STEWARDSHIP ALLIANCE:**
  www.mesaseattle.org
- **WOODLAND TRAIL GREENWAY ASSOCIATION:** www.woodlandtrail.org

# INDEX OF WALK FEATURES AND ACTIVITIES

# BEST BIRD-WATCHING

# CAMPGROUNDS

# DISABLED ACCESSIBLE TRAILS

# WETLANDS

# INDEX OF WALKS AND PARKS